PIO DEL PILAR & OTHER HEROES

ON THE COVER

Detail of a 1901 photograph of the Guam deportees: (from left) Mariano Llanera, Maximino Hizon, Artemio Ricarte *Vibora* and Pio del Pilar.

PIO DEL PILAR & OTHER HEROES

Orlino A. Ochosa

Edited,
With An Introduction & Afterword
By Frank A. Hilario

New Day Publishers
Quezon City, Philippines
1997

Published by
NEW DAY PUBLISHERS

11 Lands Street, VASRA,
Quezon City 1100, Philippines

☎ (632) 928-8046/927-5982
TeleFax (632) 924-6544

Printed in the Philippines

Editor: **Frank A. Hilario**
Book Design: **Frank A. Hilario**
Cover Design (MacGraphics): **Tony Enriquez**
Maps (MacGraphics): **Tony Enriquez**

The National Library of the Philippines CIP Data

Recommended entry:

Ochosa, Orlino A.
Pio del Pilar & other heroes / Orlino
A. Ochosa ; edited with an introduction
& afterword by Frank A. Hilario. -
Quezon City : New Day Pub., c1997
1 v

1. Del Pilar, Pio. 2. Heroes - Philippines -
Biography. I. Hilario, Frank A. II. Title.

DS676.D4 1997 959.9'092 P973000121
ISBN 971-10-1009-7

KAY
FRED PUNZALAN
(1941-1997)

AT SA LAHAT
NG MGA
"PIO DEL PILAR"
NA NAGBIBIGAY KULAY
SA KASALUKUYANG BUHAY ...

BUONG PAGSINTANG
INIHAHANDOG KO
ANG MUNTING ALAY
NA ITO.

AUTHOR'S ACKNOWLEDGMENTS

To CLIO, for the sparks.
To MERLIN, for the *drala*.
To BUGSY, BOK and SOULTWIN -- "Witches 3" -- for the never-ending brew.
To FRANK H, worping-class hero, for the precious time and energy in turning my Jurassic manuscript to Star Wars form -- with his editing, typesetting, formatting, and constructive nitpicking -- besides enriching the book with his Preface, Introduction and Afterword. And, also, for sharing my thoughts on the wisdom of using Footnotes, instead of Endnotes.
To FRED PUNZALAN, wherever he is, for his *fine* ARTS.
To TONY ENRIQUEZ, beer-drinking comrade, for his MacGraphics.
To SCOTTY, Father Dragon come back as Head Beagle (and gone once more), for his simple truths.
To GLORIA ... for believing.
To BEZALIE ... for believing still.
To BETH and DENIA, and ANNA MAE for smiling.
To all the LIBRARIES, rich and poor, for those hidden nuggets I found.
To all the HISTORIANS, great and small, for blazing the trails that led to our own chosen path.
To all the "PIO DEL PILARS" past and present, for walking with us in all walks of life.
To the HERO in all of us, for the call to accomplish things greater than with our own powers, and to fulfill our own Holy Grail quests -- like this little book on heroic History.
And last but first, to the SUSTAINER OF ALL THINGS, for all the treasures of (and not of) this earth that we're counting one by one on and on ...

CONTENTS

On Heroes

We must conclude that heroes do not have to be good, or brave, or polite, or industrious, or noble. If they are any of these things, they are them by accident ... A hero has some quality that makes him what he is ... It is in the memories of his friends, memories of what he did and what he was like, that his heroism resides.

William Wayne in
A Book of Heroes

Na sa gulong ito siyang pagcatanghal
nang taga Malibay na si Pio del Pilar,
ito'y pinuno rin na maraming caual
na natatalaga sa cacastilaan.

Si Pio del Pilar at Mariano Noriel,
Julian de Ocampo at si Leon [Joaquing]
at Isidoro Carmonang magaling
sa paquiquibaca nama'y hayag din.

From a song of the Revolution

When I have referred to men and women as heroic, it was because of their courage in battle, stoicism under torture, or willingness to make sacrifices or to risk death for the Filipino cause, not because I thought their morals were exemplary or motives unmixed.

William Henry Scott in
Ilocano Responses to American Aggression

Viva Emilio y Pio del Pilar
Vivan los soldados, valor singular.
Y ella Pio donde ataco,
Fuego derecha e izquierda,
Castila'y nagtacbo!

From another song of the Revolution

EDITOR'S PREFACE
"THE BOOK OF LIBERATION"

WE REWRITE HISTORY with this book. Orli and I embarked on a collaboration on **Pio del Pilar** (The Book) last year yet. We wanted something unconventional; we wanted a volume that would be both relevant and a revelation. A tall order of the day that became a tall order of the year. Nothing happened enroute to Damascus, no blinding light to strike us sinners atop our horses and make us redeemers. No Joseph dreams to interpret either. The windmills of the mind refused to turn. There was the desert of a thousand hours; there were no thousand flowers to bloom, no hundred thoughts to contend.

Last month, June 12, we went at it again. Now we had a good idea what we wanted to do, and we did it, which is what you're reading. And when we went over the nature of what we did, it dawned on us that together we had rewritten history; later, it dawned on us still that we did not invent the genre: Nick Joaquin did it first with his search for heroes among heroes; OD Corpuz did it in his search for the roots of the Filipino; Amado Guerrero in his search for the road not taken; Renato Constantino in his search for a release from the past; Reynaldo Ileto in his search for heroes among the masses; Teodoro Agoncillo in his search for objectivity; William Henry Scott in showing us the need to scrape the bottom of the dustbin of history; and Ambeth Ocampo in his turning history upside down, the unnoticed becoming the noticeable. Everyone trying to arrive at a common, acceptable "history from a Filipino viewpoint", in the words of Ambeth Ocampo:

> *In my case, my research on the Philippine Revolution has brought me to that great mass of documents once known as the "PIR" or Philippine* Insurgent *Records. ... Teodoro Agoncillo used to remind me that we fought a Fil-American War, not a*

> *mere insurrection as the Americans claimed. For decades, our struggle has been downgraded as an insurrection when it was a real war. Hence the PIR, now in our National Library, have been aptly renamed the Philippine* Revolutionary *Records. Another way of stressing our viewpoint in history is to refer to the Americans during the Fil-American War simply and correctly as "the enemy". This places everything in its proper context.* [1]

Before this, we were "confusing the enemy", as Ambeth Ocampo puts it: in our own history books, Filipino historians referred to us as *the enemy! So, thank you, gentlemen*. But we didn't stop there, and so we decided to give it a name. So, what would we call that genre of rewriting history we had inadvertently redefined? Today, July 30, 1997, we (Orli & Frank) have that name: **Liberation History**. So, we talk about it. It's what Benedetto Croce talks about:

> *The writing of histories -- as Goethe once noted -- is one way of getting rid of the weight of the past. Historical thought transforms it into its own material and transfigures it into its object, and the writing of history liberates us from history.* [2]

Croce is saying that if you write the right history and not rewrite it to protect your own vested interests, then that history is a liberating force. History is meant neither to raise the specter of hate nor haunt the present nor rue the past and stultify the spirit; rather, it is to confront the past to multiply our insights to address the issues of today.

It is even more than what Croce is saying. We have brought the concept to a still higher level. So, we have come to a new conceptual framework. So, we have come to the paradigm of the pyramid, with all three sides equal, and, with the whole greater than the sum of its parts. So, even before defining, we have come to understand that Liberation History is governed by three principles, which are:

First Principle: To engage in Liberation History is to write and

---

[1] *Ambeth Ocampo,* **Luna's Moustache** *(Pasig City: Anvil Publishing, 1997), pages 64-65.*

[2] *Benedetto Croce,* **History As The Story Of Liberty** *(Lanham, Maryland: University Press of America, 1984), page 44.*

deliberate on the **past** to liberate us from the present, *not* from the past. Some people would be liberated from the past by denouncing it. We are the past; we cannot denounce ourselves. We can only understand the past better, and, in so doing, understand ourselves better -- *and accept*.

Second Principle: To engage in Liberation History is to write and deliberate on the **present** to liberate us from the present. Most especially from our biases -- we all have biases -- mostly dictated either by expat experts, doctorated historians, consorting professionals or popular leaders, and unconsciously used by us as spectacles for looking at the world. And so we must understand the proper place of low and high technology in making history *and* in writing history. Technology is present history; is not Information Technology (IT) -- as exemplified by the Internet -- high technology gone above our heads? *Think locally, act globally*. Now the President is hooked to the Internet. So it must be good; so, let all high government officials *surf the Internet*. (This accepted mixed metaphor shows how IT has subtly gone from one bad phrase to another (not to mention bad metaphors like *interface* and *menu*). This is correct: <u>You Surf The Wave</u>, YOU SEARCH THE WEB, *You Explore The Net*.) Take note: The Internet is none of your business: it's somebody else's -- and there's the rub.

Third Principle: To engage in Liberation History is not only to write and deliberate on history but to make history (the present), in order to liberate us from the **future**. The future is now, the present prologue. Let us learn from the activists: "If we don't act now, who will? If not now, when?"

So then, what we have to do to engage in Liberation History we can glimpse from a proper definition of the term, and it is this:

Liberation history is setting the captives free and on fire: setting scholars free to write about past & present heroes in good will; setting writers free to use old and new information technology at will; setting users on fire to seek, to find, and not to yield.

The scholars search for *more*, the writers write about *more*; we are not all scholars or writers, but we can all use *more information*. Information is all. Information is simply something known or declared; so, in this sense, computer files are information; drugs are information. What we learn from using information is *experience*, if not *wisdom*.

So, scholars, writers, users: Liberation History is for everyone.

So, this book is history, past and present. We write about the past, and we write about present history even while we make it. But, you ask, who are we to *make* history? If you ask that, you do not understand history. So, let's hear from Manès Sperber:[3]

> *The word* ***history*** *refers to either a series of events or their methodical presentation which permits us to grasp the causes and reasons for actions and events within their proper contexts. One lives history in the first sense of the word; one writes it in the second sense. We know who writes history. But who makes history? And who doesn't?*

If that doesn't convince you, maybe this will:[4]

> *It is only when those long holidays from everyday life begin that each man realizes that, although previously unaware of it, he has always been right in the middle of things. But he forgets, as soon as order -- any order -- is restored and everyday life has become omnipotent again.*

It is time to liberate ourselves from colonialist history. Now we have a choice, and it is our very own. So now, let us choose and count our blessings from Liberation History. Here are some of them:

1. IT SHOULD LIBERATE US FROM DULL READING.

It's unfortunate that history as written usually makes dull reading for non-historians (who are the rest of us) in the Philippines (as, I imagine, elsewhere), except with *José Rizal* with his question of the status quo, except with *William Henry Scott* with his question of sources, except *Nick Joaquin* with his question of heroes, except with *Orlino Ochosa* with his question of *questioned* heroes, except with *Ambeth Ocampo* with his footnotes on heroes in question, and again, except with Orli with this book (his third) with the footnotes inputted where they were designed to be, at the foot of the page (his first, my third), and with his meaningful questions interposed between historical events in the life and times of Pio del Pilar and other heroes.

Footnotes and heroes. This is Orli's third published search for other heroes, including those considered villains and found merely in

---

[3]*Manès Sperber,* **Man And His Deeds** *(New York: McGraw-Hill Book Company, 1970), page vii.*

[4]*Sperber, cited, page vii.*

footnotes or endnotes, if mentioned at all. Now they come alive in these pages, and they are the protagonists. And they make intriguing reading.

Why should history read as prosaic as a reference book to which only the hard-pressed for additional information will turn?

Ambeth Ocampo will go down in history as the one who turned the historical footnote upside down, transformed it into the main text itself and made history as popular as the most entertaining opinion column on the editorial page. Orlino Ochosa will go down in history as one of the historians who resurrected heroes from the graves of insult and infamy, buried by colonial-minded leaders, historians and writers.[5]

Despite the popular success of Ambeth Ocampo's footnote-essays on heroes and history, the footnotes in history books remain essential to the scholar, instructor, reviewer, or curious reader (we should all be). Footnotes have their own tale to tell.

Personally, I have not been as successful with footnotes as Ambeth Ocampo either. Two years ago, I wrote the world's longest *Letter To The Editor*, to our own **The Manila Times**, all of 57 pages; I called it, of course, "Footnotes To The Times". I wrote to tell the staff that "IT WAS THE BEST OF TIMES, IT WAS THE WORST OF TIMES." I said:

> *The good news is that* THE TIMES *has very high quality, unlike the others. Quality is style and substance and impact. The bad news is that* THE TIMES *has very low quality control, just like the others. I am telling you not to insult but to inspire. I know you care enough to be the very best.*
>
> *Such style. I like the whole paper. The layout is nice, clean, cultured. I like the typeface for the text: very elegant, very readable. Such substance. When you're critical, you're detached; when you're positive, you're involved. Pardon the odious comparison, but you're a horse of a different valor. Such impact. You are a phenomenon in modern Philippine journalism. Wasn't our greatest writer, our national hero like this when he was at his best?*
>
> *... Indeed, your best foot forward is showing. So, sad to say, does your bad foot. ... I thought*

---

[5]*Local and foreign. But not, I'm glad to say, among others, Mark Twain and Reynaldo Ileto.*

> *therefore I could help you by pointing out the what where when how why. Through the art of the footnote.*
>
> *My footnotes are, please take note: for quality, not damage, control; for quality is process, not paper control.*
>
> *Having read your July 27, 1995 issue enough, if not thoroughly, for my edification, it occurs to me that you can make good use of a corporate policy of quality. Look at* ***Footnotes To The Times****, this letter to the editor, as my attempt to gaud you into jogging an exercise in utility down the road to Damascus looking out for bad grammar, faulty logic, incomplete info, and last but not least, typos.*
>
> *And yes, through a* free *demo, I could show your editors in an Executive Session what excellent writing, proofreading, editing and reviewing can be done with what ease using a personal computer and a word program. Especially executives who can't be bothered to learn new tricks. Your pleasure or mine?*[6]

Naturally, my letter had plenty of footnotes. It was a labor of love. At the end of the manuscript, I had these entries:

project started	*july 27, 1995*
project finished	*august 8, 1995*
path\filename	*c:\worbs\footimes.doc*
length of file	*17,360 words approx, 138,240 bytes*
footnotes alone	*71.5% of total*

Alas, nobody took time to send me a reaction. Nobody reads footnotes like they used to anymore? Let me remind you that footnotes are a question of scholarship -- in this case, also a question of heroes.

Footnotes and heroes. **Pio del Pilar & Other Heroes** tells of more Filipino heroes than all your other historians wrote about *combined*. This should make reading absorbing. Why should a history book not be exciting reading? Why should a biography of a warrior and of two wars not be engrossing reading? And why shouldn't the footnote

---

[6] *Frank A. Hilario, "A Footnote To The Times" (Letter to the Editor,* **The Manila Times***), August 8, 1995, 57 pages.*

add to the build-up of plot and characters[7] by being within eyeshot?

In the making of history books, there is no end. There is also no end in the trying to make good.

2. It should liberate us from high tech & high priests.

We have made history by collaborating on this book, Orli and I, also in terms of technology. Like I said, high technology is current history. He likes to point out that he is low tech and I am high tech. That is, he who deals with ancient material, the historian, composes with the Jurassic typewriter, while he who deals with the present artifact (the manuscript), the editor, proposes *and* disposes with the now-classic PC. With Liberation History but without high technology, we could not have collaborated in both quantity and quality.

After writing, editing is what I like to do. Like? Yes, *like.* I suppose you can say I like editing because I like to exercise the power of controlling. I see it differently. I like, even *love*, to edit because I like the exercise of writing -- editing to me is helping the author improve the overall structure and substance and style of a manuscript: and what is that but helping in the writing and rewriting?

In this case, as is always, my editing was both author-friendly and grammar-friendly, whichever was applicable. I would do the same for any author in the name of scholarship. I don't pick on anybody, but I'm a necessary nitpicker if you're not.[8]

In fact, I have had the singular pressure (more's the pleasure) of having "desktop-published" this book from inputting to outputting, from manuscript to camera-ready (except the photographs and covers). Since I typed and formatted the text and did the page layout, I have had the ease of manipulating the whole book onscreen: show the file in two windows side-by-side, in one window collapse the headings and/or text and review what shows on both windows while I edit. This is *outline-organizing*, which has been very helpful to me. And I used *redlining* to mark *in place* my proposed editorial changes so that the author can compare them with the original text (which remains onscreen and on file but is ~~struckthrough~~ like that) and consider each one of them -- without reading the whole manuscript trying to compare with the

---

[7] *History is, of course, among others, plot and characters.*

[8] *How do I handle grammar? I start with the assumption expressed in my favorite quote from me: "Nobody's is perfect!"*

printout -- before I finalize them. Nobody needs another body for reviewing original against edited texts: *they have become one*.

To see is to believe. And since I am *not* using a Windows version of anything, it has been a delight to be able to move from Los Baños (my residence of many years) to the Quezon City offices of New Day Publishers (newfound friends) to work from one 386-based PC to another, just bringing two 1.5 MB diskettes already with a copy of the software and the file complete in a Sony pocket-size diskcase. *That's power. That's high tech.* In information processing, high tech is *not* what the high priests of electronic files make you believe: the use of a 586- or Pentium-based PC or PowerPC or PowerMac (or faster clones); high tech is not the latest hardware but *the mastery of the basics and maximizing the power of the software of your choice*.

We may also be making history here, putting *footnotes* where they should be: *at the foot of the page*. (If your footnotes are merely citations, you don't need endnotes; the bibliography is enough.) When I read and want to know more because the footnote number implies you have more to say, I want to be able to refer to the note immediately: so don't ask me to look for Note #15 in Chapter #11 on I don't know which page (and you aren't telling me either). Just think:

Imagine the Bible without footnotes and,
instead, half a book full of endnotes.

3. It should liberate us from limiting our heroes to one or two.

About the number of heroes, my friend and I may disagree on the count: I have more heroes in his book in my list than he has in his mind, that is, *I count more in favor of rather than count more against*. (In my *Introduction*, read my list.) A radical stance that is easy to misunderstand. Be forewarned. For instance, I consider **Emilio Aguinaldo** a hero with the same stature as **Andres Bonifacio**. In fact, each considered the other counter-revolutionary and, of course, it was Aguinaldo who ordered the execution of Bonifacio who was the Father of the Katipunan and the Failed Revolution of 1896. But of course, as this book relates it although it doesn't call him such, Emilio Aguinaldo was the Father of the Continued Revolution of 1899: he came back from Hongkong to fight again, and he failed again. Then he capitulated. That's because nobody's Revolution is perfect!

This book is another question of heroes.

That's why the title **Pio Del Pilar & Other Heroes**. I was talking early this morning to Ms. Leonor Gregorio, Librarian of UP

Los Baños, a friend of many years -- she called my attention to the book review I wrote on Krip Yuson's book **Great Philippine Jungle Energy Café** (see *Afterword* for more details). She said her eyes have been opened to the richness of that book, where before it had only puzzled her and turned her off. I thanked her and said, in fact, since then I have had another insight into that Energy Café: Krip Yuson has written a history book full of heroes. And remembering that at that moment, a bold crowd of young UP Los Baños college students have barricaded the main gate to the campus to air their grievances (you heard one, you heard them all) about tuition fees and dorm fees, I said what we need is more heroes. (Also, more creative communication heroes.) Yes, she said, the youth must have other heroes to cling on to, some other heroes to emulate. I'm free to report that Liberation History gives us more heroes.

4. IT SHOULD LIBERATE US FROM STEREOTYPES.

The world is divided into two, dark and light, black and white, good and bad. The world is divided into two by convention, by people who like to classify, scientists included. To edify, the Jesuit Anthony de Mello likes to tell this story which I have given the title "Classified Information":

> *"There are, indeed, two types of human beings: the Pharisees and the Publicans," the Master says after having read one of the parables of Jesus. A disciple asks the Master, "How does one recognize who are the Pharisees?" "Simple," says the Master. "They are the ones who do the classifying!"*[9]

It is only in photography and motion pictures that we have black and white. I thank God that He designed life in living color.

Let's live it that way.

FRANK A. HILARIO
July 30, 1997

---

[9]*From "Commentaries" by Father Anthony de Mello,* **Bible Diary '96** *(Claretian Publications, 1996).*

MAKATI'S HENERAL PIO
The *Batang Makati* who later became Aguinaldo's "Beloved General" was a born leader, born winner, and--sometimes--also a trouble-maker and loser.

INTRODUCTION:
IN MY FRIEND'S BOOK ARE MANY HEROES

Two Fools

(A Parable For Our Times)

Two buffoons are shuffling back and forth in the spotlight on a dark stage, both looking intently at the floor and mumbling to each other, "Have you found the precious coin, the sacred talisman yet?" The minutes tick by. Then one of the clowns realizes that the other is off in the dark, stumbling around, still searching. Comes the question: "Why in heaven's name are you looking for the precious image in the dark where you can't see, you fool?" Comes the answer: "Why are you looking for it in the light, since it is not there?" -- Adapted from Behnken[1]

FRANK AND HILARIOUS, funny and honest, I say of *that*, a serendipitous find in an old book about writers and readers and heroes. Which reminds me: "When something is funny, search it for a grain of truth".[2] That's from the jester; now, from the philosopher: "The unexamined life is not worth living".[3] I jest not. Therefore, the unexamined hero is not worth loving, and the unexamined book is not

---

[1]*Adapted by me from an illustrative story, source unnamed, by Eloise M. Behnken,* **Thomas Carlyle: Calvinist Without the Theology** *(Columbia, Missouri: University of Missouri Press, 1978), page 1.*

[2]*If the Nobel Prize-winning British playwright and uncrowned clown George Bernard Shaw didn't say this, he should have.*

[3]*If the great Greek philosopher Plato didn't say this, he too should have. Alfred North Whitehead said of him and man: "The safest general characterization of the European philosophical tradition is that it consists of a series of footnotes to Plato."*

worth reading. I have searched this new book and found the *Orlinian* talisman. *In the dark*, it is the frontiersman's spirit to "tell it like it is"; *in the light*, it is the courage to tell the truth; and *in the light/dark*, it is the power to prick the mind by asking quite a few *sharp* questions.

Questions aside, I do declare: *In my friend's book are many heroes; here I go to prepare a place for them in your heart.*

But I must first mention that **New Day Publishers** through the person of its Executive Director, **Ms. Bezalie P. Bautista**, has been a willing (and welcome) partner in this enterprise: the search for heroes *among* the unpopular and unrecognized ones (Ochosa's) and the search for heroes *aside from* the unpopular and unrecognized ones (Hilario's). (An aside: I, a non-feminist, insist on calling her by that name, for easy recall; she, a feminist, insist on being called **Mrs. Bezalie B. Uc-Kung**, because she's married to **Al Uc-Kung**. *That's love; that's style.*)

My friend's book convinces me of the heroism of Pio del Pilar, and more than 100 heroes besides (read my list on the next page). It reconstructs the lives of brave and great *men* (*embracing women*) in that period which I prefer to call **The Fifty Years War, 1896-1946**. My view is that it was one prolonged war for liberation from colonizers: *1896-1946-was-one-continuous-war-for-liberation-from-the-Spaniards-from-the-Americans-from-the-Japanese-from-the-Americans-again.* Not revolution; for a revolution is against *duly* constituted authority; any colonizer is *unduly* constituted authority.

Pio del Pilar, a Manileño Magdalo, was one of a kind; let me quote from this book, page 35:

> *Del Pilar was one of only three important Manileños (the two others were Edilberto Evangelista the engineer and Flaviano Yengko the student) who had gone over to give succor to the Caviteños when their own part of the larger struggle had only just begun, not when victory was already theirs. The key word here is* succor -- *which is what* magdalo *signifies -- the very creed by which Emilio Aguinaldo's group of Cavite Katipuneros claimed guidance. The Magdalo fighters recognized these acts and reciprocated them by giving Evangelista, Yengko and Del Pilar responsible positions in their council -- on equal footing with such prominent native sons as Tomas Mascardo, Vito Belarmino, Pantaleon Garcia, Mariano Noriel, Daniel Tirona and Marcelino Aure.*

A SHORT LIST OF HEROES OF THE REVOLUTION

Isabelo **Abaya**
Fernando **Acevedo**
Brothers **Adiarte**
Gregorio **Aglipay**
Felipe **Agoncillo**
Henerala **Agueda**
Baldomero **Aguinaldo**
Emilio **Aguinaldo**
José **Alejandrino**
Santiago **Alvarez**
Galicano **Apacible**
Servillano **Aquino**
Deodato **Arellano**
Bonifacio **Arevalo**
Marcelino **Aure**
Felipe **Banaag**
Pio **Barican**
Mariano **Barroga**
Vito **Belarmino**
Andres **Bonifacio**
Agapito **Bonzon**
Felipe **Buencamino**
Vicente **Cabrera**
Juan **Cailles**
Telesforo **Calasanz**
Felipe **Calderon**
Lucas **Camerino**
Fernando **Canon**
Urbano **Carballo**
Isidoro **Carmona**
Francisco **Carreon**
Fernando **Caruncho**
Venancio **Concepcion**
Esteban **Consortes**
Santiago **Coronado**
Hermenegildo **Cruz**
Venancio **Cueto**
Nemesio **Cuneta**
Fr. Pedro **Dandan**
Francisco **Dayao**
Enrique **de Guia**
José **de Guzman**
Gregoria **de Jesus**
Lucino **de la Cruz**
Bartolome **de la Rosa**
Agapito **de Leon**
Isabelo **de los Reyes**
Francisco **de los Santos**
Gregorio H. **del Pilar**
Pio **del Pilar**
Rosendo **de Pajarillo**
Valentin **Diaz**
Norberto **Dimayuga**
Ladislao **Diwa**
José **Dizon**
Valentin **Esguerra**
Salvador **Estrella**
Edilberto **Evangelista**
Fernando E. **Grey**
Anastacio **Francisco**
Pantaleon **Garcia**
Julian **Gerona**
Licerio **Geronimo**
Teodoro **Gonzales**
Fernando Ma. **Guerrero**
Juan **Gutierrez**
Antonino **Guevarra**
Maximino **Hizon**
Emilio **Jacinto**
Pedro **Janolino**
Leon **Joaquin**
Feliciano **Jocson**
Leon **Kilát**
Urbano **Lacuna**
Silvestre **Legaspi**
Maximino **Letran**
Mariano **Llanera**
Lucio **Lucas**
Vicente **Lukban**
Antonio **Luna**
Apolinario **Mabini**
Lazaro **Macapagal**
Sixto **Magsaysay**
Francisco **Makabulos**
Miguel **Malvar**
Roman **Manalang**
Guillermo **Masangkay**
Tomas **Mascardo**
Arsenio **Mauricio**
Mayor of Pasig
Hugo **Medina**
Catalino **Mercado**
Ambrosio **Mojica**
Julian **Montalan**
Antonio **Montenegro**
Ildefonso **Moreno**
Julio **Nakpil**
Serapio **Narvaez**
Mamerto **Natividad** Jr.
Salvador **Natividad**
Santos **Nocon**
Apolonio **Nopuente**
Mariano **Noriel**
Cipriano **Pacheco**
Pablo **Padilla**
Julian **Paguia**
T.H. **Pardo de Tavera**
Pedro **Paterno**
José Ignacio **Pawa**
Hermogenes **Plata**
Teodoro **Plata**
Pascual **Poblete**
Lorenzo **Protacio**
Manuel **Quiogue**
Catalino **Raymundo**
Cornelio **Requiestas**
Emiliano **Riego de Dios**
Artemio **Ricarte**
José **Rizal**
Paciano **Rizal**
Joaquin **Rodriguez**
Francisco **Roman**
Narciso **Roque**
Macario **Sakay**
Felipe **Salvador**
Apolonio **Samson**
Teodoro **Sandiko**
Luciano **San Miguel**
Angelo **San Pedro**
Atilano **Santa Ana**
Alejandro **Santiago**
Julian **Santos**
Lope K. **Santos**
Rosa **Sevilla**
Lino **Taniag**
Leon **Tanjanque**
Pablo **Tecson**
Manuel **Tinio**
Candido **Tirona**
Daniel **Tirona**
Aurelio **Tolentino**
Florentino **Torres**
Isidoro **Torres**
Mariano **Trias**
Felipe **Ventura**
Ignacio **Villamor**
Ariston **Villanueva**
Fabian **Villareal**
Juan Leandro **Villarino**
Flaviano **Yengko**

Having given you *my* list of heroes, I must say this: There is an Orlinian hands-off policy here, but I can say that the aim of such an Orlinian way of writing history (historiography) is to challenge the reader to be the judge of that. He has given an entirely new sense to the biblical role of Pontius Pilate; he tells us: *Pick your own heroes. And villains*. (Okay. To me, there is only one villain in this book: *those barbaric Americans*.) That is why it is important that the presentation be comprehensive. This one *is*, about Pio del Pilar, the Hero of Makati.

Makati is in my blood, as it is in the author of the book. To me, the book represents the present trying to catch up with the past. One should not be afraid of the past, the checkered past, for every past is checkered. The City of Makati, avant garde in the arts and sciences in private and public commerce, needs to examine its checkered past to surmount the obstacles to progress and win the war against poverty -- *especially poverty of the spirit*.

The winning forms of our heroes can be seen in the songs of the Revolution. I translate from the original as the author quotes them:

Na sa gulong ito siyang pagcatanghal
nang taga Malibay na si Pio del Pilar,
ito'y pinuno rin na maraming caual
na natatalaga sa cacastilaan.

Si Pio del Pilar at Mariano Noriel,
Julian de Ocampo at si Leon [Joaquing]
at Isidoro Carmonang magaling
sa paquiquibaca nama'y hayag din.
From a song of the Revolution

In this battle did emerge as popular
The one from Malibay, this Pio del Pilar,
He was also a leader with many soldiers
Assigned to fight the Spaniards.

This Pio del Pilar and Mariano Noriel,
Julian de Ocampo and Leon Joaquin
And Isidoro Carmona all first-rated
In battle also all celebrated.
My translation

Viva Emilio y Pio del Pilar
Vivan los soldados, valor singular.
Y ella Pio donde ataco,
Fuego derecha e izquierda,
Castila'y nagtacbo!
From another song of the Revolution

Love live Emilio and Pio del Pilar
Long live the soldiers, valor singular.
And this Pio where he chose to fight,
Firing straight and left and right,
Those Spaniards all took flight!
My translation

Pio del Pilar (The Hero) showed us how to win battles (and almost the war, except that Emilio Aguinaldo hesitated at the crucial moment), with a lot of uncommon sense and without hesitation. There is a lot of uncommon sense in Makati. Orli and I learned that, oh, so long ago. We met and parted and we met again, in Makati. This time we talked about heroes, including us. We never talked like this before.

Now, how have I arrived at my list of heroes without the prior knowledge and consent of the historian? Easy. I chose them for *human* qualities: *(1) military leadership, (2) high courage, (3) indomitable will, (4) love of country, (5) martyrdom, and (6) for stubbornly not giving up when everyone else had.* Especially Pio del Pilar:

> *Pio del Pilar and his heroes have won for themselves a foremost place in the annals of the Filipino. Through the wilds of Makati, his intrepid bolomen showed their undoubted efficiency at a time when musketry is powerless to make an end of the enemy. General Pio del Pilar, with marvelous intuition, sent his bolomen against a mass of American troops, as a huntsman lets loose his hounds to drive out the wild beasts trying to hide in the depths of the woods. The episodes of those last few days had been so brilliant and so numerous that it is difficult to find a parallel in history in great military achievement.*[4]

---

[4]*Adapted from* ***La Independencia****, sometime February 1899, cited in this book, pages 84-85.*

Such testimony shows to me that Pio del Pilar's military leadership was inspired.

In fact, that in itself is an epitaph worthy of Pio del Pilar *and* many other heroes.

All heroes are made, not born, and it is us hero-worshippers who make them. We declare their greatness, then we attribute to them qualities they don't have, or exaggerate what they do. Not with **Pio del Pilar**. My good friend Orli's off-beat book is his attempt to tell the story as it was, all questions asked, not all questions answered, or can be. What this book is *is* to be *conscious* about this hero, including about his humanity.

The trouble with heroes is if they are not human. *Pio del Pilar is consciously human.* As Orli shows in his book, Pio del Pilar became the hero of Makati, warts and all. And that too is how we can judge Makati, warts and all. For you can always tell who the people are by the heroes they keep.

Which means you have to understand Pio del Pilar and other heroes in this book to understand Philippine history, especially that of the Revolution *starting* in 1896. What Orli offers is a point of view of history not offered by traditional historians, which may be stated like this:

> *History is made by men great and small, not the least being the small.*

Which means, history is both simple and complicated. It is not only the highly visible heroes like the dangerous rivals Andres Bonifacio and Emilio Aguinaldo who are heroes of historical essence but also, say, the common soldiers who did simply follow orders and did die in the trenches in the massacre in the hands of the double-dealing Americans at Pandacan on February 4, 1899 and now lie buried in unmarked graves, if buried at all. Armies are made by military officers, but battles are fought by ordinary soldiers. Now you understand how I look at heroes. (Now, with this new perspective, you may want to read again my list on page 3.)

Men respond to movements, or initiate them. Starting at least in 1896, there were at least four major movements in this country:

√ a movement for reforms by one group of Filipinos
√ a movement for independence by another group of Filipinos
√ retention of power by Spaniards over the islands, and
√ the Americans' own dreams of empire in our own world.

These four counter-movements created the tropical depression called "Insurrection" by the Americans, "Filibusterismo" by the Spaniards, and "Independence" ("Kalayaan") and "Republicanism" ("special relations" with the United States in which the Philippines is a federal part, and which I shall simply call "Kaibigan" because it's such a nice, deceptive term), by opposing groups of Filipinos. You cannot please everybody; that's why history is always in the making.

As always, wars are made by groups of conflicting interests who each think the other evil or simply misguided.

That is why there is the *sweep of history*, which is either broad or narrow, depending on the point of view of the popular leaders on one hand, and of the intellectual rebels on the other. So, *that* historical position could be restated like this:

> *History is made by men in movements great and small, not the least being the small.*

The double entendre is intentional; movements too can be great and small, except that we tend to note only the great ones.

Was Pio del Pilar a great one? Undoubtedly, Pio del Pilar had *insight* and *courage*; and so had the Makati entrepreneurs. It took boldness for the Zobels, Ayalas and Ortigases to plan on a Makati that was then largely a grassland. Look at Makati now.

You can also call it *speculation*. A hero speculates that in any battle, he will either win or lose, live or die. So does a businessman. I dare say Pio del Pilar was a good businessman, the dominant military leadership and his mistress considered:

> *Pio del Pilar's businesses were to make war and to make love -- also money. These were legitimate enterprises, given the circumstances. That is to say, he went on to relentlessly pursue and conquer the enemy; and then he went on to pursue and profess happiness.*

There are rogues and there are gentlemen who are when they want to be.[5] Being rogues do not make heroes less heroic; while we would prefer that they be not rogues, we can't have perfect heroes. Even the saints weren't always right, or likeable. *The trouble with heroes is when* we *think, or when* they *think they are always right*.

In the meantime, we need more heroes among businessmen and leaders. We can't have perfect businessmen and leaders of government and industry either, but they can at least try and be heroes themselves.

---

[5]*I suppose, it's easier to be bad: you can always claim the temptation was too great to resist.*

What about Pio del Pilar? *He was a winner. When he lost, it wasn't for lack of trying. He didn't say die until he was dead.* So, don't say cry until you've read.

I'm not surprised that my friend Orli Ochosa has been writing about his heroes, as I have been writing about mine. Heroes are personal choices, although sometimes they are thrust upon us. Last year, I met Orli again, we having last seen each other 22 years ago at Amorsolo Street at the offices of the **Pacifica Publicity Bureau** where we both started as copywriters out from the cold of our provincial naivete (he from Vigan, Ilocos Sur and I from Asingan, Pangasinan),[6] with three of our heroes in the field of advertising: **Tony Zorrilla** as Head above all, **Telly Bernardo** as Executive Vice President, and **Nonoy Gallardo** as Creative Director. I think we came to Pacifica in some of its best years, and we are glad we became part of all that. We learned some, we unlearned more -- and we enjoyed the work and ourselves. We still do.

So, in this book, two old friends meet; and, as it happens, the old meets the new, the low meets the high technology. This book was written by Orli (his third) using an old typewriter (all typewriters are now *old*). Instead of classical publishing (using the IBM Composer), I did the PC publishing (also my third such book)[7] -- I inputted, spell-checked, corrected, redlined, revised, typeset (text-formatted), composed (page-layouted), and print-outed (draft and camera-ready) -- using the personal computer (PC), a word processing program (which I

---

[6]*Two places that have given us heroes: From Pangasinan, Valentin Diaz, one of the very founders of the Katipunan; from Ilocos Sur, Isabelo Abaya the guerrilla leader and Isabelo de los Reyes, the propagandist who never said die until he was dead.*

[7]*The first one was* **Prospects and Needs of Sustainable Agriculture in Southeast Asia** *(College, Laguna: University of the Philippines Los Baños, 1993), 261 pages (Name of Editor not given, but in fact it was I). The second was O.K. Bautista (ed.),* **Introduction to Tropical Horticulture** *(College, Laguna: SEARCA and UP LOS BAÑOS, 1994), 597 pages. (I did the frontline editing of this book too.)*

prefer to refer to as a *worp*), and an HP LaserJet 4L & 5L printers. I have been *worping*, processing pages of ideas, not merely words.

With the PC, writing has been radically changed forever. It is now more mental, less monotonous and strenuous. With PC publishing, we have transcended the mechanical rites of classical publishing: typing with the typewriter, footnoting by hand, two people comparing two manuscripts to check spelling, correcting manually, retyping a manuscript X times, revising, typesetting, cutting & pasting etc. It's incredibly much faster.[8]

What exactly is a good worp good for? For one, my worp allows me to examine a manuscript of any length in terms of: outline, content, organization of ideas and flow of thought in the chapters, consistency in the usage of coined and old terms, among others, including revising extensively and intensively. *I just love it!*

Notice where the footnotes are? The worp put them there, automatically. For another, you can have "a feel" of how this Orlinian biography of Pio del Pilar reads without reading: Consider how many times key words and ideas occur and recur in the biography, among about 33,000 words in about 3,000 lines. So, my worp tells me that:

Pio with *Pioista(s), Pio del Pilar* occurs 418 times
Aguinaldo with *Aguinaldista(s)* occurs 201 times
retreat with *retreating* occurs 12 times
advance(d) with *advancing* occurs 10 times
atrocity occurs once
rape occurs once
massacre(d) occurs 5 times
hero(es) with *heroic* occurs 32 times
smile occurs *not* once
spy(ies) occurs 3 times
mistress with *beautiful mistress* with *querida* occurs 4 times
Holy Rosary occurs once
colonizers with *colonial, colonial-minded* occurs 5 times
enemy(ies) with *foe* occurs 26 times

---

[8]*For an idea how long it takes to use the old method, here's a historical note on the subject. According to Orli (*"Emilio Jacinto Pingkian", **Diliman Review**, *37(3):19) Pio Valenzuela says in his memoirs that it took the Katipuneros "about two months to finish the printing". It was only eight pages. (Don't gloat: We're* still *that slow in printing.)*

friend(s) with *friend's, friendly, friendship* occurs 21 times
contra-revolucionario(s) occurs 4 times
unsurrendered occurs once.

What about the rest of the book? Here's another list to titillate you further:

Windows occurs 11 times
Rizal with *José Rizal* occurs 68 times
PC with *personal computer* occurs 74 times
history occurs 127 times
writing with *writer(s)* occurs 55 times

Those two short lists should convince anyone that on any page, this book makes provocative reading. And that intelligent use of the personal computer is provocative, but only *after we have overcome* the *siren song of the PC.*

Shall we overcome? With the PC, we are the immovable object and there is the invitation to a dance, the irresistible force, ballroom dancing. "Music hath charm that soothes the savage breast." The wiles of information technology (IT) invite us, and we are so mesmerized that we do not notice the absence of soul. There is touch, but no intimate relationship; there is experience, but only skin-deep. We fondle the glamor of IT, not hold the heart. We fail to grasp **the heart of IT: pulsating information.** Failing in that, it's easy to be ENAMORED WITH TECHNOLOGY AND PROUD OF IT. But not, I'm glad, everyone:

> *The new generation of corporate executives has to be [not only] computer literate [but] information-systems literate. We are all in an information intensive business. Just about every business I look at suggests that information is the key.*[9]

Systems, *not* sizzles. **Windows** is hot, razzle-dazzle; Windows reminds you that everything that glitters is gold. In a little while, when your head stops spinning, you will know that you are *King Midas* in a world where everything you touch turns to gold. You will have to ask your god to take back from you the gift of gold.

Pio del Pilar wanted to be a Knight of the Round Table (Sir

---

[9]*Scott McNealy, in an interview with the Editor, "McNealy's rocket ride",* **Leaders**, *December 1995, pages 37-40. McNealy is the Chairman, President and Chief Executive Officer of Sun Microsystems Inc., a $2.8 billion company, a leader in open network computing.*

Lancelot, the most chivalrous) and King Midas too (the richest). I am *Apollo*, rider of the chariot of the gods across the sky, maker of music. Or I am *Hephaestus*, god of fire, not handsome; but I get the girl, the goddess of love *Aphrodite*; I am patron of handicrafts and protector of blacksmiths. All art is handicraft, all writers blacksmiths -- creators.

If you are unreasonable, you will always see that the PC gives you unlimited power, the power of a god: You are on top of the world, you are on top of the situation. The PC *enables* you; the PC turns you into what you never dreamed of, the best you could be -- writer, propagandist, marketing man, artist, presentor, lecturer, and editor all in one great body -- you feel invincible: you are *both* the irresistible impulse and the immovable force. Isn't it great?

When you come down to earth, you will see that with the *awesome* power of the PC, *you* are still the *exact same* person; I say:

> *With all the wonders that the PC has wrought, nothing has changed for you. For if you have been a shoddy writer, you're still a shoddy writer. If you have been an awful propagandist, you're still an awful propagandist. If you have been a rotten artist, you're still a rotten artist. If you have been a lousy presentor, you're still a lousy presentor. If you have been a sleepy lecturer, you're still a sleepy lecturer. If you have been a second-rate editor, you're still a second-rate editor.*

Except that now you are a little bit faster and fancier. You're computer literate.

Not only the heart but the *art* of the PC is what we're missing. Notice that there has not been enough creativity even to come up with a nice term for the computer user. *Computer user?* Sounds like *drug user* or *drug pusher*. On second thought, if you're not careful, the PC is exactly like a prohibited drug: *With high technology, you get high*.

So, I invent another word: *compuser*. Sounds like *confuser* (that's another) -- which is what many experts of the Information Age are. The challenge of the personal computer, with or without the Internet, with or without Pentium or Windows 97, is for me to make a *compuser* out of me, a *comprehending, competent computer user*.

Right now, I'm a compuser working on this book; I'm reading and revising for the seventh time (date: July 12, 1997 / time: 2:24 PM). I'm having a great time because it's something I like to do with something I like to do it with. I have mastered my software, my worp, so much so that, as they do it in the circus, I can make it jump through hoops if I have to. Anyway, I've been at it for 12 *happy* years.

That takes care of me; what about my friend the historian? With or without the PC -- it should be *with* -- it remains for the historian to be relevant. No problem with that, because history is always relevant. In other words, as I have said elsewhere, "*When you fail History, you are bound to repeat it*".[10] So, what is history good for, after relevance?

My friend has looked into the light and dark and gray areas in the life of the hero of Makati, Pio del Pilar, and other heroes, and saw that it was good, enough for a book. *Pioneering* (no pun intended), by method Orlinian, instead of a hagiography, he has come up with a biography. Was he a fool for doing that? No. He would have been another fool for *not* doing that. Life is not in B&W but in full color!

He throws us an Orlinian challenge in the form of a question: "Has Makati really found its hero in Pio del Pilar?"[11] Then, Pilate-like, he tells his story and doesn't stay for the answer.

My first answer is another question, "What kind of hero?" My next is: "What makes a hero a hero?" And, relevant to my search for the answer to the Orlinian question, I shall now ask a question pertinent to the times: "Has Mankind really found his hero in the Personal Computer?" **Time** even made the PC *Man of the Year* sometime ago. Or, which is the same: "Is Man, who invented the PC, the hero?"

Or considering the bugbear of being yourself a confuser (also a user who is confused) and considering the daunting prospects of ever mastering the computer, doesn't the compuser risk being a hero?

When I open my favorite software (the one I call a *worp*), it goes *Esc Window Split Vertical 22 Enter* automatically and gives me two windows of two different background colors. I collapse my outline in Window 2 and scroll the text (in interactive view) in Window 1 and either check my progress or revise the manuscript. *Now that I have written that in a book, I risk being a hero myself.*

A "hero", says the **American Heritage College Dictionary** (1993), is "a person noted for feats of courage or nobility of purpose, especially one who has risked or sacrificed his life". I have the mind to modify that to say "... one who has risked or sacrificed his life or his reputation, whichever comes first". His or her, death is either physical

---

[10]*Frank A. Hilario, "Is Bonifacio a hero? UP Diliman is upset",* TH!NK, **The Evening Paper**, *May 6, 1997, page 5.*

[11]*"Foreword", page 21.*

or psychological, the difference being trivial.

I'm risking my reputation saying I am in pursuit of happiness with a different kind of heroism, which is this: Man managing materials and *not* materials managing man. In three words: **Man over matter!**

Example: Since my interest is eclectic, I maintain five separate subdirectories of my document files and can turn to any of five different files at any time and pick up the last file I edited exactly where I stopped this morning, yesterday, or *anytime in the past*. The wonders of the power *of* technology, the wonder of the power *over* technology.

Why should we be slaves of technology? Here is where we need heroes. *Truth to tell, in nobility of purpose, we can all be heroes.*

What about the so-called Information Highway, or cyberspace: Isn't that the way of all modern-day heroes? It depends. As author and editor working with the personal computer in the last 12 years, I have relied heavily on my word processing program: I *don't* write without it. So, what about cyberspace? I say: **Cyberspace is empty until you put meaning into it.** I know; I've been there, inside and outside. I am not a computer nerd; I am a wonk. What's the difference? A nerd is a jack of all trades (programs), a master of somc. I say a wonk knows better.

Looking for heroes among the wonks, Mike Edelhart himself, Editor in Chief & Publisher of **PC/Computing**, is a wonk. He says:

> *As we consider the value of PCs as competitive tools for our companies, we must make every effort to avoid easy romanticisms and empty rhetoric.*[12]

Good point, Mr. Edelhart. It is easy to be enamored with technology -- it's the New Age way of keeping up with the Nerds Joneses. The PC is also an awesome status symbol, especially when you can ask questions very few would know enough to ask.

> *We talk so easily today about creating, moving, and evaluating information. We point to the PC as a*

[12]*Mike Edelhart, "Let's avoid easy romanticisms and get at our real business problems"*, **PC/Computing**, *April 1992, page 20.*

> *competitive panacea because it shapes information effectively, presents it handsomely, and moves it around with increasing breadth and efficiency. This view is so widespread that it's accepted as gospel.*
>
> *Hogwash. Information is not the root of our competitive problems these days.*

Neither is competition the root of our problems, Mr. Edelhart. Rather, it is the display of egoism; it is the lack of practice of heroism, the lack of heroes among us. We have yet to learn from history.

> *For a long time after the Japanese attack, historians made the same assumptions about the situation in Hawaii that we make today in business: that the right information hadn't reached the right person.*[13]

Mr. Edelhart, it is *intention*, not information, that matters, especially now that there's a lot of information and most anybody has access to it: the **Internet**, that interconnection of networks of computers all over the world. Everybody except me is hooked to the Internet; according to **Time**, even God is in and all over the Internet, according to Joshua Cooper Ramo.[14] He tells us that out there in New Mexico, the brothers of Christ in the Desert are plugged into the Internet. Yes, the Lutherans have a home page, and so do the Tibetan Buddhists, Mormons and others -- and the Vatican, starting 1995.

Which means that just about everyone is enamored with technology. Mr. Ramo says:

> *And now we stand at the start of a new movement in this delicate dance of technology and faith: the marriage of God and the global computer networks. There's no sure way to measure how much the Internet will change our lives, but the most basic truth about technological revolutions is that they change everything they touch. Just as the first telescopes forever altered our sense of where we sit in the cosmos, so the Internet may press and tug at our*

---

[13]*Edelhart, cited, page 20.*

[14]*Joshua Cooper Ramo, "Finding God on the Web",* **Time**, *December 16, 1996, pages 46-53. Ramo is a Senior Editor of Time.*

most closely held beliefs. Will the Net change religion? Is it possible that God in a networked age will look, somehow, different?[15]

Yes, and not only God -- if we continue to allow technology to dazzle us so that we do not stop and think of going back to the basics. And basics is like this, I say:

Government offices in Metro Manila have already spent at least P2,000,000,000 (two billion) for buying personal computers in flagrant violation of Philippine Government rules of auditing.

If my allegation is true, it shows that, since the birth of the first PC in 1975,[16] with Steve Jobs of Apple Computer as the undeterred, lone advocate for personal systems,[17] up to this date, July 12, 1997, we have not been thinking right about computers. We even believe that computers are becoming intelligent. In fact, "Computers cannot be intelligent because they cannot be interlocutors", says Michael Carrithers.[18] Like I'm trying to make me and you right now.

How did I arrive at my fantastic figure of two billion pesos and the flagrant violation by Government of auditing rules? Easy:

Based on the **PLDT Metro Manila Telephone Directory**, *I estimate at least 25,000 big and small national and local Government offices in Metro Manila alone. Each has 2 PCs, and that makes 50,000 PCs. Each PC costs P40,000, and that's equal to P2 billion.*

About the violation in law: In Government, when you purchase equipment, the one unbreakable accounting rule is to look for the lowest bidder (except in a negotiated bid), with the underlying assumption that there are at least three different suppliers. This is not the case with PCs. All PCs, original or clone, have

---

[15]*Ramo, cited, page 54.*

[16]*Donald H. Sanders,* **Computers Today** *(New York: McGraw-Hill Book Company, 1985), National Book Store reprint, page 210. That first PC was called the* Altair 8800.

[17]*Jeffrey S. Young,* **Steve Jobs: The Journey Is The Reward** *(New York: Lynx Books, 1988), 467 pages.*

[18]*Michael Carrithers, "Is anthropology art or science?"* **Current Anthropology** *Volume 31, Number 3, June 1990, page 278.*

> *been anomalously purchased -- because the primer of the bullet as it were, the operating system/interface of the PC (which is called* **DOS/Windows***), without which the computer is an expensive piece of junk, is supplied by only one vendor: Microsoft. This is scandalous.*
>
> *Will any whiz kid in Government now claim absence of another vendor or ignorance of the fundamental nature of PCs? Either way, it means that we have all been enamored with technology.*
>
> *It is not true that there is no other operating system/interface vendor. For one, we have* **OS/2 Warp** *by IBM, which works even better than Windows.*
>
> *This is the granddaddy of all scams, in quality and in scope (even non-Government organizations are victims, even the Americans), to think that our lives are now all affected by the personal computer whether we know it or not, whether we like it or not. The Philippine Government should stop buying PCs immediately until it has straightened its warped outlook on computers!*

That's Government basic.

Now, the private sector basic. About the sensational Internet, the mind-boggling international network of computers and telephones. If you aren't careful, you will commit *The Blindmen's Bluff* about the elephant being different things to different men, not the whole bigger than the sum of its parts.

Stripped bare of its designer wraps and underwraps, *the Internet is information at your fingertips.* A huge database of facts and fancies; even Compaq Computer Corporation agrees![19] A source, that's all. It's the fastest, it's *not the best*; in fact, because of the awe attached to it, it could be *the worst*.

So, you cannot claim that surfing the Internet is for heroes. It is more heroic to master one's own database program in a standalone PC than surf the erotic waves of the Internet.

Did I say database program? In fact, I can make my worp a database program (which it certainly is *not*) that can handle 10,000 patients (in 10,000 files) at anytime, no sweat: *Press Ctrl-Alt-H* if the

---

[19]*From Compaq Computer Corporation's "Distributed Access", an 8-page ad insert,* **Forbes**, *November 4, 1996, no page numbers assigned.*

patient's family name starts with H. In fact, I have already done it for two clinics of my favorite pediatrician. I used its own programming language, and I didn't study programming in school or office.

The Asia-Pacific Economic Cooperation (APEC) is a forum for promoting regional development. The APEC's Osaka Summit in 1995 focused on information technology, especially aiming at the expansion of interconnected information resources: computers, telephone lines, faxes, printers -- the *Internet*. I translate that as the APEC saying: *We are continuously looking for heroes to help improve the human resource using the technology resources now available.*

Why do we look for heroes? It was the writer-thinker Thomas Carlyle who promoted the role of the hero in history in his "On Heroes, Hero-Worship, and the Heroic in History" written in 1841. Carlyle

> *... believed that the world must be governed by "heroes" -- strong, just men; consequently he felt that the people should put their faith in such men and not in democracy.* [20]

Carlyle also "affirmed that work of all kinds is dignified and sacred". And "he thought that men must renounce personal happiness to obtain peace of mind".[21] I agree with him wholeheartedly (but I do *not* know about *not* believing in democracy).

In fact, Carlyle had in mind two kinds of heroes: great men of ideas, and great men of action. Heroes of the art, heroes of the act.[22]

Carlyle's perception of the hero as a man of ideas is that "he transcends the spirit of his age". In Robert Burns, Carlyle saw this:

---

[20]*Not credited, "Thomas Carlyle",* **Compton's Encyclopedia** *(Chicago: Compton's Learning Company), vol 4, page 169.*

[21]*Behnken,* **Carlyle**, *cited, page 42.*

[22]*Of course, there are exceptions: men of great mind and methods; we call them statesmen. What we need in this country right now is a statesman: Is Apo Fidel Ramos a statesman? Is any of those presidentiables a statesman? They should read more history.*

> *And thus over the lowest provinces of man's existence [Burns] pours the glory of his own soul, and they rise, in shadow and sunshine, softened and brightened into a beauty which other eyes discern not in the highest.*[23]

Of the rough Scottish life, Burns wrote in such a way that men could see its significance, says Behnken.

> *Burns, then, has insight into the divine significance of the lowly. He is a sincere and honest man who writes from the heart, and in doing so he illuminates his small corner of the world by teaching others of the dignity of the common life.*[24]

Dignity of the common life; what is that but this?

> *Then the righteous will answer Him, saying, "Lord, when did we see You hungry and feed You, or thirsty and give You drink?" And the King will answer and say to them, "Assuredly, I say to you, inasmuch as you did it to one of the least of these My brethren, you did it to Me."*[25]

Could the same be said of Robin Hood, who robbed the rich to give to the poor? It's easy to say *Yes*. But the answer is *No*. Why because you cannot right a wrong by another wrong.

To Carlyle, the German Goethe was the epitome of the hero as a man of the mind.

> *The history of his [Goethe's] mind is, in fact, at the same time, the history of German culture in his day: for whatever excellence this individual might realise has sooner or later been acknowledged and appropriated by his country.*[26]

More on Goethe according to Carlyle according to Behnken:

---

[23]*Behnken, cited, page 43.*

[24]*Behnken, cited, page 43.*

[25]*Matthew 25:37-40 (New King James Version)*

[26]*Behnken, cited, page 46.*

He was read by peasants and barons alike because his writings provided an essential recognition of what it meant to be a German; he could dig to the taproot of the culture. ... Goethe had "gifted vision", "sympathy in the ways of all men". He was the "Teacher", "exemplar of his age" because he had learned how to live well.[27]

Learning to live well, we could all be heroes of action.

Count Mirabeau was a most able French statesman of the Third Estate (the masses), defiant and courageous. He lost all his money and his wife, but he never gave up. He could have guided the Revolution well, but the King and Queen would not listen. A year after he became President of the National Assembly, he died. A great loss to France.[28]

Another Frenchman, Georges Danton was a hero:

Always his total freedom from cant is one thing; even in his briberies, and sins as to money, there is a frankness, a kind of broad greatness. Sincerity, a great rude sincerity of insight and of purpose, dwelt in the man, which quality is the root of all: a man who could see through many things, and would stop at very few things; who marched and fought impetuously forward, in the questionablest element.[29]

And Napoleon Bonaparte? His philosophy was empty, so he became a strange amalgam of the true and the false. When he was good, he was sincere; he had a feel for fact; he believed in talent, and he destroyed anarchy in France. When he was bad, he was ambitious; he was a charlatan; and he trampled on others for his own profit.[30]

So, what really makes a hero a hero? Orli's book tells us that Pio del Pilar became one by a gentleman's agreement: a law. But with

---

[27]*Behnken, cited, page 46-47.*

[28]*Not credited, "Count Mirabeau",* **Compton's Encyclopedia** *(Chicago: Compton's Learning Company, 1995), Volume 15, page 462.*

[29]*Behnken, cited, page 55. On second thought, this, to me, describes, Pio del Pilar exactly!*

[30]*Behnken, cited, page 56.*

this, his book, we don't need the law.

By divine or human dictate, the trouble with heroes is that they have human faults, but we refuse to believe that they do. And worse, they themselves refuse to believe that they do. I know, for I have known many. Carlos P. Romulo says he walked with heroes; I myself knew heroes when I was still in high school. I met them all in books.

I have always been a gambler -- in reading. Back in high school in Asingan, Pangasinan, my mother discouraged my reading except my textbooks, so I saved my pocket money for merienda and my calesa fare and walked the two kilometers to school back and forth, and, gambling that my mother would not find me out, I would buy all extracurricular reading materials I could save for: *Liwayway, Bulaklak, Kislap Graphic, Tagalog Klasiks, Pilipino Komiks, Hiwaga Komiks, Ace Comics*. Out of those, here are some heroes I remember: *El Indio, Barbaro, Kapitan Berong, Hagibis*, *Kapitan Kidlat*, *Ukala*, and *Darna*. I always won. I have always enjoyed reading.

You can have as many heroes as you want. So, the Israelites had Moses, Samson, David and a Bible-full of others. The Greeks had Ulysses and a boatful of others. The British had the most chivalrous hero in King Arthur and a Camelot-full of Knights of the Round Table. I have my own. I have always enjoyed my own heroes.

The trouble with heroes is that the way their lives are written, it's impossible to imitate them: they're too good. Not with **Pio del Pilar & Other Heroes.** As Orli puts it in one of our conversations, his **Pio del Pilar** presents "the good, the bad, and the ugly: Clint Eastwood-and-Eli Wallach-and-Lee Van Cleef all at once". Know what? *He describes my hero!*

FRANK A. HILARIO
LOS BAÑOS, LAGUNA, JULY 30 1997

FOREWORD:
PIO DEL PILAR, HERO OF MAKATI

MY FIRST IMPRESSIONS of Pio del Pilar were not so good. Back in those name-calling days when Andres Bonifacio was the "Great Plebeian" and Apolinario Mabini was the "Sublime Paralytic" and Gregorio del Pilar was the "Hero of Tirad Pass", I wondered why Pio del Pilar was not a noble someone or a hero of something. I asked myself then: Was he a relative of Marcelo and Gregorio H. del Pilar?

From the old history books, the only things I could learn about Pio del Pilar were that he was one of the Generals of the Revolution, that the war flag used by his men was part of the evolution of the national tricolor, and that he was later partly to blame for the death of Andres Bonifacio, the very founder and Supremo of the Katipunan.[1] Out of this little knowledge, I immediately got the notion that Pio del Pilar was an *Aguinaldista*, an Aguinaldo man, which was just too bad because it was a time when I was all for the Supremo and everything he stood for.

Further readings on national histories of the Revolution soon gave me a broader, though still one-sided, picture of Pio del Pilar. This time I learned about all those things we read on his Makati statue's marker. He had organized the *Magtagumpay* section of the Katipunan in Makati in 1896, had fought (my early hunch was right) under Emilio Aguinaldo's *Magdalo* army in 1897, had participated in the siege and final attack on Manila in 1898, had become a member of the Malolos Congress (which did not surprise me a bit at that time), had fought against the Americans in numerous battles all of 1899, and had been exiled to Guam together with Apolinario Mabini (the "Brains of the

---

[1] *Popular name for the* Kataastaasang Kagalang-galang na Katipunan ng mga Anak ng Bayan *(Highest & Noblest Brotherhood of the Sons of the People), Andres Bonifacio's revolutionary retort to José Rizal's reformist* La Liga Filipina.

Republic"), Artemio Ricarte ("El Vibora" or "The Viper"), and others in 1901. Reading him this way, who could not help but conclude that Pio del Pilar was, after all, a noble if unsung hero?

But my special interest in the Revolution went beyond that. Now I was interested in details, in local histories, in small names and minor events. I was now after the primary sources, the documents, the personal accounts of the participants. I was now making my own analyses and conclusions which, as things turned out, did not conform with those of many traditional historians. And now I found myself looking at, also, the ugly side of Pio del Pilar.

An old surviving photograph of the Guam expatriates of 1901 shows Pio del Pilar sporting a villainous-looking mustache and a sharp sinister look (see front cover). In real life, he did live up to this bad "ne'er-do-well" image, especially in the eyes of his American muckrakers. Indeed, he could very well exemplify the warlord-type Filipino chieftains in all the wars of '96, '98 and '99: proud, brusque, arrogant, recalcitrant, cruel and even mercenary at times.

But most of the "insurrecto"[2] leaders of this type -- men of the likes of Bonzon, Pawa, Topacio, Noriel and even Mascardo -- were no more than mere clan henchmen who had been criticized mainly for their *Cavitismo* and were thus easily identified as Aguinaldistas, or pro-Aguinaldo. Pio del Pilar, though a *Manileño*, may have been guilty of Cavitismo too, for he had been on Aguinaldo's side in all the revolutionary battles. Yet he could never be called an Aguinaldista for the reason that there were *Pioistas* -- followers of his own, fighting men who fought *for* Pio del Pilar alone -- just as there had been *Bonifacistas* and there would be *Lunistas*, *Malvaristas*, *Ricartistas*, *Salvadoristas* and so on. Besides, Pio del Pilar was more notoriously known -- and perhaps condemned -- not for Cavitismo but for the endless complaints of *salvajismo* hurled at him time and again by Spaniards, Americans and Filipinos alike.

John R.M. Taylor, compiler of the "Insurgent Records", cited and quoted Pio del Pilar more often than any other ranking "insurrecto" but he rated him down as a mere "*leader of ladrones* [who] ruled with a strong hand". [Emphasis supplied.]

William Brecknock Watson, chronicler of the early American

---

[2]*For meanings and notes on this and other non-English or non-standard terms (either in quotes throughout or set in italics on first use), see the* **Glossary** *at the back of the book.*

empire days, called him "a cattle thief and inveterate gambler". William Thaddeus Sexton forty years after the war would throw a similarly hostile line against "the bandit chieftain Pio del Pilar". And Leon Wolff in the 1960s would still share this ill-feeling for "the rather unsavory General Pio del Pilar".

Some of Pio's own contemporaries and *compañeros* in the Revolution have helped build his bad-guy reputation in separate memoirs. Julio Nakpil, for instance, hints of Pio del Pilar's sinister role (much like Gregorio del Pilar's part in the Luna assassination of 1899) as Aguinaldo's hatchetman out to assassinate Nakpil and other Bonifacistas after the Supremo's killing on 10 May 1897. General José Alejandrino, who fought the Revolution only in its second phase, clearly has no admiration for Pio del Pilar as a fellow General in the revolutionary army, much less as a fellow delegate to the Malolos Congress. Alejandrino may have had Pio del Pilar in mind when he writes of the "General who distinguished himself with his immorality and misdeeds and whom the [Malolos] government wanted to discipline by threats of dismissal from his position". And even a man of Pio del Pilar's own kind, Ricarte, has written a few unflattering lines about his fellow General and fellow irreconcilable who, many years later, in the 1970s, would be consecrated "Hero of Makati".

Has Makati really found its hero in Pio del Pilar?

THIS PAPER IS, as far as I know, the first full-length monograph on the life and times of the Hero of Makati. Being an inquiry, it raises questions, lots of questions, on whether Pio del Pilar was a true patriot genuinely fighting for <u>his</u> *Inang Bayan,* or a mere scoundrel only resorting to self-serving patriot games -- or both. But it does not answer those questions; it only offers ideas and opinions -- either in the form of interpolations of quoted works, or comments on the personalities with whom Pio del Pilar had interacted and in the events of which he was a protagonist -- in the hope that these may serve as leads or clues for future and more advanced studies on the man and his times.

No existing Pioista material available to me had been discarded or ignored, but rather scrutinized for their worth, though it must be conceded that I had not really done much "barrel-bottom scraping" as

Philippine historian William Henry Scott, for example, would have said *and* done -- on the entire collection of "insurrecto" papers in our National Library or on the mountain of people's documents in the National Archives. (I have had neither time nor budget.) And materials not accessible to me, like Record Groups 94, 350 and 395 in the U.S. National Archives, must surely yield nuggets of rich Pioista data. But then, my only purpose at this point is (to borrow a phrase from another scholar, U.P. Professor Rosario Mendoza Cortes),[3] to "break ground in an unplowed field", that is, of Philippine historiography and biography.

Breaking ground would have been impossible without all the existing and usable tools -- books, pamphlets, articles, manuscripts, scattered notes etc. -- the sources great and small that I have utilized and listed in the footnotes and *Bibliography* at the back of this little volume. Their authors all share in whatever merits this present work may earn, but I am answerable alone for its faults.

ORLINO A. OCHOSA
Marikina, 1995

---

[3] *In pioneering, Prof. Cortes has written three volumes on her father's home province which if collected would constitute one thick history book:* **Pangasinan 1572-1800**, **Pangasinan 1801-1900**, *and* **Pangasinan 1901-1986**, *all published by New Day Publishers.*

one

NATIVE OF CULI-CULI

PIO DEL PILAR did not belong to the famous, respectable Del Pilars of Bulacan, but there has been some historical confusion. Even Leon Wolff, whose views in **Little Brown Brother** are seldom found incorrect, asks his readers not to confuse Gregorio Del Pilar with "his infamous brother Pio".[1] The misconception is even worse in the works of earlier American writers: at least one famous photograph of Gregorio "Goyo" del Pilar on horseback has been wrongly captioned with Pio del Pilar's name[2] in at least two "official" accounts of the "Insurrection", as the Philippine-American War was once belittled by both colonial-minded Filipinos and their American colonizers. Even Samuel E. Kane, who was one of the *Yanquis* who fought and killed *Goyo*, the Boy General, at Tirad Pass, was as much confused. In his own memoirs, he wrote: "At Tila [sic] Pass, five thousand feet above sea level, we encountered General Pio del Pilar".[3] (Underscoring mine.)

The surname Del Pilar, it was said, was adopted by the father so as to protect himself and his family from persecution by the Spaniards, for sympathizing with *filibusteros*. But one wonders why, of all names, a dangerous name was chosen! Was the name-changing really made out of admiration for Plaridel (Marcelo II. Del Pilar)?

He was born Pio Isidro y Castañeda. The year was *1865*, according to his autobiography; *1860* according to the historical marker

---

[1]*Leon Wolff,* **Little Brown Brother** *(New York: Doubleday, 1961. Makati: Erehwon Press, 1971), pages 77 & 286. For Wolff's other references to Pio del Pilar in the same book, see also pages 134, 143, 151, 219, 224 and 248.*

[2]*See, for instance, full-page picture of General Gregorio H. del Pilar together with his Bulacan troops in José de Olivares and William S. Bryan (eds.),* **Our Islands and Their People** *(New York: N.D. Thompson Publishing Co., 1899), page 611. Note its caption which reads: "Gen. Pio del Pilar and his bodyguard". Again on page 657, full-page photo of Goyo is captioned "Gen. Pio del Pilar".*

[3]*Samuel E. Kane,* **Life or Death in Luzon** *(New York: Grosset and Dunlap, 1933). The Spaniards up to 1902 -- and the Igorots -- called the famous Ilocos Sur mountain pass "Tila".*

on his Makati statue.[4] The father was Isaac Isidro, a farmer of Makati who became *Teniente del Barrio* of Culi-Culi.[5] Pio's *mesticillo* features bore traces of the mother, a *mestiza* from the well-off Castañeda clan of Pasay. His mother did not have much schooling, though, and she made a living as a plain *bordadera.* Pio himself never had much schooling either; though he learned how to read and write and count, he never had a chance to go to any *colegio* to become an *ilustrado*. His father died when Pio was still in his early teens and he had to take over in running their farm. So, he laments in his **Biografia**: "I was not lucky enough to

---

[4]*The full text of the National Historical Committee inscription on Pio del Pilar's Makati statue marker reads thus:*

BORN ON JULY 11, 1860 IN CULI-CULI, MAKATI, RIZAL / AND NAMED PIO ISIDRO. A FARMER TURNED / REVOLUTIONARY AGAINST SPAIN, HE CHANGED / HIS SURNAME TO DEL PILAR TO PROTECT HIS / FAMILY FROM PERSECUTION. HE FOUNDED / THE KATIPUNAN CHAPTER "MAGTAGUMPAY" / AND LED A VICTORIOUS GROUP OF CAVITEÑOS AT THE BINAKAYAN BATTLE IN NOVEMBER 1896. / A GENERAL DURING THE FILIPINO-AMERICAN WAR IN 1898 HE FOUGHT AT GUADALUPE, MAKATI / BUT WAS LATER CAPTURED IN STA. ANA, MANILA [SIC] / THREE YEARS LATER. HE WAS EXILED TO GUAM. / HE DIED IN PASAY ON JUNE 21, 1931.

The statue used to stand on Ayala Avenue, until the Ayalas decided the site was more apt for Ninoy's martyr pose than Pio del Pilar's heroic "Avance!" stance (on new location, see footnote #13, Chapter 10). His birthplace was Culi-Culi, that part of Makati (called San Pedro Makati in the old days, when it was part of Manila), which until recent years had a low reputation as a whore district. Now the place had been renamed Pio del Pilar, *with a namesake elementary school on Libertad Street, but jeepney commuters have since simplified it as "Pio" -- which is, in fact, most apt because that was what Del Pilar's contemporaries, both friend and foe, called him in his heyday.*

[5]*Pio del Pilar y Castañeda,* **Biografia** *(Ms., Manila, 1929). This autobiographical account must have been written at the request of José P. Santos, to whom Del Pilar presented the manuscript. The "Ronquillo Collection" copy made available to me at the National Library seems to be incomplete. And Carlos Ronquillo himself leaves a note in Tagalog on the title page margin: "Marami sa mga talang ito ang hindi tama sa katotohanan." All quotes in English are my translations of Pio's Tagalog text.*

obtain any *titulo* from any school".[6]

But if Pio did not learn lessons from school, he learned a lot from life itself, and he learned well. At 17, he married Juliana Valeriano, a pretty lass from San Pedro Makati, of a middle-class family. The same year Juliana became his wife, Pio was conscripted (his own word was "naquintos") into the Spanish colonial army; he served in the ranks of *Batallon Primero*. An influential family friend, *Capitan* Lorenzo Protacio (who would years later become *pagador* in the Pio del Pilar Brigade), intervened in his favor, however, so that Pio's military service was soon terminated after only four months.

Pio was in his early twenties when elected *Teniente del Barrio* himself of Culi-Culi. Though poor, his *principalia* position enabled him to mix with local officials. One of these, Capitan Santiago Coronado of Mandaluyong, would become his *compadre*. It was Coronado, Pio recalls in his Biografia, who introduced him to *filibusterismo*. Del Pilar was at his compadre's house one day when who should come as a "mysterious guest" -- none other than the famous Dr. José Rizal himself! Was it when Rizal first came back to Manila in 1887 after publishing the **Noli**? Pio does not say so, only that it was from Rizal that he learned "the values of love of country and self-sacrifice". And Pio claims he helped distribute "Rizal's book" (was it the Noli?) to many friends who, in turn, passed it to their other friends. Among those he remembered helping him in this modest propaganda work were Isidoro Carmona, Valentin Esguerra and Lorenzo Protacio in Pasay; Urbano Carballo in San Pedro Makati; Lino Labao Taniag and Juan Natividad in Taguig -- all of whom would become associates of Pio del Pilar in the revolutionary army.

If his account is true, it is ironic that when the Filipinos would finally become politically conscious and began to organize, first in the reformist *La Liga Filipina* and later in the separatist Katipunan, in the early 1890s, Pio del Pilar would be left behind unaffiliated. It is even more ironic that in the inevitable witch-hunts, the non-affiliate would be among the unfortunate victims of *Guardia Civil* (police) brutality!

Though he no longer recalled the exact date, Pio would never forget the year -- 1895, when the Katipunan was still secret -- the Civil Guards tortured him for being a rebel. Was he taken for a relative of the filibustero Marcelo H. del Pilar? In any case, the Del Pilar name

---

[6]**Ibid**, *page 2. Data used for the rest of this Chapter are all taken from Pio's* **Biografia**, *pages 1-9.*

had gotten Pio into serious trouble: two *guardias* from Santa Ana whose names Pio never forgot -- Lorenzo Soliman and Tomas Reyes -- appeared at his house in Culi-Culi one Thursday afternoon, tied him elbow-to-elbow, and then dragged him into the woods in the direction of Santa Ana. On a brookside where there were no houses around, writes Pio, the Civil Guards demanded

> *that I give the names of the "rebels" in my barrio,*
> *that I should know them because I was the headman,*
> *that I bring out the documents and rosters of all the people under my command,*
> *that if I told them the truth they will see to it that I will not be harmed,*
> *that the government will even reward me for what I will inform them.*

But Pio del Pilar's Biografia says he confessed nothing; he denounced no friend. He was given two-fisted blows, then slapped, then hit with gun butts, then kicked, then plunged into a dung-filled carabao mudhole. Finally, the guardias tried to soften him with the dreaded "bamboo cure". Still, the man never softened -- and in exasperation his tormentors decided to drag him back to their headquarters in Santa Ana.

The Corporal of the Guards in Santa Ana was *Cabo* Leoncio Cayetano. The man immediately recognized the prisoner as the son of his late friend Isaac Isidro. Seeing how the two guardias had badly manhandled his old friend's son, "Cabo Tano", as Pio Del Pilar would affectionately call him, angrily scolded his subordinates, ordered them to untie their prisoner, and to make him comfortably seated on a chair. Then Cabo Tano himself brought the case to the Captain of the Civil Guards, *Señor* Alejandro Andrade. Through Cabo Tano's explanations and, later, by those of civil officials of Santa Ana and San Pedro Makati -- who all vouched for Del Pilar's good standing as a citizen -- Captain Andrade was persuaded to order Pio's release and that full medical attention be given to him. As for his erstwhile tormentors, Pio later learned that they became *castigados* -- that is, they were transferred to infantry service and sent to fight the Moros in Jolo.

Meanwhile, Pio del Pilar, punished for being a rebel, which he was not, had resolved to become a true *rebel*, which he later became in all senses of the word.

two

LAST-HOUR KATIPUNERO

ANDRES BONIFACIO headed the "revolutionary clique" of Philippine Masonry that seceded from Rizal's *La Liga Filipina* and founded the Katipunan *(Kataastaasang Kagalang-galang Katipunan ng Mga Anak ng Bayan -- Highest & Noblest Brotherhood of the Sons of the People*, also known as the KKK) in Tondo on 7 July 1892. To this group belonged such patriots as Deodato Arellano, Teodoro Plata, Valentin Diaz, Ladislao Diwa, José Dizon, Feliciano Jocson and others.

In this group of working class heroes, Pio del Pilar was never "in" with this intimate circle of Andres Bonifacio.[1] Why? First, Pio was not a Tondo boy, unlike Emilio Jacinto or Macario Sakay who were "disciples" of the Supremo: Pio was *Batang Makati*. Second, he was not an "original" *Katipunero*, unlike Francisco Carreon or Guillermo Masangkay (circa 1892): Pio was not a member of the KKK until only a few months before the Revolution began (so he was really

---

[1]*In 1892, Andres Bonifacio founded the Katipunan in Tondo together with his revolutionary faction of Rizal's* La Liga Filipina. *Tondo being the* centro *of both Liga and Katipunan activities, its* **Katagalugan** *council automatically (and theoretically) functioned as the secret brotherhood's Supreme Council, and it was the parent that gave birth to the other* **Sanggunians** *such as: "Dapitan" (Trozo), "Taga-Ilog" (Binondo), "Laong Laan" (Santa Cruz), "Karitas" (Novaliches), "Kasilawan" (Santa Ana), "Magbañgon" (Paco), "Magtagumpay" (Culi-Culi), "Uliran" (Malolos), "Magdiwang" (Noveleta), "Magdalo" (Kawit). For the pre-Revolution activities of Bonifacio and the Katipunan, see especially* **Minutes of the Katipunan** *(Manila: National Historical Institute, 1978) and John R.M. Taylor,* **The Philippine Insurrection Against the United States** *(Pasay City: Eugenio Lopez Foundation, 1971-1975), Volume 1, Exhibit 9 to 13, pages 188-255.*

I translate Katipunan *as* Brotherhood *not because I wish to emphasize the sex of the membership but because I feel that this is closest to the raison d'etre and the nature of the rites of the Katipunan.*

innocent when arrested and tortured in 1895).

By his own recollection, Del Pilar was sworn into the secret brotherhood of the "Sons of the People" sometime in May 1896. In accordance with the brotherhood's recruitment policy, he and two "brothers" from Culi-Culi had to be initiated first into the *Kasilawan* popular council of Santa Ana, whose chapter president was Telesforo Calasanz. From then on, the brothers knew Pio del Pilar by the symbolic Katipunan name *Pang-Una* (Leader).[2]

Through the triangle-cell formed by Pang-Una and his two companions, the mother council of Santa Ana soon gave birth to an offspring in Del Pilar's own Makati district of Culi-Culi: this was the *Magtagumpay* Council. This time Del Pilar remembers the full date as 28 May 1896 and Pang-Una himself was elected Secretary of the Magtagumpay section of Kasilawan.

Two weeks after the Culi-Culi chapter of the Katipunan was formed, according to Del Pilar, Supremo Andres Bonifacio personally inducted its officers in a solemn ceremony held under the auspices of the Kasilawan Council of Santa Ana. This occasion, says Del Pilar, was the very first time he came face-to-face and became acquainted with the Supremo of the Katipunan. What did he think of Bonifacio? Pio's autobiography does not tell us.

In compliance with an order of the Supremo that each section of the Katipunan create its own unit flag, new Katipuneros in Culi-Culi were initiated into the brotherhood under the Magtagumpay banner designed by Del Pilar himself (or was it really by his bordadera mother?). The flag looked like the one on the back cover.[3]

Of all the known KKK unit flags, including Llanera's *bungo* in Nueva Ecija and Goyo del Pilar's *tres colores* in Bulacan, the Magtagumpay banner was perhaps the most symbolic. This flag alone graphically captured the very Katipunan ideals and values preached by both Bonifacio and Jacinto in their writings. (Did this mean that Del Pilar had captured the spirit of the Revolution more successfully than the other leaders except the founder of the Katipunan and the brains of

---

[2]*Pio del Pilar,* **Biografia**, *page 12. It became more symbolic as the Revolution went on, for he proved to be an extraordinary leader. "Leader of the ladrones"? He was a good leader nevertheless.*

[3]*The reproduction is based on the design found in Domingo Abella's* **The Flag of Our Fathers** *(Manila: Milagros Romualdez Abella, 1977), page 61.*

the Revolution?) From Del Pilar's own explanations of the symbols of this war flag, we learn that the dominant *red* -- the standard Katipunan color -- stood for the blood that the "Sons of the People" were always ready to shed for the *Lupang Tinubuan*. *White* stood for the sacredness of their ideals and the spirit of brotherhood that united all the *kapatids* of the Katipunan. The *three Ks* stood for the major islands Luzon, Visayas and Mindanao (as all of them were considered "Katagalugan" or "Tagalogs", in Bonifacio's and Jacinto's concept word) -- aside, of course, from being the initials of the brotherhood -- and the *triangle* enclosing them symbolized the national solidarity of all Filipinos. The mountain inside the triangle stood for the ramparts of the armed struggle, and the rays of the rising sun stood for the *Liwanag* that would guide the Katipuneros onto the "true path to *Kalayaan*".[4]

It was Pio del Pilar who, as Secretary of the Magtagumpay council of Culi-Culi, received the Supremo's orders for the mass attack on San Juan del Monte on 29 August 1896. Accordingly, Pang-Una summoned the menfolk of Culi-Culi and was able to gather a thousand of them -- "while the womenfolk feverishly prayed the Holy Rosary" (his words).[5] Not one of the men of Magtagumpay carried a single gun; they only had bolos, spears and any such instruments they could use for fighting. Thus armed, the would-be fighters marched according to instructions from the Supremo to the English Cemetery in Makati, where they joined forces with the men of Kasilawan from Santa Ana.

Telesforo Calasanz was elected overall leader of both the Kasilawan and Magtagumpay groups. At the English Cemetery, they were to wait for the brothers who would come from Morong, after which they would attack San Juan del Monte as one force. In his **Biografia**, Del Pilar narrates their long wait:[6]

> *From 8 o'clock that night to 3:30 at dawn we waited at the designated place, but those who were to come from Morong never arrived, so our appointed leader Telesforo Calasanz decided to order us to return*

---

[4]*Teodoro A. Agoncillo,* **Revolt of the Masses: The Story of Andres Bonifacio and the Katipunan** *(Quezon City: U.P. Press, 1956), page 57, as he quotes Emmanuel Baja from his* **Our Country's Flag and Anthem** *(Manila: Juan Fajardo Press, 1928).*

[5]*Pio del Pilar,* **Biografia**, *page 15.*

[6]**Ibid.**

> *to our respective homes. But four of us [Calasanz, Del Pilar and two others] agreed to go on and look for the Supremo at Hagdang-Bato (Sangguniang Makabuhay). ... It was 5 in the morning when we reached Buhangin in Mandaloyon [Mandaluyong] and we found the townsfolk in chaos as the sound of battle was heard already raging at the Deposito [Waterworks] in San Juan del Monte.*

In the confusion, Telesforo Calasanz was separated from his companions who, on their part, found themselves among Katipuneros from Novaliches led by Apolonio Samson (the Bonifacista whom the Americans would hunt as a "bandit" later in the 1900s).[7] Del Pilar joined this group in the retreat to the jungles of San Francisco del Monte (in what is now Quezon City). There he found the Supremo who ordered him to go back to Culi-Culi, gather the men again, and this time bring them to the camp of Licerio Geronimo at Puray, in the hills of Montalban, where the Supremo planned to concentrate all Katipunan forces. So, Pang-Una hurried back home. But before the Magtagumpay fighters could go to Puray, Del Pilar claims in his Biografia they were

---

[7] *It was Apolonio Samson's yard in Kangkong where Bonifacio's Katipuneros together first resolved to rise in revolt. As one of the KKK Generals elected in the assembly at Balara, Samson later accompanied the Supremo to Cavite late in 1896, and was among those who were arrested and charged with sedition together with the Bonifacio brothers in 1897. Though he did not meet the fate of the Bonifacios, he dropped out of the Aguinaldo-led struggle just the same, never to emerge again until 1902 -- after Malvar's surrender -- as one of the commanders in the "bandit" army of General Luciano San Miguel. In "bandit" history, Apolonio Samson (in Constabulary records, his surname is misspelled* Sampson*) was the "terror of Novaliches" whose guerrilla raids extended to the Diliman-Caloocan area in Rizal and the San José-Norzagaray area in Bulacan. A busy street in Caloocan commemorates this plebeian hero's name -- as the 1896 Katipunero, not as the outlaw terror of the 1900s. See "Memoirs of Dr. Pio Valenzuela" in* **Minutes of the Katipunan**, *page 100; Encarnacion Alzona (ed.),* **Julio Nakpil and the Philippine Revolution** *(Manila: Carmelo and Bauermann, 1964); Artemio Ricarte,* **Memoirs** *(Manila: National Heroes Commission, 1963), pages 49, 85; and* **Reports of the Philippine Commission**, *1903 (pages 54-55) and 1904 (page 68).*

summoned by the Magdalo provincial council of Cavite headed by the Aguinaldos to report instead at Bacoor.[8]

When Andres Bonifacio came to Cavite in December, three months later, the Supremo was certainly surprised -- and perhaps dismayed -- to find Pio del Pilar *Pang-Una* among Caviteños as one of the leading figures in the victorious army of Magdalo.

---

[8]*Pio del Pilar,* **Biografia**, *page 21. (See also Kasandugo (pseud.),* **Ang Katipunan at si Gat Andres Bonifacio** *(Typescript, not dated, in the National Library).*

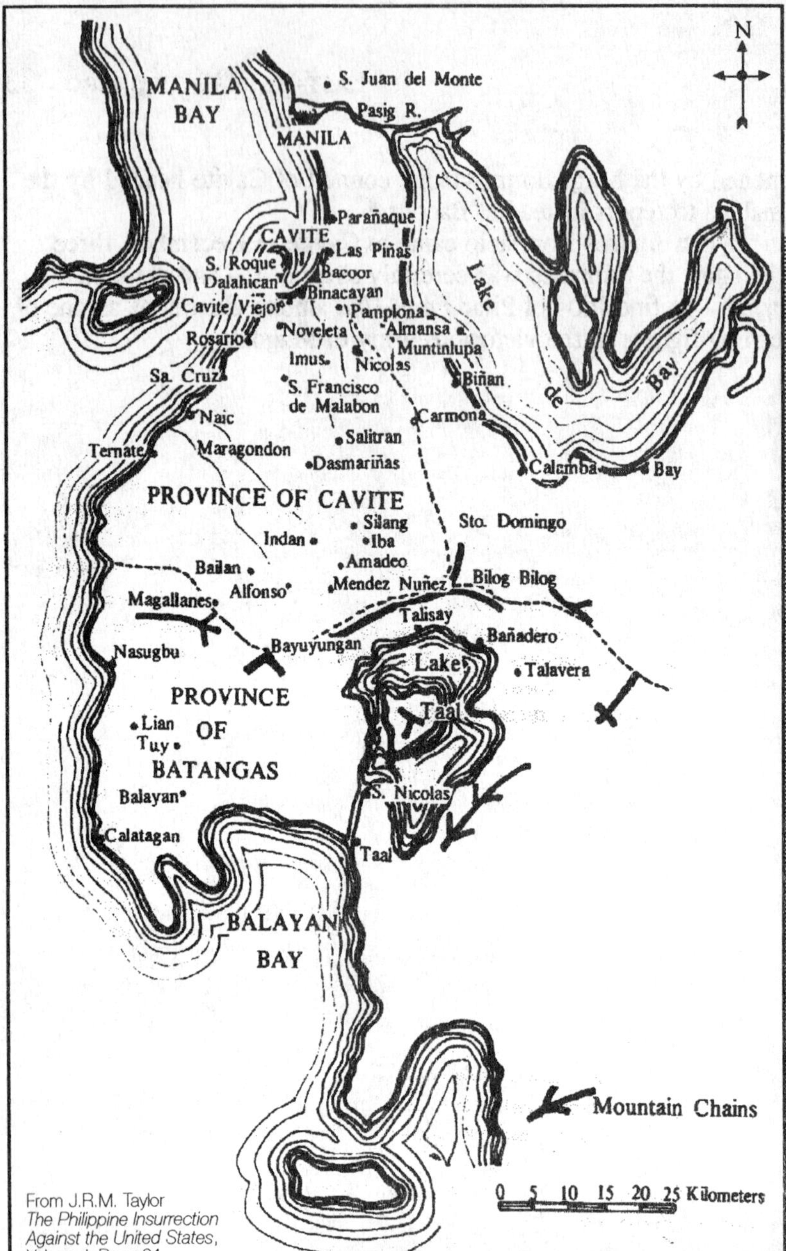

From J.R.M. Taylor
The Philippine Insurrection Against the United States,
Volume I, Page 64.

MAGTAGUMPAY VICTORIES

Pio del Pilar and his *Magtagumpay* fighters from Makati fought so well in the Cavite-Batangas battles of 1896-1897 that they were beloved by the regionalistic Caviteños.

three

GENERAL OF MAGDALO

IT IS EASY TO EXPLAIN why Pio del Pilar, among Manileños in Cavite, would be accorded so much respect in a province afflicted with regionalism. He had been among the first to go to Cavite, and not as just one more *refugee* from Manila -- not another *alsa balutan* as Bonifacio himself had been pejoratively labelled, not another one running away from his troubles.

Del Pilar was one of only three important Manileños (the two others were Edilberto Evangelista the engineer and Flaviano Yengko the student)[1] who had gone over to give succor to the Caviteños when their own part of the larger struggle had only just begun, not when victory was already theirs. The key word here is *succor* -- which is what *magdalo* signifies -- the very creed by which Emilio Aguinaldo's group of Cavite Katipuneros claimed guidance. The Magdalo fighters

---

[1]*The Magdalo heroes Edilberto Evangelista (1862-1897) and Flaviano Yengko (1873-1897) were both ilustrados. Evangelista was recently graduated as a civil engineer from the University of Ghent in Belgium and just arrived in Manila when he decided to cross over to Cavite to join Aguinaldo's Magdalo* revolucionarios. *He rose to the rank of Lieutenant-General and would have been elected President of the Revolutionary Government at Aguinaldo's own motion, historians claim, had he not fallen at the Battle of Zapote River on 17 February 1897. Flaviano Yengko was a 24-yeur old BA graduate of Letran, holder of a teacher's diploma from Escuela Normal, and a law student at Santo Tomas when he joined the Revolution -- and, according to General José Alejandrino, a dandy who "joined the roughest combats, neatly dressed and even perfumed". He was already a Brigadier-General of Magdalo when he fell at the Battle of Perez Dasmariñas on 3 March 1897. (See José Alejandrino,* **The Price of Freedom** *(Manila: M. Colcol Press, 1949), pages 15-19 and 27-28; Gregorio F. Zaide,* **Great Filipinos in History** *(Manila: Verde Book Store, 1970), pages 167-173 and 633-637; and Hector Villaroel et al.,* **Eminent Filipinos** *(Manila: National Historical Commission, 1965), pages 99-100 and 288-289.*

recognized these acts and reciprocated them by giving Evangelista, Yengko and Del Pilar responsible positions in their council -- on equal footing with such prominent native sons as Tomas Mascardo, Vito Belarmino, Pantaleon Garcia, Mariano Noriel, Daniel Tirona and Marcelino Aure.

In the rival Magdiwang provincial council of Cavite headed by the Alvarezes, the Ilocano Artemio Ricarte *Vibora* was among its generals. In his memoirs written in prison in 1904, Ricarte puts Pio del Pilar in the list of lower echelon leaders of the Magdalo army in 1896.[2] But Aguinaldo himself, writing his reminiscences of the Revolution 65 years later, regards Pio as one of his trusted commanders. Aguinaldo recalls with fondness and pride the many glorious campaigns he shared with his "Beloved General" from Makati.[3]

The fond affection was not without reason. Pio del Pilar and his Magtagumpay bolomen had scarcely arrived in Cavite when Aguinaldo ordered them to join the Magdalo rebels in attacking the Spanish outpost in Almanza, southeast of Las Piñas. If this baptism of fire was Aguinaldo's test for the men from Makati, then they passed that test with flying colors, so to speak. The attack had been successful, Del Pilar and his men captured their first rifles, and the Magdalo army was afforded the chance to construct a long line of "Evangelista trenches" in that strategic area.[4]

On 3 October 1896, Aguinaldo attacked in three columns and besieged the headquarters of Spanish Regiment No. 72 in the Batangas border town of Talisay. "The fourth column led by General Pio del Pilar", writes Aguinaldo in his memoirs, "waited in ambush in the outskirts of the town ... in case reinforcements came from the [Spanish] Rios Brigade in Tanauan".[5] On the second day of the siege, the expected enemy reinforcements from Tanauan, Batangas came. On this occasion Del Pilar's men did a fine guerrilla job, ambushing the enemy

---

[2]*Ricarte,* **Memoirs**, *page 14.*

[3]*Emilio Aguinaldo,* **Mga Gunita ng Himagsikan** *(Manila: Cristina Aguinaldo Suntay, 1964). (Subsequent quotes in English are my translations.) For Aguinaldo's fond recollections of Pio del Pilar, see especially pages 104, 108, 112, 113, 124, 137, 149, 163 and 174.*

[4]*Aguinaldo,* **Gunita**, *page 108.*

[5]**Ibid.**, *page 112.*

column and almost annihilating the enemy troops, capturing their guns. On the third day, a stronger force from Tanauan arrived. But again, Aguinaldo fondly recalls, "they walked straight into the new trap I had ordered General Pio del Pilar to set and once more the enemy received a merciless blow".[6] Again, Pio del Pilar was the hero of the day. Again, the Spanish forces and their mercenaries ran away from the Indio General and his fighters from Makati. Among the countless casualties suffered by the enemy in this battle was the intrepid (but misoriented) mestizo from Pampanga, Captain Eugenio Blanco, whose fellow Macabebes he commanded as mercenaries[7] in the Spanish Army.

Early in November, Aguinaldo attacked the detachment of *cazadores* (Spanish infantry) then stationed at Bañadero, near Tanauan. "I brought along my two seasoned Generals, Candido Tirona and Pio del Pilar", the Old Warrior of Kawit recalls. And Aguinaldo again had his "two seasoned Generals" by his side at the famous Battle of Binakayan on 10 November 1896: "On the left or western flank I placed the column of General Candido Tria Tirona; and on the right or eastern flank, the column of General Pio del Pilar", writes Aguinaldo.[8]

Aguinaldo lost Candido Tirona at Binakayan. But he still had his Pio del Pilar. Together they attacked and occupied the lakeshore Morong towns of Muntinglupa, Taguig and Pateros during the first week of January 1897. This time, according to Aguinaldo, Pio miscalculated: his commando style of fighting did not work out well. So, in the afternoon of 3 January, it was his men's turn to be chased by a swarm of cazadores and Civil Guards who had crossed the lake from Laguna and landed at Napindan.[9]

Pio del Pilar's greatest battle was, perhaps, the defense of Bacoor on 16 February 1897. Here he was in command of the rebel advance lines together with Colonels Mariano Noriel and Agapito Bonzon. The defense of Bacoor was a joint effort of the Magdalo and Magdiwang forces, and among its defenders were Andres Bonifacio's personal troops from Tondo and Balara under General Lucino de la Cruz. Although the rebels suffered heavy losses, particularly at Zapote

---

[6]**Ibid.**, *page 113.*

[7]*Reader, remember the Macabebes!*

[8]**Ibid.**, *page 127.*

[9]**Ibid.**, *pages 147-149.*

Bridge where the ilustrado-engineer General Edilberto Evangelista died in action, the Filipinos never abandoned their trenches. Finally, General Pio del Pilar led his Magtagumpay troops in a brilliant flanking action, hacking and firing their way into the very lines of the enemy and engaging the Spaniards in what was probably the fiercest running fight ever recorded in the history of the "first war".[10] And that night -- almost all night -- Aguinaldo and his Pio del Pilar stayed awake deliberating on their next moves.[11]

If Aguinaldo was all praise for his favorite Manileño, Ricarte was not so impressed. The Vibora blames Pio for the defeat at San Francisco de Malabon, capital of the rival Magdiwang army to which Ricarte belonged, when Bonifacio's group defended the town during the first week of April 1897. Ricarte writes in his memoirs:[12]

> *General Pio del Pilar, with a large body of [his] men, supported by a small body of men from Imus under the command of a Major, went to the defense of San Francisco de Malabon, but before the struggle began, they departed without warning those who were [posted] in Tarique. As a result, the Spaniards seized the town and burned several houses therein ...*

And yet, Pio del Pilar was the very man whom Bonifacio would want to install as Commanding General of the rebel forces after the Supremo's downfall at the assembly in Tejeros![13]

---

[10]**Ibid.**, *pages 163-172; Ricarte,* **Memoirs**, *page 33. When Pio del Pilar was good, he was the best!*

[11]*Aguinaldo,* **Gunita**, *page 172.*

[12]*Artemio Ricarte,* **Memoirs**, *page 44. Santiago Alvarez corroborates this in his own memoirs,* **The Katipunan and the Revolution** *(Quezon City: Ateneo University Press, 1992), page 89: "Gen. Pio del Pilar and his troops, along with a small detachment from Imus, came to help in the defense of San Francisco de Malabon, but for some unknown reason he withdrew even before the enemy could attack. He made his withdrawal without notifying those inside the [rebel] fort."*

[13]*When Pio del Pilar was bad, he was very bad?*

four

THE RELUCTANT GENERALISSIMO

WAS IT GENUINE ADMIRATION for the man -- or was it really to sow intrigue and dissension in Cavite -- that led the Supremo of the Katipunan to choose Pio del Pilar to lead the "contra-revolucionario" forces after Bonifacio lost to Aguinaldo at Tejeros?[1]

Andres Bonifacio, who never won any battle in Manila, never won any battle in Cavite either. And while Bonifacio led the Magdiwang (which, at first, took his side as Supremo and allied itself with the Tondo-based Katipunan Supreme Council or the "Haring Bayang Katagalugan") into a series of defeats, Aguinaldo and his Magdalo troops (including Pio and his Magtagumpay fighters) scored victory after victory -- in their own Cavite territories, in Batangas, and even in the very suburbs of Manila where Bonifacio had once stood helpless.

The choice of Aguinaldo over Bonifacio as head of the Revolution in the assembly of patriots at Tejeros in March 1897 was therefore inevitable. And whether Daniel Tirona[2] insulted Bonifacio or

---

[1] *On the Tejeros Convention, see José Alejandrino,* **Price of Freedom,** *pages 47-55. (See also Epifanio de los Santos,* **The Revolutionists: Aguinaldo, Bonifacio and Jacinto** *(Manila: National Historical Commission, 1975), pages 10 and 120-124; Gregorio F. Zaide,* **The Philippine Revolution** *(Manila: Modern Book Company, 1954), pages 146-147; Carlos Quirino,* **The Young Aguinaldo** *(Manila: Regal Printing Co., 1969); and Agoncillo,* **Revolt of the Masses,** *pages 232-235 and 298-299.*

[2] *Daniel Tirona, one of Bonifacio's first Caviteño recruits in the Katipunan, was a brother of the hero General Candido Tirona (1866-1896) who fell while fighting alongside Aguinaldo and Pio del Pilar at the Battle of Binakayan. Standard histories of the Revolution point to Daniel Tirona as having started all the trouble in Tejeros (and before) when he questioned the election of Andres Bonifacio as Secretary of Interior on the ground that the post required someone who was university-educated -- a slur on the character of the self-taught Supremo. Later in the Philippine-American War, as*

not, the split with the Supremo -- or between "pro-*Republicanos*" (Magdalo-Magdiwang Caviteños) and "true Katipuneros" (Katagalugan Manileños) -- was just as predictable.

General Pantaleon Garcia,[3] a Magdalo adherent, who later played a principal role in the court martial of the Bonifacio brothers, sums up in his own memoirs the Supremo's reaction and course of action after the mess in Tejeros.[4]

> *In desperation Andres Bonifacio decided to completely break away from the newly acclaimed [Republicano] leadership. Andres Bonifacio talked to General Pio del Pilar and offered to make him Generalissimo or overall commander of the revolutionary army which was accepted [by Del Pilar].*

Commanding General of the Filipino forces in the Cagayan Valley, Tirona shamed his family's name, defamed his fellow Caviteños, and riled Aguinaldo himself (who was hurrying up to join him somewhere in Isabela) by surrendering to the Americans without firing a single shot. For Tirona's trouble-making role in Tejeros, see Ricarte, **Memoirs**, *pages 39-40; and Alvarez,* **The Katipunan**, *pages 85-86. For his heart-breaking Cagayan surrender, see Simeon A. Villa,* **Aguinaldo's Odyssey: As Told in the Diaries of Col. Simeon Villa and Dr. Santiago Barcelona** *(Manila: Bureau of Public Libraries, 1963; with annotations and Introduction by Carlos Quirino), pages 27-28.*

[3]*This handsome, mustachioed, Spanish-looking mestizo from Imus was a schoolteacher when he joined Aguinaldo's Magdalo Army. He later accompanied Aguinaldo in the retreat to Biyak-na-Bato and, still later, in exile to Hongkong. In the siege of and attack on Manila in 1898 he commanded the Filipino Fourth Zone, the same territory he defended and lost to the Americans in the early battles of the Philippine-American War. He was for a while chief of staff of Aguinaldo's* Republicano *Army up to the time he was relieved by General Venancio Concepcion shortly before Aguinaldo fled to the North. Garcia was Commanding General of all guerrilla forces in Central Luzon when he was captured in Jaen, Nueva Ecija on 4 May 1900. For his role in the "first war", see his* **Maikling Ulat ng Himagsikan** *(Manila: José Paez Santos, 1930). For his part in the "second war" and in the Philippine-American War, see Taylor,* **Philippine Insurrection**, *Volume 2, passim.*

[4]*Garcia,* **Maikling Ulat**, *portions of which are reproduced as Appendix E in Agoncillo,* **Revolt of the Masses**, *pages 393-398.*

> *Nobody knows why, when this [agreement] was about to be carried out, General Pio del Pilar changed heart. He went to General Emilio Aguinaldo and denounced the plot of Andres Bonifacio ...*

Andres Bonifacio's apparent "Save-the-Katipunan" plan had been well evidenced by the so-called Naik Agreement in which 44 signers including Pio del Pilar himself agreed first of all: "All the combatants, by means of persuasion or force, will be organized into an army corps and placed under the command of General Pio del Pilar".[5]

Aguinaldo, when all the protagonists but himself were dead, would claim he caught the plotters in the act; and he would recount his shock at seeing "my two Beloved Generals" -- Pio del Pilar and Mariano Noriel -- in league with the "contra-revolucionario" Bonifacio. General Pio del Pilar would himself admit to Aguinaldo, the latter writes, that he had been induced to switch loyalty by means of anonymous letters (*carta anonima*) shown him by the Supremo.[6] Unfortunately, this can not be supported by Pio's own **Biografia**, as the existing manuscript ends after Pio and his men crossed to Cavite in 1896.

Whatever really motivated the Naik Council of War that gave birth to the Naik Agreement, General José Alejandrino in his own memoirs can not see any good in it. Alejandrino thinks Del Pilar's appointment as Generalissimo was "the most tactless and unwise action that could have been taken in those critical days when Andres Bonifacio and Emilio Aguinaldo were the only leaders who enjoyed sufficient prestige to make all the other chiefs submit to their authority". And he concludes with an analogy in the next war with the Americans.[7]

> *The appointment of Pio del Pilar without doubt would have caused insubordination and indiscipline in our ranks. A similar case occurred when [in 1899] General Luna was appointed Chief of Operations at*

---

[5]*See full text in Alejandrino,* **Price of Freedom**, *pages 53-54; De Los Santos,* **The Revolutionists**, *pages 122-123; Ricarte,* **Memoirs**, *Appendix C, page 99; and Agoncillo,* **Revolt of the Masses**, *pages 231-232.*

[6]*Aguinaldo,* **Gunita**, *page 201.*

[7]*Alejandrino,* **Price of Freedom**, *page 54.*

> *Caloocan, and very few of the other generals wanted to submit themselves to his command as to recognize his authority, despite [imminent danger to life and limb due to] the presence of the enemy [i.e., the Americans] before them.*

Maybe so, but Pio del Pilar in Cavite, unlike Luna in Caloocan, was at least a battle hero who enjoyed considerable prestige among his fellow Magdalo fighters, if not in the whole of Cavite, including the territories of Magdiwang. What Alejandrino probably means is that the leaders of Magdiwang -- the Alvarezes, the Villanuevas, the Mojicas, the Nocons -- would certainly have begrudged in their hearts having to take orders from a Magdalo man *who was not even a Caviteño*. At any rate, Del Pilar had sense enough to "change heart" and reject Bonifacio's plan.

Most historians have made Pio del Pilar a scapegoat in their efforts to lessen the guilt of either Bonifacio or Aguinaldo in the internecine intramurals within the revolutionary ranks. Gregorio Zaide, in his **The Philippine Revolution**, comments that "for some reason or another, General Pio del Pilar, instead of accepting Bonifacio's offer to command the revolutionary forces, went to Aguinaldo and revealed Bonifacio's plan" -- without any explanation why Pio should be doing that. [8] Teodoro Agoncillo, too, in his **The Revolt of the Masses**, is unfair to Del Pilar when he describes him as "originally a Bonifacio man" and when he includes him among the "admirers of the Supremo ... [who] turned against him".[9]

The gravest mistake of all is to call him a Bonifacio *disloyal* -- because Pio del Pilar, though a Manileño, was never a Bonifacista (and he probably never even admired Bonifacio more than he admired Rizal). There could have been only one reason why Pio acted the way he did, and that reason was obvious enough. From the day he crossed over to Cavite in 1896, Pio was a Magdalo, a very staunch one, and he had merely defended Magdalo interest by choosing not to accept Bonifacio's offer. By doing so he saved himself, he saved his Magdalo

---

[8]*Zaide,* **Philippine Revolution***, page 147.*

[9]*Agoncillo,* **Revolt of the Masses***, pages 298, 302.*

friends, and, though he may not have realized it, *he saved the Revolution*. What more could one man have done?

Perhaps, too, Pio del Pilar came to realize he was not really qualified for such a grand enterprise. Perhaps he saw through the subtleties of the Supremo's schemes. Whatever his true reasons, or intentions, were, Del Pilar went up to his Magdalo chief, revealed the "seditious" plans of Magdiwang (or Bonifacio's?), washed his hands off any part of it, and himself cried for the blood of the Supremo.[10] The rest, as we already know, led to the regrettable incident at Limbon -- and to the sadder end of the Bonifacio brothers at Maragundon, where they were both executed.

Those were, indeed, troubled times. It was so for Bonifacio's orphaned "true Katipuneros" struggling for survival -- against both comrade and foe -- away from their native Tondo and Balara, as it was for the Caviteño Republicano factions now fighting as one for their own Cavite. Not only was the Revolution being internally devoured by its own children squabbling for leadership but was also being threatened, from without, by an angry *Madre España* who vowed to crush it. And though he won that battle for leadership of the Revolution, Aguinaldo lost the war in Cavite. Now it was his turn to abandon his home territory: in reverse, he crossed over from Cavite to the dead Supremo's domain.

And it was the Magdalo *brother* from Culi-Culi who escorted the warlord of Cavite in his flight through the mountains of Talisay and Tagaytay -- then to Malapad-na-Bato, then to Puray -- and, finally, to Biyak-na-Bato.[11]

---

[10] *For Aguinaldo's version, see his* **Gunita**, *page 226.*

[11] *Ricarte,* **Memoirs**, *pages 52-53; and Aguinaldo,* **Gunita**, *pages 235-242.*

PIO'S "MI PRESIDENTE"
Emilio Aguinaldo *Magdalo* poses for this 1897 photograph taken at Biyak-na-Bato, seat of his "republic" after the death of the KKK Supremo.

five

HATCHETMAN? HIGHWAYMAN?

FIVE REBEL GENERALS ACCOMPANIED Aguinaldo in his strategic retreat to the North in June 1897.[1] Four were his *comprovincianos* from Cavite: Baldomero Aguinaldo, Vito Belarmino, Pantaleon Garcia and Mariano Noriel. The fifth was Pio del Pilar himself -- the "beloved" Manileño, the ever trusty Pang-Una.

It was Pio del Pilar's assigned job as chief security officer to determine and clear the areas through which the Generalissimo and his small retinue would pass. In this work he had the good sense to use as guides a few former followers of the fallen Supremo, among them the young Tondo revolutionary Arsenio Mauricio (who would later become one of the leading Pioista commanders).[2]

Aguinaldo recalls having had high fever while they were at Malapad-na-Bato (what is now Fort Bonifacio). "But General Pio del Pilar", says Aguinaldo of his favorite Manileño, "insisted that he bring me to a shack on the road near the [Pasig] river which we were to cross".[3] Undetected by the Spanish sentries, they all arrived safely at Licerio Geronimo's rebel camp in Puray.

Earlier, to this same camp the Supremo had ordered Pio del Pilar to bring the men of Culi-Culi in 1896, after the rout in San Juan, but instead, he and his Magtagumpay Katipuneros crossed over to Cavite and joined Aguinaldo. Now, almost a year after, he had brought to Puray not just himself and his men but even the new leader of the

---

[1]*Aguinaldo,* **Gunita**, *page 236.*

[2]*Both Ricarte (***Memoirs**, *page 31) and Alvarez (***The Katipunan**, *pages 76-77) mention Mauricio as a veteran of the 1897 Cavite-Batangas campaigns, leading mixed troops from Manila and Bulacan that fought under Magdiwang. And Ricarte (***ibid.**, *page 49) cites him again -- along with Francisco Carreon, Apolonio Samson, Alejandro Santiago and Antonino Guevarra -- as among Bonifacistas arrested with their Supremo in Limbon (Indang, Cavite).*

[3]*Aguinaldo,* **Gunita**, *page 241.*

Revolution. Going there in 1896, the unseasoned Pio del Pilar would have been, at best, one of Geronimo's subordinates. Arriving there in 1897 as a veteran of the Cavite campaign, "Heneral Pio" was the co-equal of "Heneral Serio". And at Puray on 14 June, these two unschooled (but skilled) Indio Generals commanded side-by-side to face three Spanish commanders leading separate columns -- and almost massacred one of the columns, led by Lieutenant-Colonel Dujiols.[4]

It was also in Puray where Manileños led by Feliciano Jocson organized the so-called Departmental Government of Central Luzon, including the provinces of Laguna and Morong.[5] The Bonifacista Julio Nakpil writes that although he was not present in Puray (he was then in Laguna with Emilio Jacinto), this departmental government named him one of its ministers. Nakpil claims he declined; instead, true to his Supremo, he advocated continuance of the Katipunan. Says Nakpil in his memoirs: "Señor Aguinaldo took this ill and without any further explanation ordered ... Pio del Pilar to assassinate me". Nakpil is quick to add, however, that "Pio del Pilar did not obey such orders, for he

---

[4]**Ibid.**, *page 242; and Ricarte,* **Memoirs**, *page 53. Says Ricarte of the Battle of Puray: "As a result of this triumph, the name of Licerio Geronimo, who was promoted to Lieutenant-General of the Army, was heard everywhere." See also Teodoro A. Agoncillo,* **Malolos: The Crisis of the Republic** *(Quezon City: U.P. Press, 1960), pages 7-8.*

[5]*The guerrilla padre, Pedro Dandan y Masangkay, was elected President of this regional government, with Jocson himself as one of the Secretaries. De Los Santos (***The Revolutionists**, *pages 11-12) gives the full list of officials elected in Puray: Padre Pedro Dandan (Cavite), President; Dr. Anastacio Francisco (Manila), Vice-President; Paciano Rizal (Laguna), Secretary of the Treasury; Cipriano Pacheco (Morong), Secretary of War; Teodoro Gonzales (Morong), Secretary of Interior; and Feliciano Jocson (Manila), Secretary of Welfare. Mamerto Natividad Jr. and Mariano Llanera, both representing Nueva Ecija, commanded its armed forces as Lieutenant-Generals; and under them were such other Generals as Licerio Geronimo (Morong), Isidoro Torres (Bulacan), Salvador Natividad (Nueva Ecija) and Francisco Makabulos (Tarlac). The Departmental Government of Central Luzon covered the same territory where Bonifacio in April 1897, as Supremo, assigned Emilio Jacinto as "Generalissimo of the North Zone". (For facsimile of Jacinto's appointment paper, see Agoncillo,* **Revolt of the Masses**, *page 187.)*

considered them infamous, unjust and without motive whatsoever."[6]

If Nakpil's allegations are true, Pio could not have carried out the orders even if he had wanted to, because Aguinaldo himself claims his tireless fighting General had gone with him to Biyak-na-Bato and was busy leading guerrillas against enemy strongholds. As proof, Aguinaldo cites two actions in Central Luzon where General Pio del Pilar and his Manila-Morong troops took part -- San Rafael in Bulacan and Aliaga in Nueva Ecija. In order to provision their Biyak-na-Bato camp, Aguinaldo ordered a foraging assault on San Rafael during the first week of August 1897. "I instructed General Pio del Pilar and his soldiers to make the frontal assault, while Gen. Salvador Estrella would ambush or block the enemy that might come [as reinforcements] from Baliwag" -- Aguinaldo recalls.[7] And in the three-day Battle of Aliaga on 5-7 September, also with the objective of getting food supplies, General Pio del Pilar was again in the thick of the fight commanding side-by-side with General Manuel Tinio, General Noriel and others.[8]

The only thing that is hazy here is that, if one ever misses the Aguinaldo version, there appears a gap on Pio del Pilar's activities between the months of June and December in 1897 -- from Aguinaldo's escape from Cavite, to his acceptance of the peace agreement in Biyak-na-Bato. Before the Aguinaldo memoirs came out in 1965, the national histories of the Revolution by Kalaw (1925), Zaide (1954) and Agoncillo (1956 and 1961) -- as well as the 1926 Ricarte and 1927 Alvarez memoirs before them -- were all silent on Pio's presence at

---

[6]*Alzona,* **Julio Nakpil**, *page 45. Nakpil, who later married Bonifacio's widow (Gregoria de Jesus) in 1898, was not a Katipunero but a Mason and La Liga Filipina member who was among Manileños who evacuated to Bonifacio's camp in Balara during the Spanish witch-hunts in August 1896. He did not fight in the Philippine-American War and was, in fact, one of the founding members of the Americanista* **Partido Federalista** *in 1900. Nevertheless, had Bonifacio survived and won his independence war, Nakpil's musical composition* **Marangal na Dalit Nitong Katagalugan** *could have been our national anthem.*

[7]*Aguinaldo,* **Gunita**, *page 250.*

[8]**Ibid.**, *page 255.*

Puray, or his participation in the battles in Central Luzon.[9] And indeed, if Aguinaldo's own allegations are true, one wonders why Pio del Pilar was not among the signers of the "Biyak-na-Bato Constitution" drafted in November (was he out fighting?) or why he was not among the close Aguinaldo associates who went to Hongkong after the "Pact of Biyak-na-Bato" was concluded in December (was he still out fighting?).

But anyway, at least one document of Aguinaldo's Biyak-na-Bato "Republic" lists Pio del Pilar as one of three Lieutenant-Generals (the others being Mariano Llanera and Miguel Malvar) of its armed forces -- and, possibly, he had taken over the place of Lieutenant-General Mamertito Natividad who was killed in action in November.[10]

On the other hand, the "Insurgent Records" reveal him as one of the recipients of the Biyak-na-Bato money distributed in January 1898, when Aguinaldo was already in Hongkong. Surely he had ceased fighting then, and in six official receipts -- numbered 12, 13, 14, 29, 34 and 36 -- jointly signed with Urbano Lacuna (who was then still in the service of Spain), he was supposed to have received a total of 20,400 pesos to pay for the guns of the men who surrendered with him.[11] And Ricarte, who should know because he was there in Biyak-na-Bato as Commanding General of the revolutionary army, reports that when the surrendered rebels were being provided with safety passes by the Spanish Government so that they could return unmolested to their homes, the sole exception was "Pio del Pilar who, on account of his

---

[9]*Agoncillo (***Malolos***, page 31), for example, writes that at about this time, Pedro Paterno "went to Morong to interview Pio del Pilar". (Underscoring mine.)*

[10]*For the list, see Teodoro M. Kalaw's footnotes in his* **Life and Death of a Boy General** *(Manila: National Historical Commission, 1974), pages 60-61.*

[11]*Taylor,* **Philippine Insurrection***, Volume 1, Exhibit 78 and 79, pages 462-466. See also Teodoro Agoncillo,* **Malolos***, Appendix B ("Distribution of the P200,000 Given to the Biyak-na-Bato Rebels by Primo de Rivera as Second Installment"), pages 750-752. Pio himself surrendered few arms, as follows: six Remington rifles with 70 bullets, four muskets, one revolver, and two native cannons called* lantakas.

animals -- horses and carabaos -- met with difficulty in securing a pass".[12]

Where did all those animals come from? And where did all that "peace" money go?

---

[12]*Ricarte,* **Memoirs**, *page 88. Ricarte's words are similar to those of Santiago Alvarez in his own memoirs,* **Ang Katipunan at Paghihimagsik**: *"... si Hral. Pio del Pilar natagalan bago nakaalis sa Biak-na-Bato dahil sa pagaayos ng kapahintulutan (pases), at ng marami niyang hayup na iuuwi, baka, kalabaw, kabayo." Paula Carolina Malay translates it out of context in* **The Katipunan**, *page 198: "Gen. Pio del Pilar was assigned the task of issuing the passes, and because he was also in charge of transporting the many livestock -- cows, carabaos, horses -- he was among the last to leave Biak-na-Bato." William Henry Scott, in a letter to me dated 20 August 1988, calls my attention to a bit of "incidental intelligence" (his words) in connection with Pio's livestock holdings, attributing its source to a Jesuit's 1898 diary: "Pio sold [the Jesuits] some cows at P 200 each on 6 August (when even all horses in Manila had been butchered)." Scotty is obviously referring to Miguel Saderra Maso's diary, portions of which (22 April to 13 August 1898) were published in 1989 as "The Fall of Manila: Excerpts from a Jesuit Diary" by José S. Arcilla, in* **Philippine Studies 37** *(1989), pages 192-214. Maso writes in his 3 August entry: "Pio del Pilar has volunteered to bring in food stuffs [through the cordon], selling us cows and carabaos"; and again on 6 August: "Pio del Pilar has allowed to pass into the city some cattle at P 200 each. In peace time, cattle cost between P 20 and P 30 each." (Arcilla,* **ibid.**, *page 210.) And Arturo Ma. Misa, in a 1972 magazine article, puts Pio in good light by saying that he helped Emilio Jacinto put up a cow meat business by supplying the Pio del Pilar Brigade, among other clients, with genuine "bakang Batangas" -- and for this charitable assistance, says Misa, "General Del Pilar refused to get a centavo worth of commission." Misa based his data on an interview with a surviving cousin of Emilio Jacinto. (See Misa's "Emilio Jacinto as the Meat Merchant",* **Sunday Times Magazine**, *6 June 1972.) For interpolations on Misa's views, see my "Emilio Jacinto* Pingkian", **Diliman Review**, *37:3 (1989), pages 17-26.*

SPANISH VOLUNTEER MILITIA
Organized to fight the Americans, and composed mostly of *creoles* and *mestizos*, many defected to the rebel side to fight as Pioistas.

SIX

MERCENARY? BOUNTY HUNTER?

RECALCITRANT REBELS with a cause like Makabulos, Torres, Manalang and Jocson would renew their guerrilla activities in Central Luzon and around Manila, but Pio del Pilar remained true to the provisions of the Biyak-na-Bato "pact".[1] It was for a good reason too, because he was among the "ex-rebel" leaders who were given commissions in the Spanish Volunteer Militia.[2] This was in April 1898. And it was probably in the performance of his duty as militia officer of the Spanish Army in the Philippines that he figured in a controversial confrontation with Feliciano Jocson.

---

[1] *Francisco Makabulos Soliman led the uprising in Tarlac and Pangasinan and, in April 1898, formed the "Central Executive Committee" that coordinated all revolutionary activities in the same provinces covered by the shortlived Departmental Government of Central Luzon. Theoretically, the resistance movements led by Feliciano Jocson in the Manila-Morong area, Roman Manalang in the Zambales-Pangasinan area, and Makabulos himself in the Tarlac-Pangasinan area were under this central committee's single control. On his own, Emilio Jacinto continued his "Katipunization" drives in Laguna, particularly in the Bay-Nagcarlan-Magdalena area. The possibility of any of these personalities having influenced the 1898 local outbreaks led by Isabelo Abaya in Ilocos, Ildefonso Moreno in Bicol and Leon Kilát in Cebu is remote but not altogether improbable. See Agoncillo,* **Malolos**, *pages 64-70; Zaide,* **Philippine Revolution**, *pages 166-168, 288; Ricarte,* **Memoirs**, *pages 65-67; Leandro Fernandez,* **The Philippine Republic** *(New York: Columbia University Press, 1926), pages 50-51; John Foreman,* **The Philippine Islands** *(Hongkong: Kelly and Walsh, Ltd., 1906), pages 401-408; and Renato Constantino,* **The Philippines: A Past Revisited** *(Quezon City: Tala Publishing, 1976), pages 195-197.*

[2] *Taylor,* **Philippine Insurrection**, *Volume 2, page 8. The other revolutionary leaders appointed to the Spanish Volunteer Militia included Mariano Trias, Emiliano Riego de Dios, Ambrosio Mojica, Licerio Geronimo and Artemio Ricarte.*

Jocson was one of the few ilustrados (he was a pharmacist graduated from Santo Tomas) who joined the Katipunan before 1896 and who, early in 1897, joined the exodus to Cavite too. But he did not hold any military rank in either armies of Magdalo or Magdiwang, choosing to serve the revolutionary cause alone and even volunteering to go to Hongkong (partly at his own expense) for the purpose of purchasing arms and ammunitions for the use of both rebel groups.[3] Later, back in Cavite, he would clash with Bonifacio (probably on the question of money), and Jocson from then on tended to side more with the Magdalo. Still later he would disagree with Aguinaldo on the conduct of the peace negotiations at Biyak-na-Bato, and he refused to lay down his arms when the peace treaty was finally signed.[4]

In 1898, this ilustrado Katipunero called upon the old followers of Bonifacio to join him in his cause. A few minor leaders (like Cenon Nicdao and Nicomedes Carreon, both of whom Jocson appointed as "Generals") did answer his call, but it is unlikely that he worked in concert with Emilio Jacinto who continued his Katipunan activities in Laguna after Bonifacio's death -- even as he and Nakpil and Sakay and other Bonifacistas were hunted down as "contra-revolucionarios" by the Republicano factions. On the contrary, Jacinto must have scorned this pretender who was trying to usurp the Supremo's title, of which he (who was later in history dubbed, and quite correctly, the "Brains of the

---

[3]*A good account of Jocson's 1896 gun-smuggling activities in Hongkong, in behalf of both the Aguinaldo and Bonifacio factions, may be found in Alejandrino,* **Price of Freedom**, *pages 29-31. In contrast, Alvarez (***The Katipunan**, *pages 119-120) is unimpressed by Jocson, and even insinuates mishandling of rebel funds by him: "It will be recalled that this gentleman solicited a great sum from the Magdiwang and Magdalo governments and from the Katipunan [Supreme] Council, with the understanding that he would use the money for buying arms and ammunition. But no guns or ammunition materialized, and neither was there an accounting of the money collected for the purpose."*

[4]*Ricarte (***Memoirs**, *page 65) says the reason for Jocson's recalcitrance was because he was not consulted during the peace negotiations at Biyak-na-Bato. And Alvarez (***The Katipunan**, *page 196) tells us Jocson tried to "explain his reasons for objecting to the pact, but Aguinaldo paid little attention to him".*

Katipunan"), was its rightful heir.[5]

This interim between the "First War" of 1896 and the "Second War" of 1898, or the time Aguinaldo was in Hongkong and Pio del Pilar was once again in the service of Spain, was a confused period in the first place. And when Jocson's own attempted uprising in Manila failed after Nicdao's house on Calle Camba was raided by Spanish troops, the confusion became even worse.[6]

No one will perhaps ever know exactly what Feliciano Jocson's true motives were, or how he really died. But Ricarte may have the last word. He says in his memoirs that after the fiasco in Manila, Jocson fled to the Laguna Lake town of Bay. It was a bad choice for the unlucky Jocson, for Bay swarmed with Bonifacistas (Emilio Jacinto and Julio Nakpil were there) who had never quite given up the independence goals of the Katipunan. On his arrival Jocson was arrested by Venancio Cueto, the Katipunan chieftain in Laguna. Cueto, says Ricarte, had earlier received "orders from General Pio del Pilar requesting the arrest of Jocson ... which orders contained the statement that this man was paid by the friars to renew the revolt". Ricarte also says that Jocson was at first treated well on the advice of the patriot

---

[5]*Emilio Jacinto knew from the letters of his friend Bonifacio's wife, Gregoria de Jesus, that Jocson was one of the Supremo's deadly enemies in Cavite. And there are reasons to believe that Jacinto, in line with his sustained efforts to "Katipunize" the Laguna Lake region according to original Katipunan plans, was himself in Manila while Jocson was appealing for support right in Bonifacio's Katagalugan center of Tondo. Was Jacinto partly instrumental in the making of the Jocson fiasco? For evidence of Jacinto's presence in Manila at the time of Jocson's failed revolt, see Francisco Carreon's account in José P. Santos,* **Tatlong Napabantog na "Tulisan" sa Pilipinas** *(Tarlac: José Paez Santos, 1930), pages 71-72. For letters of the Bonifacios to Jacinto, see Teodoro A. Agoncillo,* **The Writings and Trial of Andres Bonifacio** *(Manila: Bonifacio Centennial Commission, 1963), pages 13-22; De Los Santos,* **The Revolutionists,** *pages 108-118, 124-128; and Agoncillo,* **Revolt of the Masses,** *Appendices H and I, pages 403-419. For sympathetic views on Jocson, see Ricarte,* **Memoirs,** *pages 65-67; Alejandrino,* **Price of Freedom,** *pages 29-31; and Alzona,* **Julio Nakpil.**

[6]*Alvarez,* **The Katipunan,** *pages 201-202. Alvarez calls this movement the "Jocson Katipunan".*

Apolinario Mabini, who was then also hiding in Bay. But:[7]

> *As soon as Pio del Pilar learned of the capture of Jocson, he went in haste to Bay, in [the] company of his ever-beautiful mistress, Monica, and under a solemn promise made in the presence of Mabini and Paciano Rizal that he would not surrender Jocson to the Spanish government, and would not permit him to be maltreated in word or in deed by anyone, received the two prisoners [Jocson had a companion] from Cueto. They went willingly with General Pio del Pilar, on whom [ultimately] lies the responsibility for the almost mysterious disappearance of Jocson.*

The irony of it is that, shortly after this, Emilio Aguinaldo returned from exile to renew the Revolution. Would Pio del Pilar now make haste to where Aguinaldo was hiding to discourage this new "violator" of the "pact"? Would he (again?) play bounty hunter and deliver Aguinaldo into the hands of the Spanish authorities? Says Taylor: "Pio del Pilar who had fought for Spain for some days, on 31 May joined Aguinaldo".[8]

Taylor cites a letter Pio sent that day to Aguinaldo, signed with

---

[7]*Ricarte,* **Memoirs**, *pages 66-67. Alejandrino (***Price of Freedom**, *page 31) says: "His death until now [1933] is a mystery to be cleared up, for some [asserted] that he was killed by those who were interested in complying with what was agreed upon with the Spanish government to deliver all the arms in our possession." Alvarez (***The Katipunan**, *pages 202-204) more or less agrees with Ricarte's story, although he would like his readers to "understand the role of Gen. Pio del Pilar in this affair [as to] why he assumed the unpleasant responsibility of having a brother-in-arms arrested [and executed?]". (***Ibid.**, *page 202.) Alvarez also contributes this interesting detail: "For a long time [Jocson's friends] received no news at all about Jocson. Finally, a sad rumor reached them that a body was discovered near the cemetery of the Catholic church in Mandaluyong, Rizal. People who knew him identified the dead man to be Feliciano Jocson." (***Ibid.**, *page 204.) And Julio Nakpil thinks it was "a great error to have him killed for the mere fact of having induced the revolutionists to rise in arms after the conclusion of the peace of Biyak-na-Bato". (Alzona,* **Julio Nakpil***)*

[8]*Taylor,* **Philippine Insurrection**, *Volume 2, page 25.*

his symbolic Katipunan name Pang-Una, and his rank as Lieutenant-General in the Biyak-na-Bato "Republic":[9]

> *31 May 1898*
> *Hon. President Emilio Aguinaldo:*
>
> *I have the honor to advise you that today, Thursday, the 31st of May, I am here in the town of Las Piñas with 500 volunteers, all members of the Katipunan, under my command, and wait for your orders as to what we shall do. The names of the town under my jurisdiction are noted in the margin [which are: Las Piñas, Parañaque, Malibay, San Pedro Makati, Mandaluyong and Muntinglupa]. In case you take one of these towns I would wish to have an agreement with you in order to avert collisions with us. The volunteers who are garrisoning the town of Tagui-ik [Taguig] are all favorable to you and ready to obey your orders; their chief Fernando Acevedo, a native half-caste, is one of us and has 400 volunteers under his command.*
>
> *While I am awaiting for your orders, I wish that God may keep you in good health for many years.*
> *Las Piñas, May 31st, 1898.*
>
> *(Sgd) PANG-UNA (PIO DEL PILAR)*
> *Lieut. General*

That same day, Aguinaldo replied to Pio del Pilar's letter with an order to attack the positions of the Spanish forces. Said Aguinaldo to his "Beloved General" of 1896:[10]

> *... If the troops in the trenches in front of Zapote Bridge, jurisdiction of Las Piñas, are really our enemies, they will be attacked from the rear; those in the town of Las Piñas will also be attacked and as far as Malibay, Pateros, Tagui-ik and Pasig. You will stop all operations against Santa Ana, Pasay, San Pedro*

---

[9]**Ibid.**, *Volume 3, Exhibit 13, page 39.*

[10]**Ibid.**, *pages 40-41.*

> *Makati and Mandaluyong which towns we will attack together. In case Pasig has already surrendered, you will build fortifications there, to defend the town against the forces of the enemy which might come from San Juan del Monte, and likewise you will fortify the other towns to protect them against those which might come from Manila. You must not leave Las Piñas and Parañaque. Do your best to carry out our plans in the most successful manner -- if possible, without firing a shot -- by next Friday, the 3rd [of June] inst. On making the movements the forces of Tagui-ik and Pasig will follow those of the above-mentioned towns. On hearing the shots the forces of Bacoor will come to their aid, so that you will have four columns under your command ...*

It was a time when even Ricarte, Trias and Riego de Dios were still undecided on whether to remain loyal to Spain or to rejoin their former chief. There were rumors, in fact, that Trias, who was a Major in the Spanish volunteer militia, "had promised to bring Aguinaldo's head to the Spanish Governor-General for 100,000 pesos"[11] -- a fortune in those days! So, even as Pio del Pilar volunteered his services to Aguinaldo, the latter must have had his doubts on the former's true intentions. And yet, Del Pilar was true to his word. Again, let us hear it from Taylor:[12]

> *Pio del Pilar who had fought for Spain for some days, on 31 May joined Aguinaldo. Three quarters of the native militia under him and [Felipe] Buencamino followed their commanders to the hostile [i.e., Filipino] camp. The small Spanish force at Zapote had to fall back; the road was opened to the insurgents in Cavite province, and the next day a swarm of insurgents surrounded Manila.*

By the time *independencia* was declared in Kawit on 12 June 1898, "all the commanders of the militia, except Licerio Geronimo who

---

[11]**Ibid.**, *Volume 2, page 25.*

[12]**Ibid.**

remained loyal with Spain until the end, had joined the insurgents", says Taylor.[13]

Meanwhile, true revolutionary that he was, General Pio del Pilar and his men, no longer guarding Manila but advancing on it, had closed in to as near as San Pedro Makati, ready to pounce on the capital city in the name of the Revolutionary Government.

---

[13]**Ibid.**, *page 26.*

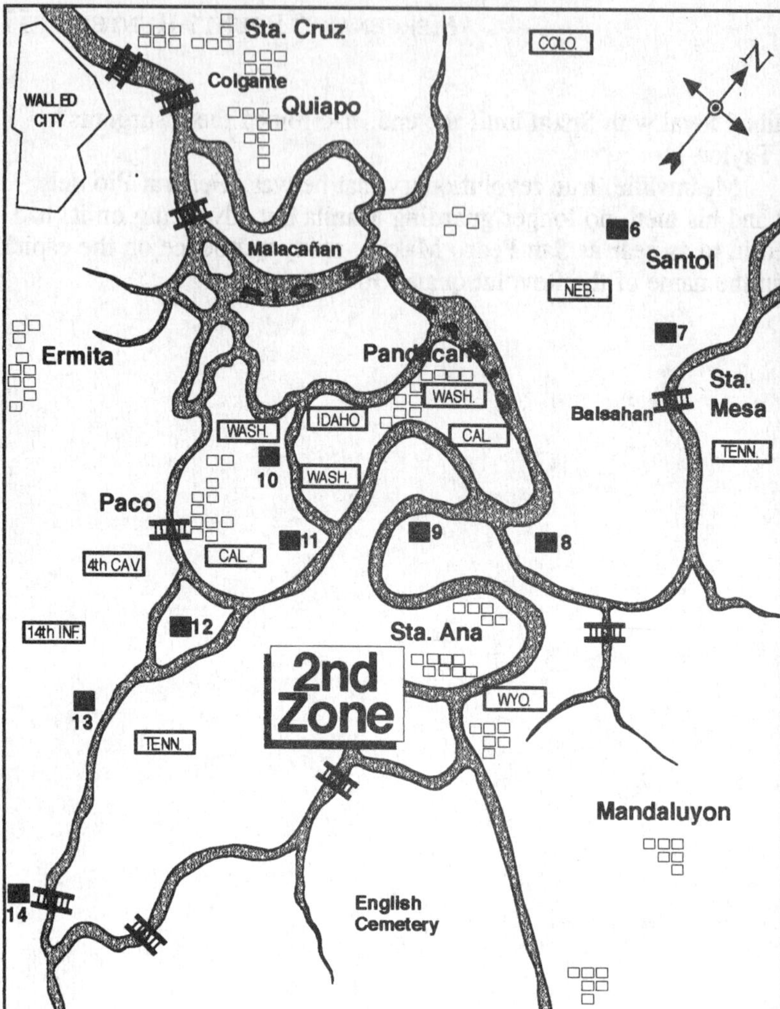

SEGUNDA ZONA
The rebel Second Zone of Manila was where Brigada Pio del Pilar was born during the "second war" of '98 when Aguinaldo returned.

seven

BRIGADA PIO DEL PILAR

BRIGADA PIO DEL PILAR was born during the siege of Manila. Its birthplace was that part of the city which Aguinaldo designated as *Segunda Zona*. And it grew out of Pio's old Magtagumpay veterans of 1896, of the mestizo officers and men of the Spanish volunteer militia who followed Pio's example, and of the various units from other military organizations attached to its zone.

As organized in June 1898, the Second Zone was commanded by General Pio del Pilar himself, with Colonel Luciano San Miguel as his second-in-command.[1] Aside from San Pedro Makati, the zone headquarters, its territory covered Paco, Pandacan, Santa Ana, Guadalupe, Pasig, Pateros and Taguig -- from which places many of Pio's officers and men had been originally recruited as Katipuneros. The strength of the forces of the Manila Second Zone by 1899 reached a peak of 2,688 officers and men who comprised 11 companies of regular troops armed with guns, including a few artillery pieces. Two companies of Infantry and one of Engineers were unorganized -- that is, they were lacking in arms and equipment -- and functioned in the capacity of reserves. Two more companies from Cavite (one each from Indang and Noveleta) were attached to Pio's command.[2]

A few words on the personalities who served briefly in the just-born Pio del Pilar Brigade in the Manila Second Zone:

Among the troops of the zone in 1898 were some ex-militia volunteers, under Juan M. Gutierrez, who had deserted their own

---

[1]*Taylor,* **Philippine Insurrection**, *Volume 3, Exhibit 37, page 127; Exhibit 129, page 219. The other Manila zones and their respective chiefs were: First Zone (Pasay-Malate area) under General Mariano Noriel; Third Zone (San Juan-Marikina area) under Colonel Antonio Montenegro, then Colonel Luciano San Miguel, then General Licerio Geronimo; and Fourth Zone (Tondo-Caloocan area) under General Pantaleon Garcia.*

[2]**Ibid.**, *Volume 3, Exhibit 489 ("Forces around Manila"), page 638. Taylor gives the peak strength in Volume 2, page 216.*

commanding officer, Colonel Pintos, and joined Del Pilar's mutiny in May. Gutierrez, an Ilocano mestizo, was promoted to First Lieutenant in June for his brilliant showing in Del Pilar's successful attack on and capture of Guadalupe.[3] Gutierrez was later transferred to the Tinio Brigade in Ilocos where he rose to become commander of that brigade's La Union Battalion. Still later, in 1901, shortly after Aguinaldo's fall, Gutierrez was captured by the Americans, tried by a U.S. military commission, and then hanged in San Fernando for having ordered his guerrillas to execute two American prisoners of war in the heat of an American army "search-and-destroy" operations.[4]

One of Pio's staff officers when his brigade headquarters were moved to Santa Ana was Urbano Lacuna. He, too, had been an officer in the Spanish volunteer militia who went over to Aguinaldo's side in 1898. Returning home to Nueva Ecija after the outbreak of the war with the Americans in February 1899, he led the "Gapan Volunteers" who fought so well in the Central Luzon campaigns they became famous. He would be linked to the murder plot against Luna, would become a Brigadier-General, and would be famous as the guerrilla leader "involved" in the capture of Aguinaldo. It happened that the Americans used Lacuna's captured stationery and forged his signature in a fake letter sent to Aguinaldo at his Palanan headquarters. The letter announced that Lacuna was sending reinforcements to Palanan, which were in reality the Macabebe mercenaries led by General Funston.[5]

Luciano San Miguel was Pio's second chief in the Second Zone during the siege of Manila. He was among the '96 Magdiwang veterans who dropped out of prominence during the Biyak-na-Bato phase of the

---

[3]**Philippine Insurgent Records**, *"Pio del Pilar Papers", RL-14, RL-15 and RL-16, in the National Library Filipiniana and Asia Division rare books section.*

[4]*See my* **The Tinio Brigade: Anti-American Resistance in the Ilocos Provinces, 1899-1901** *(Quezon City: New Day Publishers, 1989), pages 223-224.*

[5]*For a brief but fine biographical account of Urbano Lacuna, see E. Arsenio Manuel,* **Dictionary of Philippine Biography** *(Manila: Filipiniana Publications, 1957), Volume 1, pages 239-241. For Lacuna's anti-American guerrilla activities, see especially Frederick Funston,* **Memories of Two Wars** *(New York: Charles Scribner's Sons, 1911),* passim*; and Taylor,* **Philippine Insurrection**, *Volume 2, passim.*

Revolution. When Aguinaldo returned from Hongkong, San Miguel was surprisingly the first ranking officer to report to him for orders. And one sees here the spectacle of a former Magdiwang man rallying the Magdalo forces in Cavite for the "Second Revolution" -- while Pio del Pilar and the others were still dilly-dallying in the Spanish militia. But now in the Second Zone -- now that Pio was back on Aguinaldo's side -- he who was of Magdalo became the first chief. Later, when Colonel Montenegro was ousted as chief of the Third Zone, San Miguel was relieved of his post in the Second Zone to take command of the Third. At the height of the fighting in Central Luzon, in the war against the Americans, Aguinaldo made him a Brigadier-General and then named him Chief of Operations in Zambales. In the guerrilla war, the Magdiwang veteran would fall back on Katipunan doctrines, would not surrender with Aguinaldo in 1901, would not surrender with Malvar in 1902, and, taking command of the Revolution himself, would die fighting for independencia at the Battle of Corral-na-Bato near Marikina on 27 March 1903 -- at a time when Pio del Pilar was among those irreconcilables exiled in Guam. San Miguel was an "insurrecto" to the end, but "official history" never acclaimed him as a hero.[6]

Now, about those true-blue Pioistas themselves. They were a motley bunch of curious characters, those men who fought with the Pio del Pilar Brigade from beginning to end. There was the scarfaced Colonel Julian Paguia -- once a ferocious *Guardia Civil*, now a ferocious "insurrecto" -- who would become Pio's second-in-command. There was the Creole renegade, Major Fernando E. Grey y Formentos, who would become Pio's chief of staff. There was the notorious Major Isidoro Carmona of Pasay -- the "Isidoro Carmonang magaling" of revolutionary legend and song -- a vicious man who feared no other man. There was Major Arsenio Mauricio, the young ex-Bonifacista-turned-Pioista from Tondo. There was the well-bred Batangueño Major Vicente Cabrera, and the spirited Lagunense Major Felipe Banaag. And there were respectable names such as Caruncho, Cuneta, Raymundo, Carballo, De la Rosa, De la Paz, Magsaysay, Quiogue, Tanjanque,

---

[6]*For biographical notes on this hero, see my "Gen. Luciano San Miguel: A Rebel to the End",* **Mirror Magazine**, *27 November 1965; my "Himagsikan ng mga Tulisan",* **Diliman Review** *37:3 (1988); and my "San Luciano San Miguel", in my* **"Bandoleros": Outlawed Guerrillas of the Philippine-American War, 1903-1907** *(Quezon City: New Day Publishers, 1995), pages 1-45.*

Nopuente, Joaquin, Taniag and others to belie the "ladron" label from Spaniards and Americans alike.[7]

FROM ITS MAKATI HEADQUARTERS, the Pio del Pilar Brigade widened its liberated territory in the Second Zone. After the capture of Guadalupe in June, Del Pilar's men attacked the Spanish positions at the English Cemetery and at Blockhouse No. 11 in Makati on 21 July.[8] The following day, Aguinaldo received a telegram from Ricarte with "our warmest congratulations for the capture of the English Cemetery". The message ended with a cheer: "Long live General Pio del Pilar!"[9]

Some 3,000 rebel troops (half of them armed with guns) were by now concentrated in San Pedro Makati -- all set and eager to attack Manila. But the men had little or no cartridges for their rifles and their food supplies were fast running out. On 29 July, *Presidente Local* (head of town or Mayor) Catalino Raymundo (who later joined Del Pilar's staff) made an appeal to the Presidente Local of Pasig to help him provision the troops in Makati; he asked him to send two cavans of salt and two cans of lard so that the soldiers would at least have rice and salt (for *sinangag*?) to sustain them for the siege.[10]

Meanwhile, Aguinaldo's American "allies" were all this time increasing their military strength in Manila. The Filipinos were puzzled to see the arrival of huge land forces sent to augment Admiral Dewey's squadron in Manila Bay. Three big American forces arrived in groups on different dates: General Anderson's on 30 June, General Greene's on 17 July, and General Merritt's on 25 July. On 29 July, General Greene's division managed to get hold of strategic positions in the advance rebel lines, having tricked General Noriel's men from some of

---

[7]*Scattered notes on these men are found in* **Philippine Insurgent Records**, *"Pio del Pilar Papers", National Library.*

[8]*Taylor,* **Philippine Insurrection**, *Volume 2, page 27.*

[9]**Ibid.**, *Volume 3, Exhibit 74, page 177.*

[10]**Ibid.**, *Exhibit 160, pages 276-277.*

their trenches in the "insurrecto" First Zone.[11]

It was probably to even the score that Pio del Pilar on 30 July, according to Taylor, notified the Spanish commander at Santa Ana about the presence of American troops opposite his lines. Del Pilar warned that the Americans intended to attack the Spanish positions on 2 August. If the Spaniards would fall back to the city walls and leave Santa Ana to him -- Del Pilar offered -- "he would hold it with his own men". The Americans did not attack, and the Spanish commander must have been thankful he had not given up Santa Ana to Del Pilar.[12]

Another big American expeditionary force, commanded by General Arthur MacArthur, arrived on 7 August amid strong winds and heavy rains. The weather was indeed -- literally and figuratively -- getting stormy in Manila during those first two weeks of August in 1898. On 8 August, in anticipation of the "storm", Aguinaldo named General Artemio Ricarte -- The Viper -- overall Chief of Operations for Manila. [13] On the same day, Pio del Pilar received a note from his mestizo friend Fernando Acevedo warning that the Americans planned to double-cross the Filipinos by capturing Manila all by themselves the next day. Acevedo therefore urged Pio that "it is requisite and necessary before the attack takes place tomorrow that you tomorrow or tonight annihilate them, sparing no one for the way they have deceived us". [14] Del Pilar must have been bothered by Acevedo's intrigues because on 10 August, he sent three telegrams to Aguinaldo:[15]

---

[11]**Ibid.**, *Volume 2, page 81.*

[12]**Ibid.**, *page 65.*

[13]**Ibid.**, *page 63.*

[14]**Ibid.**, *page 71. For full text, see* **ibid.**, *Volume 3, Exhibit 134, pages 236-237. Of Fernando Acevedo, the Jesuit Miguel Saderra Maso wrote in his diary on 18 August 1898: "This very morning, the [rebel] leader Pio del Pilar was in our villa house [in Santa Ana], visiting* Señor *Acevedo, the commander of the militia volunteers from Bayambang. The latter, at the same time that he shows his loyalty [to Spain], is the object of Aguinaldo's and his men's sympathies, and he is even rumored to have been named [a revolutionary] Lieutenant-General." (Arcilla, "Fall of Manila",* **Philippine Studies 37**, *page 212.)*

[15]*Taylor,* **ibid.**, *Volume 3, Exhibit 92, 93 and 94, page 192.*

> *[10: a.m.] Information received that 10,000 German soldiers disembarked in Subig [Subic] to aid the Spaniards and to seize the country from us. Request you tell me confidentially what our situation is. These things dishearten us and we have no cartridges. If we had cartridges, would by this time have entered Santa Ana, but in spite of this we are close to the Spanish Battery. I hope you will attend to this.*
>
> *[4:30 p.m.] Urgent: Comandante Acevedo writes that the Spaniards are about to surrender because they want to turn over the place; the Americans want them to leave only the batteries and say that they will station themselves in said batteries. It appears that they want to deceive us;*[16] *they do not want to give us arms, and if they do not give us arms we shall attack them and drive them out. I await your reply.*
>
> *[8:00 p.m.] Urgent: I would wish to have placed at my disposal, if you see fit, the launches* Cavadonga, Nueva Yor [York] *and* Suerte *to attack and take the gunboat* Otalora *as they say she carries much money.*

Acevedo's warning of the American attack on the 9th failed to materialize, but only because of discordance in strategy among the American generals. But on the 13th, it became a reality. Aguinaldo narrates (in 1898) in his **Reseña Veridica**:[17]

> *I noted a general movement of attack against Manila on the part of the American squadron and of the land forces under the command of General Anderson in Parañaque. Immediately I ordered my troops to attack along the whole line. General Pio del Pilar succeeded*

---

[16]*Pio del Pilar had good information.*

[17]*Emilio Aguinaldo,* **Reseña Veridica de la Revolucion Filipina** *(Tarlac: Imprenta Nacional del Zacarias Fajardo, 1899), based on an English translation in* **Historical Bulletin**, *XIII:1-4 (1969), page 301. For other English translations, see* **The Philippine Social Sciences Review** *(May 1941), pages 179-223; and Taylor,* **Philippine Insurrection**, *Volume 1, Exhibit 71, pages 443-448 and Volume 3, Exhibit 2, pages 2-47.*

> *in entering Sampalok and attacked the Spanish troops that were defending the suspension bridge. These fell back toward the bridge of Spain ... In Santa Ana, General Ricarte, aided by the troops of General Pio del Pilar, succeeded in cutting off five columns of Spaniards.*

In all four zones, the Filipino forces simultaneously struck against the Spanish defenders of Manila. And in this final attack on 13 August it was Brigada Pio del Pilar who got nearest the Walled City (Intramuros) -- fighting their way through Santa Ana and Pandacan, then to Paco on the northwestern limits of their zone. By 2:00 p.m. of the 13th, they were already in the district of Concepcion. If the Pioistas did not move any further, it was only because General Pio del Pilar was waiting for Aguinaldo's orders to cross the Pasig River and pounce on Intramuros itself. Excitedly, Del Pilar wired Aguinaldo: "Permission [to attack] and rounds of ammunition are very necessary. Do not fail to reply immediately. Congratulations to all".[18] (Was complete victory within reach?)

But, sadly, Aguinaldo the compromiser dilly-dallied. Did he trust the Americans more than his own "Beloved General" Pio del Pilar? So, as Pio del Pilar closed in with his troops on the city walls that afternoon of 13 August 1898, the U.S. forces under General Greene blocked their advance. The American General in effect served notice that the American Army "now held Manila and the suburbs and were guarding the roads", in Taylor's words. Therefore, Greene said, Del Pilar "should instruct his men not to fire towards Manila, nor cross the Pasig River with arms".[19]

Mad as a raging bull, Pio del Pilar wanted to fight the Americans right then and there. That same afternoon he wired Ricarte to come "or there will be trouble, since they are driving me away".[20] And the following morning of the 14th, he telegraphed Aguinaldo himself: "Most urgent: Ask send General to arrange avoid conflict

---

[18]*Taylor,* **ibid.**, *Volume 3, Exhibit 106, page 202.*

[19]**Ibid.**, *Vol 2, page 88.*

[20]**Ibid.**, *Volume 3, Exhibit 107, page 202.*

which is probable".[21] Aguinaldo, as we know, wavered and let the Americans take over the capital city -- to the indignation and dismay of warriors like Pio del Pilar.

And so, as "friendly relations" between the American and Filipino "allies" became strained, the "special ties" between Emilio Aguinaldo and Pio del Pilar also began to unravel. Karl Irving Faust thus observes that in 1899: "There was intense dissatisfaction on the part of a large segment of the insurgent command ... [and] Gen. Pio del Pilar was the leader of this faction".[22]

---

[21]**Ibid.**, *Exhibit 185, page 307. (See also Leon Wolff,* **Little Brown Brother**, *page 134.)*

[22]*Karl Irving Faust,* **Campaigning in the Philippines** *(San Francisco: Hicks-Judd Company, 1899), page 110.*

eight

THORNS IN THE FLESH

HIS SILENT RIFT with the President of the *Republica Filipina*, his Commander-in-Chief, revealed yet another side of Pio del Pilar. The Manileño who idolized Aguinaldo in 1896 and sided with him -- versus a fellow Manileño (Bonifacio) in Aguinaldo's 1897 confrontation with the Supremo of the Katipunan -- was not, after all, an Aguinaldista. He was a Magdalo adherent, yes, but he obviously never adhered to Cavitismo. **Harper's Weekly** correspondent Marrion Wilcox said something about Aguinaldo suspecting, because of a controversy with General Makabulos in 1898, that "while the Commander-in-Chief in name, he [Aguinaldo] was, in the opinion of many of his generals, only a partner in the enterprise".[1] One of the Generals whom Wilcox had in mind must surely have been Pio del Pilar.

Thorns in the flesh of the just-born Republica Filipina the Pioistas would become in 1899. A mean, private army called Brigada Pio del Pilar would presume to turn into the Army of the Republic. For Aguinaldo, it must have been even more painful because Pio del Pilar was a personal friend, an old beloved comrade from the very "first war".

Gambling was, for instance, among the vices Presidente Aguinaldo had strictly prohibited in the revolutionary army, under pain of dismissal from service.[2] But Taylor notes that Pio del Pilar, after the Americans occupied Manila -- as if to show his displeasure at the leadership of the Revolution -- "established himself in Pasig where his mistress [would she be the same "ever-beautiful" Monica whom Ricarte mentions in his memoirs?] lived upon the returns of the gambling

---

[1]*Marrion Wilcox (ed.),* **Harper's History of the War in the Philippines** *(New York: Harper and Brothers, 1900), page 67.*

[2]*Taylor,* **Philippine Insurrection**, *Volume 2, page 68.*

houses of the town, whose monopoly Pio secured to her".[3]

And when Aguinaldo, against the advice of Mabini, consented to concede some of his trenches to the Americans, Pio sneered at the presidential orders and refused to obey. As a disciplinary action against him, some people around Aguinaldo thought it best "to remove [from the Manila Second Zone] his men ... gradually by organizations, and thereafter punish him for his disobedience".[4] Again, Apolinario Mabini counseled against such a move, and, instead, on 20 August wrote Aguinaldo that it was "absolutely necessary, if you think well enough of it, for us to promote General Pio and make him your second in command". Mabini felt that this was the only way -- the most prudent way -- to remove Pio from Manila without using force, and to control him. "And do not reprimand him", the Brains of the Republic advised his Presidente.[5]

On 31 August, the day General Elwell S. Otis began his duty as the first American Military Governor, Pio defied territorial regulations by going on a visit to Pasay fully armed together with one of his aides. American sentries at the Paco Bridge naturally stopped him -- to his rage and fury -- and the incident created some stir in the high commands of both Filipino and American camps.[6] And that was just the start.

Del Pilar soon retaliated by blocking navigation by Americans on his zone's side of the Pasig River. This led Teodoro Sandiko (later General, but at the time an "insurgent mole" inside American lines) to warn Aguinaldo early in September: "I make known to you that they [the American authorities] are all offended with Pio del Pilar's conduct at preventing the navigation of an American launch and for stopping the engineers in their work in spite of their having a pass signed by you, and for asking officers for passes".[7]

On 13 September, Aguinaldo moved his capital for strategic

---

[3]**Ibid.**

[4]**Ibid.**, *page 137.*

[5]*Apolinario Mabini,* **Letters** *(Manila: National Heroes Commission, 1965), page 54. (See also Taylor,* **Philippine Insurrection,** *Volume 3, Exhibit 197, page 314.)*

[6]*Taylor,* **ibid.**, *Exhibit 220, page 331.*

[7]**Ibid.**, *Exhibit 224, page 335.*

reasons from Bacoor to Malolos. Finally, the Filipino troops made a general withdrawal from the much-contested trenches around Manila -- all except the Pio del Pilar Brigade in Paco and Pandacan. As American author Leon Wolff puts it, Del Pilar "clung like a leech to every inch of his trenches, fortifications and blockhouses".[8] And on the effect of this defiant action on the Americans, the military historian Sexton writes:[9]

> *The insurgent lines in Pandacan were just across the river from the Malacañan, Otis's quarters, and the undisciplined Philippine soldiers [under Pio] used their proximity to the city as a means of provoking the Americans at every opportunity. Pilar's troops entered the American lines at night, engaged in highway robbery, kidnapped Filipinos unfavorable to their cause, and in some cases created disturbances within a block of Otis's quarters.*

Complaints against Pio del Pilar poured into Malolos. A *quilez* owned by one Señor Dueñas, a Spaniard, was reported stolen -- then it was allegedly found in Pio's possession.[10] One "cruel officer" in his brigade, Major Isidoro Carmona, was denounced for alleged "barbarous treatment" of Spanish and Macabebe prisoners of war as well as of suspected "contra-revolucionarios".[11]

Pio's men as a rule were accused of numerous provocative acts committed against the Americans. Pioista recalcitrance wrought so much tension in the Manila Second Zone that Sandiko had to repeat his warnings to Aguinaldo:[12]

> *I fear that the continuous arrests made by the Second Zone in the jurisdiction of the Americans will*

---

[8]*Wolff,* **Little Brown Brother**, *page 151.*

[9]*William T. Sexton,* **Soldiers in the Sun** *(Harrisburg, Pennsylvania: The Military Service Publishing Co., 1939), page 67.*

[10]*Letter of Teodoro Sandiko to Aguinaldo, dated 28 September 1898, in Taylor,* **Philippine Insurrection**, *Volume 3, Exhibit 263, page 372.*

[11]*Letter of Teodoro Sandiko to Aguinaldo, dated 24 September 1898,* **ibid.**, *Exhibit 259, pages 362-363.*

[12]*Taylor,* **ibid.**, *Exhibit 269, page 381.*

> *result in their requesting us to [again] evacuate Paco. Major Carmona whom you suppose at the present time to be in Malolos under trial, is here in Paco issuing warrants of arrest within the American jurisdiction, as two of his officers and some soldiers are [detained] in different [U.S. Army] barracks and in Bilibid now on account of it. For this reason I believe it would be advisable to renew orders to the Generals of the different zones, and especially to General Pio del Pilar, to cease issuing warrants of arrests with[in] American jurisdiction.*

Sandiko's letter was dated 4 October. Less than a week later, on 9 October, came what Sexton considers the "prime provocation from Pilar's troops".[13] This was when the steam launch *Cañacao*, flying the U.S. flag, was stopped while entering the "insurgent" side of the Pasig River. Del Pilar's guards then arrested the American officer they found on board, who turned out to be none other than General Thomas Anderson -- the American Division Commander himself!

This time it was Dr. T.H. Pardo de Tavera, head of the Filipino commission sent by Malolos to confer with Otis, who was bothered by Del Pilar's heavy-handed methods. "Last night Major Bell [of General Otis's staff] spoke to me highly enraged", the European-educated Creole wrote in a grumbling letter to Aguinaldo from Manila on the 11th of October. "Señor Bell says that the Americans do not exhibit such conduct in their treatment of us; but that nevertheless General [Del] Pilar treats the Americans not as friends and allies with whom we have fought against Spain, but rather as avowed enemies".[14]

If the Americans were enraged, ilustrados (like T.H. Pardo de Tavera) who had joined the Revolution were certainly repelled by Pio's

---

[13]*Sexton,* **Soldiers in the Sun**, *page 67. On this incident, General Anderson wrote his superiors: "It is respectfully submitted that whether this act of [Pio del] Pilar was authorized or not by the assumed insurgent government, it should, in any event, be resented." See "Documents on the Philippine-American War",* **Historical Bulletin**, *XII:1-4 (1969), page 455.*

[14]*Taylor,* **Philippine Insurrection**, *Volume 5, Exhibit 582 (Addendum to Volume 3), page 86. As later events would show, Pio was right!*

brash behavior. At that time diplomatic agents of the Republic were busy "selling" the Philippines abroad, in a bid for participation in the Treaty of Paris. Felipe Agoncillo, head of the Hongkong Junta, had been designated leader of the Filipino commission in Paris and Galicano Apacible in September arrived in Hongkong to take over his place in the Junta. Agoncillo in Paris somehow got wind of Pio del Pilar's mutinous stance and on 22 October, in a telegram to Apacible, he advised that no dissension in the Filipino ranks should hinder his negotiations: "All should be of one mind".[15] Apacible then notified Malolos, and Aguinaldo three days later replied to Agoncillo and denied the whole thing: "What you telegraphed to Señor Apacible regarding General Pio del Pilar and [Gen. Francisco] Makabulos is incorrect".[16]

Even ilustrados in the Republicano Army must have shared this antipathy for Pio. General José Alejandrino, for one, the European-trained engineer who constructed all those fine trenches and fortifications in the Manila Fourth Zone, showed no admiration for Del Pilar, the unschooled veteran campaigner. Somewhere in his memoirs, Pepe Alejandrino mentions a fellow General "who distinguished himself with his immorality and misdeeds". Hearing the Malolos government threaten him with dismissal, Alejandrino tells us, this Filipino General publicly uttered in defiance: "I have earned these insignias thru shots and bolo strokes and if they want to take them away from me it should also be thru shots".[17]

Could Alejandrino be really making allusions to General Pio del Pilar?

In **Malolos: The Crisis of the Republic**, historian Teodoro Agoncillo devotes one whole chapter to "internal conflict".[18] Yet, the conflict he sees was only that of the "executive force" clashing against the "legislative force" -- or, as Agoncillo varies it, the Aguinaldo-Mabini group vs. the Paterno-Buencamino group, or the "have-nots" vs. the "haves", or what comes out later as the *independistas* vs. the *autonomistas*. It seems Agoncillo fails to discern the *inner* conflict from

---

[15]**Ibid.**, *Exhibit 520 (Addendum), page 15.*

[16]**Ibid.**, *Volume 3, Exhibit 275, page 390.*

[17]*Alejandrino,* **Price of Freedom**, *page 113.*

[18]*See Chapter 10 in Agoncillo,* **Malolos**, *pages 373-408.*

below with the real "have-nots" -- in the persons of those unschooled (but not "true Katipunero") Generals of the Republica, like Pio del Pilar and Francisco Makabulos. In this conflict, just this once, the "executive" and "legislative" forces were certainly united. And in this one conflict, the Malolos government (or was it Mabini alone?) showed remarkable prudence and sophistication in handling the Pioista "problem".

The Republicano government in Malolos did not have to do anything "thru shots". The first thing done was to appoint Del Pilar in November as a *diputado* to the Revolutionary Congress to represent Negros Oriental, which did not elect a delegate to Malolos.[19] And the next thing Malolos did was to assign him (a new hatchetman's role?) in December as Post Commander at San Fernando de la Union (Ilocos Region), apparently as a precaution against rumored peasant agitations among the *Guardia de Honor* fanatics in Pangasinan and southern La Union.[20] The whole thing was meant, of course, to quietly expel Pio del Pilar from Manila, specifically out of the Second Zone.

It is doubtful that Del Pilar ever participated in the deliberations of the Malolos Congress or that he ever complied with his new, cursory assignment to San Fernando. But he was positively in Malolos when the Revolutionary Congress drafted the Constitution on 23 January 1899, as his signature appears on the original document.

Some people will claim that Pio del Pilar's presence in the Malolos Congress attests to the democratic character of our first legislative body, but no: the truth is, he was an anomaly among those distinguished *Señores* of that era. True, he was one of the four delegates appointed from the Army to represent some provinces without representatives. But General Antonio Luna was a cosmopolite who had known bohemian days in Europe; and General Isidoro Torres had gone to the University of Santo Tomas; and even General Vito Belarmino,

---

[19]**Ibid.**, *Appendix D, page 786 and Appendix E, page 789. (See also Taylor,* **Philippine Insurrection**, *Volume 4, Exhibit 674, pages 126-130 for full list of Revolutionary Congress members as of 6 October 1899.)*

[20]*Taylor,* **ibid.**, *Volume 3, Exhibit 488 ("List of Military Chiefs and Their Stations [in 1898]"), page 637.*

who did not go to college, was described as "urbane and cultured".[21] He was alone in his class.

True, he might have been the only delegate in the Malolos Congress truly representative of the masses. But the question is, *which mass* did he represent? Certainly not the revolutionary masses oath-bound to the Katipunan, for he had not been a worthy Son of the People in the eyes of *true* Katipuneros. And certainly not the simple patriotic masses sworn to the Republicano Army, for his own fellows saw a scoundrel through Pio's *rayadillo* uniform.

Were the Americans right, after all, in classifying Pio del Pilar as leader of the "ladron" element of the Revolution?

---

[21] *Ulpiano Herrero y Sampedro,* **Nuestra Prision en Poder de los Revolucionarios Filipinos** *(Manila: Imprenta del Colegio de Santo Tomas, 1900), page 135. Herrero was one of the friar-prisoners of the revolutionary forces in 1898. Vito Belarmino, a Caviteño from Silang, was a non-ilustrado* **principal** *who became Commanding General of the Bicol provinces until his surrender in 1901. He later became blind, but reportedly gained supernatural powers as a psychic healer. (See Hector R. Villaroel et al.,* **Eminent Filipinos**, *pages 60-61.)*

SEPULCHRES OF HEROES
On 4 and 5 February 1899, the Pio del Pilar Brigade's Manila Second Zone became one whole blazing combat arena.

nine

MASSACRE IN PANDACAN

THE AMERICANS' HATRED for Pio del Pilar and his "arrogant and hated troops"[1] was unmistakable. This was proven later in all the battles that occurred in the Second Zone immediately after the first exchange of fire on the night of 4 February. Those Yanquis -- those barbarians! -- opposing General Pio del Pilar's men always made it a point not to take prisoners alive and wanted to wipe out the Pio del Pilar Brigade to the last man if possible. When the fighting finally subsided on the 5th, the American forces had virtually turned the Filipino trenches in Santa Ana, Paco, Pandacan and San Pedro Makati into veritable sepulchres.

In Pandacan alone, 700 Pioistas were driven to the Pasig River and massacred. The American military historian Sexton himself shows no sympathy for Del Pilar or his soldiers as he sums up the mass slaughter that took place in the Second Zone on 5 February:[2]

> *On Anderson's left (east) flank, in the Pandacan District, a sharp bend in the Pasig River placed the troops of the Washington and Idaho Volunteers within a stone's throw of the insurgent troops under the command of General Pio del Pilar. [Del] Pilar was an erstwhile native bandit who had brought his gang into Aguinaldo's army. Poorly disciplined, [Del] Pilar's troops had particularly antagonized the American troops opposite. By unmistakable gestures and taunts, they had displayed their low regard for the potential fighting ability of these western volunteers.*

---

[1] *Words of Wolff in* **Little Brown Brother**, *page 224. Taylor, Sexton and other American authors may have expressed it differently, but they shared the same* antipatico *feeling for Pioistas in general and for Pio in particular.*

[2] *Sexton,* **Soldiers in the Sun**, *pages 94-95. (See also Wolff,* **Little Brown Brother**, *pages 224-226.)*

An order to attack was what the troops opposite [Del] Pilar's brigade wanted most. On signal, the Idaho and Washington Volunteers left their positions and, with shouts which resembled everything from a cowboy's "yippee" to an old Civil War rebel yell, and supported by Hawthorne's mountain battery, viciously charged [Del] Pilar's redoubt in Pandacan. In the face of muzzle blast from Krupp artillery pieces which the insurgents had mounted in one particularly strong redoubt, the Idaho troops, at the cost of many casualties including a battalion commander [this was Major Edward McConville], chased the insurgents out of their trenches at the point of a bayonet and pushed them back to the bank of the Pasig.

[Del] Pilar's dispositions had not anticipated a retreat. When his troops reached the river bank, they realized that they were in a cul de sac, Americans to their front, the river to their rear. Many attempted to swim the river or cross in the few boats available: few elected to surrender. Consequently, big game hunting, which the western volunteers had often found a practical necessity while at home, turned into pot shooting at insurgents attempting to cross the river. The marksmanship of the western volunteers was so accurate that not a single [rebel body] was seen to reach the opposite bank. It is estimated that some seven hundred insurgents were killed, captured, wounded or drowned in this quick bloody attack.

While the Idahoans were chasing the insurgents into the river, the California regiment on the right of the brigade charged and took the town of Santa Ana, capturing in it an arsenal containing a large supply of rice, eight cannons, seventy-eight rifles and 34,000 rounds of ammunition. The optimism of the insurgents before the battle started is indicated by the fact that they stored a large amount of war materials immediately in rear of their front lines.

The Californians then assisted by a battalion of the First Wyoming Volunteers and a company of Engineers, moved south and took the town of San Pedro

Makati, about two miles distant. By noon [of the 5th], the insurgents on the left of Anderson's line had been entirely dispersed.

American historians from Taylor (1904) to Sexton (1939) to Wolff (1961) are one indeed in their accounts of how the Pio del Pilar Brigade bore the brunt of the initial battles of the Filipino-American War -- the "Philippine Insurrection" in their books. Yet, not one of them makes it clear that General Pio del Pilar himself may have been absent in all these actions.

The rebel leadership had maneuvered for Pio to turn over his zone (and his brigade) to General Artemio Ricarte, overall Chief of Operations in Manila, late in 1898. Presidente Aguinaldo, probably on Mabini's advice, had appointed Pio to the Revolutionary Congress as representative of the province of Negros Occidental in a tactful move to get him out of Manila and out of mischief-making. When the Malolos Constitution was signed in January 1899, he was one of the 65 signers. Pio was positively in Malolos when the month of January ended; possibly he was still there when the fighting broke out.[3]

In fairness to Ricarte, it must be said that he, too, was on official business in Malolos on that Saturday night of 4 February when the hostilities began (by the Americans), and he had nothing to do with the near annihilation of the Pio del Pilar Brigade the next day.[4]

Just the same, the officers and men of the Second Zone fought well, according to eyewitness accounts. The first shots that came from the Nebraska Volunteers at San Juan Bridge[5] around 10 p.m. quickly

---

[3]*Taylor (***Philippine Insurrection***, Volume 3, page 190) comments: "On 31 January [Generals] Luna, Ricarte, Llanera, Rizal, Alvarez, Macabulos, Trias, Mascardo, Garcia, Torres and Pio del Pilar were in Malolos." (Underscoring mine.)*

[4]*You have to hand it to Pio del Pilar: his brigade kept on resurrecting -- as later history would show.*

[5]*Faust,* **Campaigning in the Philippines***, page 129. From most American sources, we know the first shot actually came from Private Willie Grayson of the Nebraska Volunteers. And from the "Insurrecto Papers", we learn that the first Filipino casualties were Captain Serapio Narvaez's company of the Morong battalion assigned in the Santa Mesa outpost of Colonel San Miguel's Third Zone of Manila. For a lengthy and very interesting "revisionist" account of the first battles of the Philippine-American War, see Benito J.*

spread that same night to three points in Manila: La Loma in the north, Santa Mesa in the northeast, and -- across the Pasig River -- Santa Ana on the southwest. Around 3:30 dawn of the 5th, firing spread further south in the Second Zone when the Filipinos fired on Blockhouse No. 11 near San Pedro Makati.

In Santa Ana, the "insurrectos" initially clashed with the troops of the California and Wyoming Volunteers. The British residents there were caught by the war inside the Filipino lines, for they had preferred to stay there during all those past troubled months. It puzzled them how the Filipinos could have started the war -- as Otis made it appear -- when their Generals were not even there. To seek safety from the bullets of both sides, these European neutrals all gathered in the stone house of the McCleods. One of them was Richard Brinsley Sheridan who later in 1900 wrote **The Filipino Martyrs**. In describing that particular scene of the Battle of Santa Ana in his book, Sheridan's sympathies are clearly for the Filipinos:[6]

> *The English residents of Santa Ana had the most trying time on the night of the 4th, and had it not been for the kindness and generosity of the Filipinos, many British subjects would, no doubt, have been killed by the bullets of the Americans ...*
>
> *All through the night the men stood [sic] covering the bodies of the women [Sheridan's own wife was there] who remained bravely motionless, awaiting their expected end. The bullets were pattering on the walls, and whistling through their rooms and around the house. The groans of the wounded and the dying could plainly be heard.*
>
> *The Filipino officers frequently came to them and offered them encouragement, altered their positions as the firing changed, and generally inspired them with renewed hope and consequently renewed strength to bear the terrors of their position.*

Legarda, "The first shot that triggered the Philippine-American War in Feb. 1899 was fired in Balic-Balic, not San Juan (a neighborhood chronicle)", **Mr. & Ms. Magazine**, *2 & 9 February 1988.*

[6]*Richard Brinsley Sheridan,* **The Filipino Martyrs** *(London: The Bodley Head, 1900; Manila: Malaya Books, 1971), pages 164-165. Page numbers used here are those in the Malaya edition.*

Sheridan subheads his book, "A story of the crime of February 4, 1899".[7] To him it is a simple case of the Americans having *wronged* the Filipinos -- and the non-American nationals as well. Sheridan continues:[8]

> *... Santa Ana is situated on the Rio Pasig, which was now patrolled by a small American armed launch [this was the* Laguna de Bay *which had brought in more U.S. troops to Santa Ana during the night] and its guns were directed and fired upon the town. This shelling of the European and native houses added to the fears and dangers of the people huddled together in Mr. M___'s [McCleod's] house.*
>
> *It was well known that General Otis had maps of Santa Ana, in which all the European houses were marked and their positions located, and it was therefore scandalous that shells should have been unnecessarily thrown into the houses of British residents.*
>
> *When the Filipinos were closely pressed for the want of ammunition, the officers informed the M___'s [McCleod's] party they had only ammunition enough to cover their retreat, and their trials were now ended, as the town would soon be in the hands of the Americans.*
>
> *The Filipinos retired from Santa Ana in perfect order, fighting all the time, with determination, energy and courage. In this fashion did the Americans take Santa Ana.*

Sheridan's account tells only of what he saw and what he heard while holed up in the McCleod house as night fighting raged in Santa Ana. On the Filipino behavior right in the trenches, here's what General Thomas Anderson testified the following day: "The Filipinos made a brave defense; as the Scotch Guard at Flodden Field formed an unbroken line around their king, so these misguided insurgents fell where they fought, filling the trenches with an unbroken line of killed

---

[7]**Ibid.**, *see the book's inside title page.*

[8]**Ibid.**, *pages 165-166.*

and wounded".[9] Anderson had commanded all U.S. forces south of the Pasig and had personally supervised operations against the Filipino Second Zone on the 4th and 5th of that bloody February of 1899.

Surprisingly, the "insurgent" lines in Paco had been quiet during the night Santa Ana and Santa Mesa were blazing combat zones. But when the Americans entered that part of Manila the next day, Filipino riflemen began to fire from concealed positions on the U.S. ammunition carts and hospital ambulances. The "insurrectos" were using smokeless Mausers, which made it difficult for the Yanquis to detect their line of fire. To dislodge these snipers, the American commander, Colonel Duboce, ordered all nipa shacks burned, resulting in the roundup of some 50 prisoners. Next target was the Paco stone church, near the bridge where Pio del Pilar had been disarmed by American sentries the previous year. An American battery shelled the church until it burned. Around 60 "insurrectos" came out of the flames and took refuge in the tower. Now followed a shooting contest "between desperados in the tower and our artillery" (Anderson's words) which lasted for several hours.[10] Shells from the American battery failed to discourage the "desperados" -- Sheridan found them still holding out in the tower when he arrived in Paco, and he observed that they fired only on passing American officers, but not on privates.

"As a matter of fact", Sheridan concludes, "the tower was not destroyed, and the Filipinos escaped that night".[11]

Lope K. Santos, who later became Senator, was then in his late teens.[12] Two older friends from Santa Ana -- José de Guzman and Felipe Ventura, whom he described as "like parents to me" -- convinced him to work with them at the Aduana under the Americans. It turned

---

[9]*Faust,* **Campaigning**, *page 136.*

[10]**Ibid.**, *page 139.*

[11]*Sheridan,* **Filipino Martyrs**, *page 161.*

[12]*Lope K. Santos would at war's "official" end become a famous vernacular writer and poet, editor of the nationalist paper* **Muling Pagsilang**, *and co-founder of the radical and anti-American* Partido Nacionalista *in the league of Macario Sakay, Aurelio Tolentino, Santiago Alvarez, Pascual Poblete and others. His biography had been compiled, edited and published by his daughter Paraluman S. Aspillera as* **Talambuhay ni Lope K. Santos** *(Manila: Capitol Publishing House, 1972).*

out that his two friends were really "insurrectos" who must have been ordered to work as moles inside the Aduana. For when the shooting war began and all three of them went over to the "insurgent" lines at Santa Ana, Ventura turned out to be a Captain and De Guzman a Lieutenant in the Pio del Pilar Brigade. Lope K. Santos recounts in his autobiography that he served with that Brigade's military administration and saw the first battles with his own eyes. He writes in his memoirs:

> *While the firing went on [in Santa Ana], we were at the Archbishop's residence preparing food to be delivered to the soldiers at the firing line. One of those who came to us suffering from multiple wounds was Major Isidoro Carmona [remember the cruel one?]. There I also heard the news that Captain Sixto Magsaysay was left for dead ["nakabulagta"] at the battlefield in San Piro, near Santa Ana. Accordingly, the battle became fierce that night and by dawn our soldiers could not help returning the continuous fire from across the river at Santa Ana where the Americans were. We who were quartered at the Archbishop's residence joined the retreat towards San Pedro Makati. We passed by the church and the barrio of Saboy going to San Piro. Such was the surprise of the people at this panic from the scene of battle.*

Lope K. Santos later joined the retreat to Pasig, then to Pateros. He did not know that what was left of the Pio del Pilar Brigade -- walloped at every turn in its zone: in Paco, in Pandacan, in Santa Ana, in San Pedro Makati -- finally opted for survival and found refuge in the hills of Antipolo. He did not know that Captain Magsaysay survived his wounds after he was picked up from where he fell and carried off to Antipolo. And he did not know that Pio del Pilar, returning from Malolos, would in a few days reappear in that mountain shrine-town of Morong where the miraculous image of the *Nuestra Señora de la Paz y Buenviaje* was, as is now, venerated by pilgrims.[13]

---

[13]*From Pateros, Lope K. Santos accompanied a small group that went to San Pablo, Laguna, joining General Cailles, serving in its propaganda corps. (Aspillera,* **Talambuhay**, *pages 16-20)*

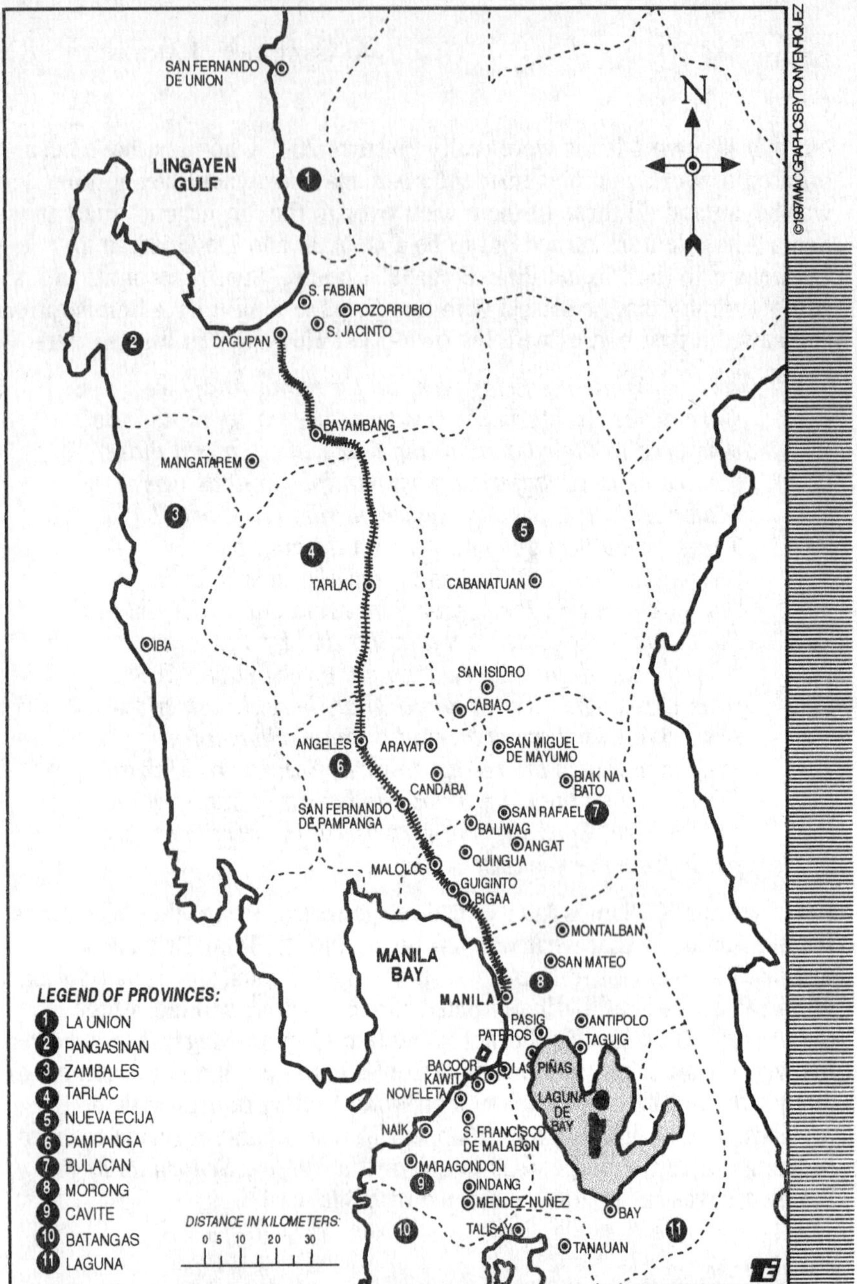

PIO'S BATTLES IN LUZON

Pang-Una lived up to his KKK name in all the battles fought by the Pioistas in Cavite, Batangas, Manila-Morong, Bulacan and Nueva Ecija, from 1896 to 1900.

ten

MIRACLE IN ANTIPOLO

THE SECOND ZONE OF MANILA had been its cradle and grave, while the hills of Antipolo was where Brigada Pio del Pilar miraculously "resurrected". To Antipolo the remnants of the Second Zone forces had fled after the initial shocks of defeat of 4 and 5 February. And to Antipolo a raging Pio del Pilar had rushed from Malolos to gather again, animate again, and organize again his surviving Pioistas.[1]

From Antipolo, on 11 February, General Del Pilar notified the Secretary of War in Malolos:[2]

> *I have today taken command of the [Morong] regiment of the Second Zone of Manila, which is at present concentrated in this town of Antipolo; its battalions are utterly disorganized. I do not know why; but I can inform you that they have lost heavily, especially many rifles, cannons, much ammunition, cannon balls, arsenal repair shops and materials. And I accordingly send herewith rolls of the members of the companies present in order to show the state in which these battalions are; and I have today ordered my Captains to enlist such men as are willing to serve the country as soldiers with an indefinite term of service.*

---

[1]*Antipolo was even then already famous for its Maytime festivals. As the mountain pilgrimage shrine of the miraculous* **Nuestra Señora de la Paz y Buenviaje** -- *Our Lady of Peace and Good Voyage -- it was referred to as "the pearl of the Philippine curacies" and, as a parish, it had been much-contested by the Secularization Movement led by Fathers Pelaez and Burgos in their struggle against* **frailucracia** *in the 1860-1870s. (See Nick Joaquin,* **A Question of Heroes** *[Makati: Ayala Museum, 1977], page 14.)*

[2]*Taylor,* **Philippine Insurrection**, *Volume 4, Exhibit 826, page 575.*

> *But I must tell you that every soldier has only five cartridges; hence it is of the most urgent necessity for the office of [the Secretary of] War to send me at once by the Captain who carries this letter 300 rifles, 20,000 Remington cartridges and 5,000 Mauser cartridges. I beg you not to delay in sending these rifles and cartridges ... because the condition of these* pueblos *today is a critical one.*

Only two weeks later, one is astonished to find Pio del Pilar succeed in gathering back the strength and courage of his previously battered, demoralized troops. Without doubt he had used force and, as Taylor puts it, he must have really "ruled with a strong hand" -- commandeering work animals here, punishing collaborators there, pressing the people all around.[3] But the way he handled the situation to bring back the morale and enthusiasm of his nearly annihilated troops, and turning them into fighting men again, was something to marvel about -- a feat unmatched by any other leader anywhere. Sexton was probably right in saying that Pio del Pilar was "one of the few insurgent leaders capable of keeping his troops together".[4]

By 18 February, Del Pilar had gathered enough strength to come down from Antipolo with most of his men armed only with bolos for an attack on Malapad-na-Bato (the present-day Fort Bonifacio) and Guadalupe.[5] General Antonio Luna, by this time Chief of Operations north of Manila, hearing of Del Pilar's bold exploits, wired Aguinaldo on the 20th: "I congratulate General Pio".[6] And the revolutionary paper **La Independencia** reported:[7]

> *Pio del Pilar and his heroes have won for themselves a foremost place in the annals of the present generation. Through the wilds of Malapatnabato [sic],*

---

[3]**Ibid.**, *Volume 2, page 68.*

[4]*Sexton,* **Soldiers in the Sun**, *page 150.*

[5]*Taylor,* **Philippine Insurrection**, *Volume 4, Exhibit 609, page 23; Exhibit 834, page 586.*

[6]**Ibid.**, *Exhibit 609.*

[7]*Quoted by Edwin Wildman in his* **Aguinaldo: A Narrative of Filipino Ambition** *(Boston: Lothrop Publishing Co., 1901), page 108.*

his intrepid bolomen showed once and for all their undoubted efficiency at a time when musketry is powerless to make an end of the enemy. General Pio del Pilar, with marvelous intuition, sent his bolomen against a mass of American troops, as a huntsman lets loose his hounds to drive out the wild beasts trying to hide in the depths of the woods. The episodes of the last few days have been so brilliant and so numerous that it is difficult to find a parallel in history in great military achievement. [8]

The brutal but courageous Major Isidoro Carmona was back in the front, though his many wounds had not yet healed. Fellow "insurrectos" would hear about and speak of his valor even as far south as the Visayas: one news dispatch in Iloilo reported an amputation of one leg. [9] And there was Captain Sixto Magsaysay who was seen falling seriously wounded at the Battle of Santa Ana and who many, including Lope K. Santos, thought was dead -- like a miracle, he "rose again from the dead" with his brigade in Antipolo to fight again at Guadalupe.[10]

On 22 February, Washington's birthday to the Americans, General Luna carried out his own grand assault on Manila. This was the day the *Sandatahanes* of Manila -- the bolomen enlisted from the old Katipunan councils -- would have risen inside the American lines at the same time Luna's troops in the north zones, simultaneous with those in the south zones, moved in for the big kill. The action began with the burning by the Sandatahan of Santa Cruz district and parts of Tondo and Binondo. This was the signal for the Filipino troops to attack in full force.

Luna's personal troops, led by the mestizo officers Francisco Roman and Rosendo Simon de Pajarillo, were able to enter the city as far as Tondo and Santa Cruz in the Fourth Zone. Noriel's troops in the First Zone reached up to Ermita, while Geronimo's men in the Third

---

[8] *Hurray for Pio del Pilar!*

[9] *Taylor,* **Philippine Insurrection,** *Volume 5, Exhibit 1242, page 499.*

[10] **Philippine Insurgent Records,** *"Pio del Pilar Papers". As of March 1899, Captain Sixto Magsaysay was reported in Pasig, and Pio on 5 March ordered Lieutenant Antonio Nopuente to hand over to Magsaysay all remaining rifles of the First Company.*

Zone and portions of the Pio del Pilar Brigade in the Second Zone fought their way to as far as the districts of San Miguel and Sampalok. But though promising at first, the whole operation soon fell apart after the Americans counter-attacked with vigor and the Filipinos on their part were hampered with dissensions in their ranks -- such as the refusal of the unruly Kawit companies to obey Luna's orders, on the poor and dangerous pretext that there were no orders from Aguinaldo himself. By 24 February, Luna's troops had fallen back to their old lines -- as did those in the south sectors -- except the Pio del Pilar Brigade which kept on advancing against the enemy.[11]

On 25 February, Del Pilar's men recaptured Guadalupe.[12] The Americans, on retreating, burned down the houses in the town proper. The "insurgents" then proceeded to besiege San Pedro Makati to isolate the Americans stationed at the English Cemetery from his hordes of fanatical Pioistas, many of whom were themselves Makati-born.[13] By 1 March, General Pio del Pilar had regained partial control of his Second Zone, had in fact mobilized a force stronger than what he had when the war broke out -- now 2,688 officers and men, 1,695 of whom were concentrated in Pasig, according to Taylor's account -- and had become too much of a threat to be ignored by the American high command in Manila.[14]

Now it was General Otis's move. Hastily he formed a provisional brigade, since then famous as "Wheaton's Flying Column", commanded by the American General of that name. Its mission was to

---

[11]*For accounts of Luna's 22 February attack on Manila, see Agoncillo,* **Malolos**, *pages 501-502; Sexton,* **Soldiers in the Sun**, *pages 101-102; Taylor,* **Philippine Insurrection**, *Volume 2, pages 204-205; Le Roy,* **Americans in the Philippines**, *Volume 2, page 26-27; Faust,* **Campaigning**, *pages 144-146; Wilcox,* **Harper's History**, *pages 137-142; and Zaide,* **Philippine Revolution**, *pages 306-308.*

[12]*Taylor,* **Philippine Insurrection**, *Volume 4, Exhibit 834, page 586.*

[13]*It could be that, unknowingly, the Ayalas of Makati had really moved Pio's statue from its original site on Ayala Avenue to the intersection of Makati Avenue and Paseo de Roxas at the very spot where the "Hero of Makati" must have waved his sword while crying out "Avance! -- Sugod!" to his hordes of fanatical Pioistas, many of whom were themselves Makati-born.*

[14]**Ibid.**, *Volume 2, page 216.*

clear and regain the area about the Pasig occupied by the Filipinos and vital to them as a communications link between their northern (Luna) and southern (Ricarte) commands. Taylor summarizes these operations as follows:[15]

> *During the week beginning 10 March (1899), General Wheaton, in command of a provisional brigade, cleared the south side of the Pasig River and occupied the towns of Pasig, Pateros and Taguig. The line of the Pasig River was occupied and communications between the insurgent forces on the north and south was permanently interrupted ... General Otis reported that General Wheaton between 10 and 17 March 1899 inflicted a loss of more than 200 killed and wounded upon the insurgents in Guadalupe Ridge, Pasig, Pateros, Cainta and Taguig and driving them from the line of the Pasig River. The insurgent reports state that the casualties in Guadalupe were 11 killed and 41 wounded, at Ugong and San Felipe (Neri?] 3 killed and 28 wounded, and at Taguig 6 killed and 11 wounded. On 25 March Pio del Pilar lost [sic] 3 dead and 4 wounded at Pasig.*

In these actions, General Wheaton had with him the 20th U.S. Infantry, the 22nd U.S. Infantry, two battalions of the 1st Wyoming Volunteers, seven companies of the 2nd Oregon Volunteers, one squadron of the 4th U.S. Cavalry, Lieutenant E.D. Scott's platoon of the 6th U.S. Artillery, and the gunboat *Laguna de Bay*.[16] Finally, in April, after a month of hard fighting, the Americans forced the Pio del Pilar Brigade to fall back once more to its Antipolo stronghold. But this did not mean it was the end of Pio del Pilar's control over the Manila Second Zone.

Meanwhile, intrigues against Pio, denouncing his harsh methods, rained again at Aguinaldo's headquarters in Central Luzon. From Antipolo, Colonel Lazaro Macapagal Lacandola, chief of the Morong Battalion which was "conscripted" into the reorganized Pio del Pilar Brigade (and the same Macapagal, incidentally, who executed the

---

[15]**Ibid.**, *page 208.*

[16]*Faust,* **Campaigning**, *pages 148-149.*

Bonifacio brothers in 1897), wrote to Aguinaldo complaining of the many abuses -- robbery, rape, cruelty etc. -- committed by the Pioistas, which he said were tolerated by their General. "I very much dislike to be in the company of these people and ... I would like to be with you and die by your side" -- Macapagal tells Aguinaldo in a typical gesture of Cavitismo.[17] And from Pasig, the ilustrado partisan Señor Bonifacio Arevalo denounced the widespread *monte* gambling "authorized by General Pio, who received bribes, the proceeds of which the said General employs to maintain his mistress [was she the same Monica of 1898 notoriety?] who lives here in Pasig".[18]

These and many other complaints against Pio del Pilar by citizens and by his own comrades in the Republicano Army must have led the American military commentator, Sexton, to observe with typical anti-Pioista bias:[19]

> *During the latter part of May [1899] it was reported that the native inhabitants of the Mariquina Valley were suffering heavily on account of various crimes committed by the insurgents in the area under the nominal command of General Pio del Pilar ... who, prior to the insurrection enjoyed the reputation of being the bandit chief in that section of the country. Either through fear or because he was one of the few insurgent leaders capable of keeping his troops together, [Del] Pilar stood high in Aguinaldo's favor and the many depredations which his troops committed on the native citizenry were accomplished in the name of the insurgent government. After Wheaton had driven the bandit away from Manila and Pasig in March, [Del] Pilar had simply transferred his activities further east.*

The "bandit" was again the object of an American manhunt in

---

[17] *Taylor,* **Philippine Insurrection**, *Volume 4, Exhibit 637, pages 71-72.*

[18] **Ibid.**, *Exhibit 638, page 73.*

[19] *Sexton,* **Soldiers in the Sun**, *pages 149-150.*

June, this time led personally by Major-General Henry W. Lawton. This American officer had just come from a similar mission in east Central Luzon in support of General MacArthur's main thrusts against Luna's army along the railroad line. While he was at San Isidro (Nueva Ecija), Lawton on 18 May telegraphed MacArthur at San Fernando (Pampanga) that "previous to the capture of Calumpit, Aguinaldo had given Pio del Pilar orders to move from Antipolo to the assistance of Gregorio del Pilar at Baliwag".[20] This particular Pio del Pilar story turned out to be fictitious, for the "bandit" had never gone to Bulacan (at least not this time) but had instead moved in again on the Pasig River area. It was for this reason that Lawton was aching to face him.

Lawton's move on Antipolo began on 3 June from San Pedro Makati. His command took the towns of Cainta and Taytay, and then Morong and Taguig, as if the "insurgents" did not care to defend those towns. And even the "vigorous resistance" expected for Antipolo itself -- being sacred ground to Filipinos -- took only a few hours for the Americans to "demolish" with no loss on the Filipinos. The Americans had expected the Filipinos to defend Antipolo with utter fanaticism. Such half-hearted Pioista resistance was unusual and the reason behind this could be logistics -- that is, lack of it -- for Taylor reports that Pio on 14 May was requesting Ricarte's south command for its Imus arsenal to "supply him 300,000 cartridges", the ammunition his brigade needed so that every *soldado* can carry 50 cartridges in his belt, with another 50 in reserve. Avoiding pitched battles, the Pioistas merely moved out of Antipolo, went down to the lowlands again, and then massed around San Pedro Makati -- Pio's own home ground -- where Lawton's troops had come from. On 7 June, Lawton was ordered to concentrate 4,000 men in that section.[21] And Karl Irving Faust, in his **Campaigning in the Philippines**, records a skirmish at Guadalupe on the 10th of June:[22]

---

[20]*Faust,* **Campaigning**, *"A Mythical Insurgent Army", page 220; Sexton,* **ibid.**, *pages 134, 149-150; and "Documents of the Philippine-American War",* **Historical Bulletin**, *XIII:1-4 (1969), page 505.*

[21]*Wilcox,* **Harper's History**, *pages 211-212; Taylor,* **Philippine Insurrection**, *Volume 2, pages 232-233; and Faust,* **Campaigning**, *page 233.*

[22]*Faust,* **ibid.**, *page 234.*

> *Lieut. Scott's first shot from the [6th U.S.] artillery [was directed] at the line of insurgent defense. He hit close to it and exploded some shells right over them. But sly Pio del Pilar was too old a rat to be caught in a cheese trap like that. You could see his men vamoose over the hill, and no cannon could shoot away a hill. Not yet, [Pio del] Pilar, whether you are a traitor or patriot, shall Yankee hands be laid on you.*

Not yet. "Sly Pio del Pilar" would not allow another Pandacan or Santa Ana massacre. The good leader that he was, once more he saved his brigade. And Sexton makes this conclusion on Lawton's Morong campaign in these words: "Considering its purpose to be that of cooping [Del] Pilar's forces up to the Morong Peninsula, that [American] expedition had been a failure".[23]

---

[23]*Sexton,* **Soldiers in the Sun**, *page 152.*

eleven

Excursion To Bulacan

LUNA'S MURDER IN JUNE and the strong signals of pro-Luna partisanship that followed, compelled Emilio Aguinaldo to take personal command of the Republicano Army.[1] The first thing he did was to purge it of Luna diehards -- the mestizos enlisted from the Creole army ("native" volunteers) and the Ilocano troops summoned by Luna from the North -- expectedly replacing them with men of his own confidence, particularly the men of Cavite and of 1896.

Aguinaldo set up his new headquarters at Tarlac town, in a province controlled by General Francisco Makabulos, a '96 veteran of

---

[1]*Lieutenant-General Antonio Luna, Emilio Aguinaldo's Undersecretary of War and Acting Commander-in-Chief of his army, was murdered in Cabanatuan on 5 June 1899 together with his senior aide, Colonel Francisco (Paco) Roman, by Caviteño soldiers belonging to Colonel Agapito Bonzon's Kawit Battalion -- specifically the company commanded by Captain Pedro ("Kastila") Janolino. Luna had answered what appeared to be a government summon for a conference in that Nueva Ecija town, then the capital of Aguinaldo's* Republica. *Luna's "war" with the Kawit soldiers must have began during his 22 February mass attack on Manila, after Luna disarmed several companies of them for refusing to obey his orders to attack (for the flimsy reason that those orders did not come from Aguinaldo himself). Of course, Luna's accusation that they were cowards was belied by the many instances of bravery the men of Kawit -- and Bonzon especially -- displayed in the 1899 battles in the Southern Tagalog Region and in Central Luzon, not to mention the 1896-1898 campaign in Cavite of which they were all veterans. For contrasting views on the "tragedy of Cabanatuan", Agoncillo's* **Malolos** *and Vivencio R. José's* **The Rise and Fall of Antonio Luna** *(Quezon City: The U.P. Press, 1976) are recommended. (See also their Luna "debate" published in* **Solidarity***: Agoncillo, "General Luna Reconsidered" (March-April 1976); José, "The Bankruptcy of the Subjectivist Conception of History" (September-December 1976); and Agoncillo, "On Distorting Historical Facts" (January-February 1977).*

considerable prestige -- though, like Pio del Pilar, of unpredictable character (nobody knew for sure if he was pro- or anti-Luna). To insure his control over the different brigades, at least those which were defending Central Luzon, he appointed another '96 chieftain and a staunch Magdalo, General Pantaleon Garcia, as his Chief of Staff. And to punish or quiet down the *Lunistas*, the hatchetman's role attributed to Pio del Pilar in the hunt for anti-Aguinaldistas in 1897 was assigned to a younger Del Pilar -- and Aguinaldo's new "Beloved General" -- General Gregorio H. del Pilar.[2]

But Aguinaldo had not really forgotten the Pio del Pilar of '96, even though he had turned into the unruly subaltern he now was. In the middle of June, Aguinaldo personally directed his troops in a general attack on San Fernando de Pampanga. It was a tactical failure. The Generalissimo's only gain in this drive was in having alarmed the American commander, General Arthur MacArthur, who found it necessary to send out his Iowa and Kansas troops in full force for a vigorous counter-attack. For the rest of the month and throughout the next, the Filipinos launched small sorties and skirmishes meant to annoy the *Americanos* who were already hard-pressed by the rains. In August, heavy fighting raged again when the Americans renewed their attacks on the Filipino lines which at this time extended from the barrios of San Fernando in Pampanga to the barrios of Baliwag in Bulacan. Aguinaldo's San Fernando line was well defended by the

---

[2]*Goyo del Pilar, to repeat, had no blood relations with Pio del Pilar. He was a mere boy of 21 when he joined Aguinaldo at Biyak-na-Bato in 1897. Returning from Hongkong for the "Second Revolution" in 1898, he liberated his native Bulacan from the Spanish forces and became Commanding General of its provincial brigade. By 1899, and especially after Luna's death, he had become Aguinaldo's hatchetman and he stayed by his* Presidente's *side in the retreat to the North. He died in action at the Battle of Tirad Pass ("Tila" to the Igorots and the Spaniards) -- at a time when Pio del Pilar himself, back in Antipolo, ceased to be in the rolls of Generals of the Republic. For contrasting views on "Heneral Goyo", see Teodoro M. Kalaw's* **Life and Death of a Boy General**, *already cited, and Nick Joaquin's "Was the Hero of Tirad a Hatchetman?" in his* **A Question of Heroes**, *pages 183-202. A recent work by Isaac C. Cruz,* **General Gregorio H. del Pilar: Idol of the Revolution** *(Bulacan, Bulacan: Samahang Pagkalinangan ng Bulacan, 1985), deifies the hero and contains many useful local history materials not found in Kalaw's and Joaquin's works.*

Mascardo, Aquino and San Miguel brigades. But the Baliwag line was defended only by a few troops of Gregorio del Pilar's Bulacan Brigade under Colonel Pablo Tecson, as the main force of this brigade went with their Boy General in the hunt for hostile Lunistas in the North. In Tarlac, Aguinaldo had Garcia, Bonzon and Goyo del Pilar by his side. In Pampanga, he had Mascardo and San Miguel as guards.

But in Bulacan, he needed another "trusty henchman" to hold that part of the "insurrecto" lines.[3] It was a job for Pio del Pilar. And the maverick warrior returned to the fold, so to speak, to come nearer and be reconciled with "mi Presidente".

At this point, it would do well to have a look at some of the men who rode with "Heneral Pio". The Pio del Pilar Brigade, when this marched to the rice paddies of Bulacan that August of 1899, had a strength of twelve organized infantry companies divided into two battalions. The brigade had a general staff and lineup of field officers, as follows:[4]

General Staff

Major Fernando E. Grey, Chief of Staff
Capt. Catalino Raymundo, Aide-de-Camp
First Lieut. Benito Raymundo, Aide-de-Camp
Capt. Fernando Caruncho, *Comisario*
Capt. Alejandro de la Rosa, *Interpretor*
Capt. Lorenzo A. Protacio, *Cajero*
Capt. [no name in document], *Medico*

Field Officers

Colonel Julian Paguia
Lieut. Col. Isidoro Carmona
Major Valentin Esguerra

---

[3]*The other Bulakeño General, Isidoro Torres, who was not on friendly terms with Goyo del Pilar, seems to be inactive at this time. But in the guerrilla phase of the war, as will be seen in subsequent pages of this work, Torres would be in the thick of the anti-American resistance in Bulacan. (See Taylor,* **Philippine Insurrection**, *Volume 2,* passim, *for his guerrilla activities; Volume 5,* passim, *for his "insurrecto" papers.)*

[4]*This list I completed from separate muster rolls of the various units of the Pio del Pilar Brigade, in* **Philippine Insurgent Records**, *"Pio del Pilar Papers", RL-14, RL-15 and RL-16. Taylor (Volume 2, page 246) places the total Pioista strength at 1,283 officers and men as of 30 October 1899 in San Miguel de Mayumo.*

Major Vicente Cabrera
Major Arsenio Mauricio
Major Felipe Banaag
Major Maximino Letran
Major Bonifacio de la Cruz

[1st Battalion]

Capt. Catalino Mercado, 1st Company
Capt. Lino Labao Taniag, 2nd Company
Capt. Manuel Quiogue, 3rd Company
Capt. Rufino Concepcion, 4th Company
Capt. Urbano Carballo, 5th Company
Capt. Bonifacio Molina, 6th Company

[2nd Battalion]

Capt. Blas Lapeña, 1st Company
Capt. Cosme G. Cruz, 2nd Company
Capt. Agapito de Leon, 3rd Company
Capt. Narciso Molina, 4th Company
Capt. Enrique Serrano de Guia, 5th Company
Capt. Angelo San Pedro, 6th Company

[Attached]

Capt. Isidoro Hernandez
Capt. Mateo Cruz
Capt. Pascual Jasmin

Field Commander Colonel Julian Paguia wore an ugly scar on his face. It was not a badge of courage, but a grim reminder of his infamous 1896 *Guardia Civil* days when he was a scourge of the Katipuneros. Having been one of those sent to chase the rebels fleeing from their San Juan disaster towards Marikina, his detachment of civil guards clashed near Barangka with Katipuneros led by Julian Santos (who would become a notorious "bandit" in the early 1900s). In a *manu-mano* combat, a patriot hacked Paguia on the face with his bolo, but the celebrated *Guardia* survived and escaped.[5] When he surfaced again -- after the peace of Biyak-na-Bato -- Julian Paguia had joined the ranks of the "insurrectos" and was all ready to atone for his past misdeeds. Pio del Pilar saw his potentials as a good fighter and made him his *segundo jefe.*

---

[5]*Kasandugo,* **Ang Katipunan**, *page 395.*

Lieutenant-Colonel Isidoro Carmona and Major Valentin Esguerra were Pio's contemporaries and townmates in Culi-Culi.[6] Carmona, especially, had gained a reputation as an arrogant and cruel officer. When his brigade was in Santa Ana, many complaints were hurled against him -- he was especially harsh on Spanish and Macabebe prisoners. But the man was a brave and fierce fighter: later in the war against the Americans, Carmona's fame as a *valiente* would be heard far and wide as he got wounded again and again in battle after battle.

The chief of staff of the Pio del Pilar Brigade was Major Fernando E. Grey y Formentos. We know by the sound of his name that he was Spanish -- he was, in fact, a Creole officer of volunteers in the Spanish Army who went over to the Filipino side to fight against the Americans. He was at first appointed third in command to Colonel Luciano San Miguel in the Manila Third Zone and became sort of famous for having personally supervised the defense of the compromised Santa Mesa area during the initial actions on 4 and 5 February, in the absence of his superior officers.[7] He joined the retreat to Antipolo and from then on was of Brigada Pio del Pilar.

Major Vicente Cabrera commanded the brigade's First Battalion. He was a '96 veteran who had fought with Pio del Pilar in the early battles in Cavite and Batangas. Then he joined the flight to Puray, then to Biyak-na-Bato in 1897. Cabrera, like his chief, had been commissioned an officer in the Spanish Volunteer Militia in 1898, serving as First Lieutenant in the Zapote Line.

---

[6]*In his* **Biografia** *(page 4), Pio del Pilar mentions the pre-Revolution anti-Spanish activism of Isidoro Carmona and Valentin Esguerra.*

[7]*Thus, Fernando Grey became especially famous to us students of the "insurrection".*

A street along Santa Mesa has been named after Grey. Not far from this area, Grey had supervised the defense of the Manila Third Zone while his superior chief, San Miguel, was in Malolos "paying homage to Terpsichore", in the words of Dr. Santiago Barcelona (see **Aguinaldo's Odyssey: As Told in the Diaries of Col. Simeon Villa and Dr. Santiago Barcelona**, *already cited, page 106). That very night of 4 February when the Philippine-American War began, Grey wired Malolos: "At nine sharp tonight, American camp started hostilities. Our forces answered enemy fire. All in their post without fear. Await orders." (See Agoncillo,* **Malolos**, *page 453.)*

And there was Major Arsenio Mauricio. He was from Tondo and had been, at first, a Bonifacista who was among those arrested and tried with the Supremo for the "crime" of counter-revolution in Cavite in 1897. But Pio del Pilar took the young Manileño and the Katipuneros under him into his force, brought them along to Puray, and then to Biyak-na-Bato. In the end, the ex-Bonifacista turned into a staunch Pioista.

Captain Raymundo of the staff was the fugitive Presidente Local of San Pedro Makati. Del Pilar's paymaster, Captain Protacio, was the same gentleman who worked for Pio's discharge from military service in the Spanish Army back in the 1880s. Captains Taniag and Carballo were two more contemporaries of Pio and his fellow *propagandistas* in the dissemination of Rizal's works in pre-Katipunan activist days. Captain Rufino Concepcion, who replaced the promoted Major Bonifacio de la Cruz as Commander of the Fourth Company of the First Battalion in October, preceded Pio del Pilar in the Katipunan and was, in fact, among those who convinced him to become a Katipunero.

First Lieutenant Joaquin Rodriguez was a *Sargento* in General Salvador Estrella's forces in Cavite when the "Second Revolution" began in May 1898. His Cavite company was later attached to the Second Zone of Manila where, during the siege of the city, he rose to Second Lieutenant of Engineers (reserves) in the Pio del Pilar Brigade. He was finally reactivated as a regular officer during the brigade's reorganization at Antipolo in March 1899. And for his good showing in the next battles, Pio del Pilar made him a First Lieutenant in May.

And among the host of other First Lieutenants and Second Lieutenants who fought as Pioistas were: Victorino L. Adriano, Ricardo Alano, Carmelo Basa, Andres Cabrera, Dionisio Capistrano, Anselmo Cruz, Nemesio Cuneta, Francisco Dayao, Fortunato Dinguinbayan, Tomas Evangelista, Agapito Jabalan, Leon Joaquin,[8]

---

[8]*A contemporary revolutionary awit (metrical romance) entitled "Casunod ng Buhay ng Ating Manga Kapatid" sings of some of the martial exploits of Pioistas, as in Stanza 118 where Lieutenant Leon Joaquin's name is mentioned but misspelled: "Si Pio del Pilar at Mariano Noriel / Julian de Ocampo at si Leon Juanching / at si Isidoro Carmonang magaling ..." (See full text in Reynaldo Ileto,* **Pasyon and Revolution**, *Appendix 4, pages 325-330.)*

Eduardo José, Maximino Lopez, Hugo Medina, Gregorio Natividad y San Pedro, Juan Natividad, Apolonio Nopuente, Fausto Ordiales, Marcelo de la Paz, José Reyes, Modesto Salgado, Gregorio Sarmiento, Agaton Taba, Leon Tanjanque, Eusebio Tejada and Fabian Vasquez.[9]

Under these officers, and in compliance with orders from Tarlac, the Pio del Pilar Brigade moved out of Antipolo on 10 August 1899 -- to the relief, no doubt, of the "abused" populace and the indigenous troops of Colonel Lazaro Macapagal Lacandola. Their destination was San Rafael, Bulacan. Their mission: To create a new front and relieve the American pressure on Aguinaldo's Pampanga defense lines.

One of the "insurgent records", **Diario de Operaciones del Ejercito Durante el Mes de Agosto, 1899,**[10] gives a day-to-day account of this operation (or was it, more aptly, an excursion?) of the Pio del Pilar Brigade in Bulacan. The Pioistas set out for San Rafael taking the same route they took during the retreat from Puray to Biyak-na-Bato in 1897. For many of them, it was a coming back -- a sort of sentimental journey -- to Bulacan. At a place called Caingin (which must be in the vicinity of Kakarong), Pio del Pilar left behind some of the troops to stay there overnight with the intention of proceeding the next day to Bintog -- to attack nearby Quingua (now Plaridel) from the northeast. Pio placed Major Valentin Esguerra in command of this column. The main force of the brigade headed for San Rafael, reaching their destination on the 11th.

At San Rafael, General Del Pilar lost no time in sending his scarfaced Colonel Paguia with another column on a circuitous march to reconnoiter the barrios of Angat, Pulong Buhangin, Santa Maria, Santa Clara and Pandi. Paguia rested his men for the night at Pandi, in preparation for attacks on the towns of Guiguinto and Bigaa.

On the 12th, Del Pilar ordered the Esguerra column at Bintog to attack. But on setting out for Quingua, its left flank skirmished with an American scouting party which the Filipinos lured into a *tambang*

---

[9]*All these foregoing data I took from scattered notes in* **Philippine Insurgent Records**, *"Pio del Pilar Papers", RL-14, RL-15 and RL-16.*

[10]*Taylor,* **Philippine Insurrection,** *Volume 4, Exhibit 903 ("Statement of the Operations of the Army during the Months of August 1899"), pages 677-681.*

position. The ambuscade was not a complete surprise, however, and the Americans were able to flee, with the entire Esguerra column hot on their heels. The American garrison at Quingua now came out in force to the rescue of their endangered comrades -- and it was now their turn to run after Esguerra's men, who scurried back to Bintog. Subsequently, in an attempt to drive the "insurrectos" out of their lair, the Americans were in turn ambushed with many casualties which included one officer and nine men killed. The Americans returned to Quingua beaten.

Meanwhile, the Paguia column was also busy fighting some American detachments in Bigaa and Guiguinto. In several barrios in these towns, hit-and-run engagements were fought in the rice paddies which lasted until midnight of the 12th. The following day, 13 August, Paguia's fighters resumed their attack on Guiguinto, destroying the railroad between this town and Bigaa. And that same day, in the outskirts of Quingua, the Esguerra column ran into a small patrol of the U.S. Cavalry. Surprised and outnumbered, the American cavalrymen galloped away, chased by the Filipinos. Some of the Americans dashed into the Quingua River and drowned.

The Pioistas sustained a total of fifteen casualties -- and this includes one Captain and three Lieutenants -- in this action-packed four-day sortie around San Rafael.[11] After these actions, Pio del Pilar brought his troops to San Miguel de Mayumo, near the border of Nueva Ecija.

For the last quarter of 1899, San Miguel would be the headquarters of the Pio del Pilar Brigade.[12]

---

[11]**Ibid.**, *page 681.*

[12]**Philippine Insurgent Records**, *"Pio del Pilar Papers"*.

twelve

THE FAILED GUERRILLERO

THE BULACAN OPERATIONS of the Pio del Pilar Brigade in August were carried out simultaneously -- and obviously in concert -- with the Pampanga operations of the Aquino, Mascardo and San Miguel Brigades.[1]

It was during this same period that attempts were made by the Paterno-Buencamino wing of the "insurgent government" (or what Teodoro Agoncillo calls the "legislative bloc") to revive the Revolutionary Congress and resume its sessions in Tarlac. But Mabini, retired in Rosales (Pangasinan), had protested the move for its bad timing in a seemingly sour-graping article in **La Independencia** -- which particular copies Aguinaldo had ordered confiscated.[2]

Yet, Mabini himself probably missed the point: it would have been best had he objected on the ground that the revived Congress would adversely affect military operations. If Mabini only took a good look at the composition of the "new" Congress in August, he would have seen a long list of military leaders appointed to fill the vacant seats.[3] Luna had been murdered, and that was one military man out. But the new names of Generals Pantaleon Garcia, Tomas Mascardo, Luciano San Miguel, Servillano Aquino, Maximino Hizon, Francisco

---

[1]*Details of these military operations are contained in a single report, the already mentioned "Statement of the Operations of the [Filipino] Army During the Months of August 1899", Exhibit 903 in Taylor's* **Philippine Insurrection**, *Volume 4. (See also Nick Joaquin's hindsight account in his* **The Aquinos of Tarlac** *(Manila: Cacho Hermanos, 1983), Chapter 5, pages 57-58.*

[2]*Taylor,* **Philippine Insurrection**, *Volume 2, page 234; also Volume 4, Exhibit 683, pages 146-149. Mabini was in Rosales for treatment of his paralysis.*

[3]*For complete list of members of the "revitalized" Revolutionary Congress at Tarlac, see Taylor,* **ibid.**, *Volume 4, Exhibit 674, pages 126-130; and Agoncillo,* **Malolos**, *Appendix E, pages 787-791.*

Makabulos, Daniel Tirona, Antonio Montenegro, Venancio Concepcion, Fernando Canon and José Alejandrino had been added to the old names of Vito Belarmino, Isidoro Torres and Pio del Pilar. Mabini's argument should have been simple enough: If these Generals were to attend the congressional sessions, who would attend to their brigades? But anyway, Pio del Pilar for one would rather chase *Yanquis* in the rice paddies than spend his time deliberating in Congress with *burguesos* who had little or no regard for his character in the first place -- the feeling was mutual.

Aguinaldo at this time had his headquarters in Tarlac and was himself preoccupied with the defense of the Paruao River Line.[4] This was Aguinaldo's personal project. Patterned after the now-famous "Evangelista trenches" in Cavite, he had it constructed soon after Luna's own Bagbag River Line fell, and he had hoped to make the Americans bleed through its bamboo palisades before they could take his capital. But Aguinaldo had not intended these trenches to stop the enemy's advance. He had realized after his massive but fruitless attack on San Fernando (Pampanga) in June that it was futile to hold Central Luzon by means of pitched battles. And he was convinced, rather too late, that the best way to fight the Americans was the way he fought the Spaniards in 1897: in the same mountains, with the same men, by the same guerrilla methods. The Paruao defenses were only meant to delay the American northern advance long enough to give the "insurgent army" ample time to prepare for *that* guerrilla war.

---

[4]*On the Paruao River Line, Epifanio de los Santos comments: "[After Luna's death] Aguinaldo mobilized his men and constructed the famous Paruao Line, in order to check as much as possible the enemy's invasion [of Northern Luzon]. The bamboo palisades ... antedated the famous barbed wire entanglements successfully used during the Russo-Japanese War." (See De los Santos' "Aguinaldo and His Times", in* **The Revolutionists**, *page 47.) On the importance of this defense line to the American high command, Don Panyong writes: "The American army, wishing to terminate the Revolution, planned to capture Aguinaldo and his forces before the latter had time to complete the Paruao Line and the defense system of the Bambang [Tarlac] hills." (See his letter to the Editor,* **Philippine Magazine**, *13 April 1926, cited as footnote in Simeon Villa, "The Flight and Wanderings of General Emilio Aguinaldo from Bayambang to Palanan: A Diary", in* **Historical Bulletin**, *XIII:1-4 [1969], pages 87-88.*

The need to bide for time became so imperative to Aguinaldo that he even took advantage of the anniversary of the Cavite uprising (31 August) as an occasion to send commissioners to Manila to confer with Otis, on the pretext of releasing some American prisoners. The news of a Filipino commission coming to Manila in September was accompanied with a rumor that Pio del Pilar would come on his own to make trouble. Says Taylor:[5]

> *General Pio del Pilar may have thought Aguinaldo preparing to sell out and determined to make an offer himself before that of his superior could reach the American commander; for General Otis reported that in September 1899, an insurgent officer wrote to a friend in Manila who must have been close to the American commander and who must have informed him of the proposal, that [Del] Pilar and his troops would capture that city by January [1900] at the farthest, and would take into captivity the archbishop and the American commander; but that for $1,000,000 [wow!!!] he would hand over Aguinaldo and his entire government.*

This could not have been true -- or Pio del Pilar was, in fact, double-dealing -- because the "insurrecto papers" also tell us that on 10 September he was recommending to Aguinaldo a plan for guerrilla warfare for the whole province of Bulacan, with him as overall commander.[6] Pio proposed to harass the Americans in that province by means of *gapang* (surprise raids) and *tambang* (ambuscades) -- for which, Aguinaldo knew, Pio was a master of the art.

To this Aguinaldo replied on 19 September through his Chief of Staff, General Pantaleon Garcia, who transmitted the Presidente's approval of Pio's guerrilla plan and his appointment as Chief of Operations, but *only* for that part of Bulacan east of the railroad line. Only the troops and military chiefs in that area were to be under his orders.[7]

---

[5]*Taylor,* **Philippine Insurrection**, *Volume 2, page 244.*

[6]*Chief-of-Staff Garcia to Secretary of War,* **ibid.**, *Volume 4, Exhibit 694, page 167.*

[7]**Ibid.**

But on 20 October, a month later, Garcia notified the Secretary of War at Bayambang that "by reason of the exigencies of the war in Bulacan", Pio del Pilar had been reappointed "Chief of Operations of said entire province" -- with supervisory control over the commands of Colonels Pablo Tecson and Julian (brother of Goyo) H. del Pilar.[8] And the next day, from Tarlac, Aguinaldo rushed this long telegram to Pio del Pilar, giving his full instructions:[9]

> *You must already know that the enemy is at San Isidro [Nueva Ecija] and that some ten thousand of his forces are concentrated at [the Pampanga towns of] Santa Ana, Arayat, Angeles and neighboring territory. According to our spy [in Manila?] they will land some of their troops at Dagupan [Pangasinan] so as to capture our government and myself, as though they thought I had lost both of my legs and no one could come to my help. For these reasons I deem it necessary for you to be there [in Bulacan] and organize as many guerrilla bands as possible and promote disturbances in the province ... and also to scatter our forces throughout the territory so as to keep [the Americans busy] locating and chasing our guerrillas. The latter must likewise try to cut the railroad and derail the trains used for military operations, and especially when crossing the bridges toward the town of Victoria [Tarlac].*
>
> *You must act at once and not wait for further instructions which will not reach you quickly on account of the distance. I shall expect all the soldiers of your command to conduct themselves properly toward the inhabitants of the towns and desire that the guerrillas shall not operate in the inhabited districts and thus [not] expose the same to the attacks of the Americans, thereby [not] causing discontentment toward our troops among those who, because of the*

---

[8]*Chief-of-Staff Garcia to Secretary of War,* **ibid.**, *Volume 4, Exhibit 946, page 730.*

[9]*Aguinaldo to Pio del Pilar,* **ibid.**, *Volume 4, Exhibit 703, page 183.*

outrages committed, are somewhat displeased with the conduct of those Filipinos [i.e., Macabebes] who are serving in the American Army. It is necessary for us to organize a party of four hundred armed men in the city of Manila, who must operate there according to the instructions sent by me some time ago.

I shall expect you all to give the enemy no rest and that you conduct the campaign in combination with the forces of Gen. Licerio [Geronimo] and those of Col. [Teodoro] Gonzales, who is in Novaliches; I charge you with guarding the ordnance stores in Biac-na-Bato [sic] as well as the commissary stores there. I wish you would also try to capture the launches [of the Americans] lying in the lake [i.e., swamp] of Candaba.

This telegram was "to be forwarded to San Miguel de Mayumo by the [Presidentes Locales] of the towns en route". But the action was futile; the last-minute instructions it contained were inutile, for Pio del Pilar may have not have received them or received them too late. For the truth is, the Pioistas were the very troops who had been badly beaten trying to defend San Isidro where, by accident, while foraging for supplies, they clashed with the Americans in that Nueva Ecija border town.[10]

The American offensive in the North had begun during the first week of October, immediately after the peace commission headed by General José Alejandrino came back from Manila. Mabini, as usual, had misgivings about the "armistice", fearing that the Americans would only see through Aguinaldo's ploy and discover the weakness of his army.[11] And he was probably right again, because Otis right away pursued his long-pending "Get Aguinaldo" plan.[12]

---

[10]*Sexton,* **Soldiers in the Sun**, *page 177. See also American correspondent William Dinwiddie's account in Wilcox,* **Harper's History**, *page 301. Dinwiddie describes the San Isidro encounter as "among the liveliest engagements of the campaign". On the Filipino rout, he comments: "The enemy's loss is known to have been very heavy. General Young [commanding Lawton's cavalry] estimates the forces in front of him at almost a thousand under Pio del Pilar."*

[11]*Alejandrino,* **Price of Freedom**, *page 165.*

[12]*For summaries of Elwell Otis's "Get Aggie!" campaign of*

Aguinaldo's spies were right about the Yanqui plans to land troops at Dagupan (Pangasinan). And Aguinaldo himself was correct in estimating that they were out "to capture the government and myself". On 12 October, General Lawton, Pio del Pilar's recent antagonist in Morong, led a strong division of infantry, cavalry and Macabebe mercenaries from Baliwag in Bulacan, took Arayat in Pampanga, then proceeded to Cabiao in Nueva Ecija. The 22nd Infantry, old enemies of the Pioistas, did very well in this movement. And on 19 October, according to Sexton, this regiment "marched into San Isidro, after routing some 900 insurgents under the control of General Pio del Pilar". [13]

Or was it, as some writers think, *Gregorio* del Pilar?[14]

No; the others were mistaken and Sexton was right. It was Pio all right, because Goyo del Pilar was at that time in Tarlac by his Presidente's side.

But what was Pio del Pilar doing in Nueva Ecija when he should be operating in Bulacan?[15]

1899, see Taylor, **Philippine Insurrection**, *Volume 2, pages 251-258; Le Roy,* **The Americans in the Philippines**, *Volume 2; James Blount,* **The American Occupation of the Philippines** *(New York: G.P. Putnam's Sons, 1912; Manila: Malaya Books, 1968), pages 233-247; Sexton,* **Soldiers in the Sun**; *Uldarico S. Baclagon,* **Philippine Campaigns** *(Manila: Graphic House, 1952), pages 114-119; Zaide,* **Philippine Revolution**, *pages 327-329; Agoncillo,* **Malolos**, *pages 540-545; Wolff,* **Little Brown Brother**, *pages 277-285; Stuart Creighton Miller,* **"Benevolent Assimilation": The American Conquest of the Philippines** *(New Haven, Connecticut: Yale University Press, 1982), pages 95-97; Richard E. Welch Jr.,* **Response to Imperialism** *(Chapel Hill: University of North Carolina Press, 1987), pages 30-32; and my own* **The Tinio Brigade**, *pages 69-77.*

[13]*Sexton,* **Soldiers in the Sun**, *page 177.*

[14]*Agoncillo (***Malolos**, *page 542), for one, says it was "General Gregorio del Pilar's forces" whom the Americans clobbered at the Battle of San Isidro.*

[15]*Frederick Funston writes in his memoirs: "It was known that the notorious Pio del Pilar ... was hiding in the mountains along the boundary between the [Central Luzon] districts commanded by General [Frederick] Grant and myself, but just what authority he exercised was not known." (***Memoirs of Two Wars**, *page 337.)*

One looks at a map of Central Luzon and sees that the Nueva Ecija border towns of Cabiao and San Isidro are just a short distance away from his base, the Bulacan border town of San Miguel de Mayumo. So he could have gone there for provisions as had become customary when Aguinaldo made Biyak-na-Bato, not too far away, his headquarters back in the days of 1897. Otherwise, Pio del Pilar was on his way to join Aguinaldo in Tarlac -- contrary to the latter's instructions -- when the San Isidro disaster took place.

Aguinaldo himself was shortly after driven further north by General MacArthur's division. The American advance toward Tarlac began on 5 November; the "insurgent" capital fell on the 12th. By then, Aguinaldo had already transferred his capital to Bayambang where he called a council of war of a few Generals (Alejandrino among them) that decided -- then and there -- to officially wage guerrilla warfare. Meanwhile, another American division under General Wheaton had landed on Lingayen Gulf -- at San Fabian, and not at Dagupan as rumored -- on 7 November, advanced to San Jacinto on the 11th, and pushed eastward to Pozorrubio on the 14th. This move sought a link somewhere near Pozorrubio with Lawton's own thrust from San Isidro, with the aim of sealing off Aguinaldo's escape route to the North. But Aguinaldo escaped with Goyo del Pilar and his troops to the Ilocano provinces. On 2 December, the younger and more famous Del Pilar was martyred in Ilocos Sur in the now-famous sacrificial Battle of Tirad Pass. Though he died a hero, he was a failure as Presidente Aguinaldo's protector.[16] The "lesser" Del Pilar -- "sly Pio del Pilar" -- lived. But he, too, was a dismal failure. Beaten at San Isidro, his troops -- whipped, mauled and crippled -- fell back once more to San Miguel de Mayumo. They were still there, licking their wounds, when October ended. But the Pio del Pilar Brigade, now too decimated to even carry out their projected guerrilla war "to promote disturbances" in Bulacan, never lived up to their Presidente's expectations. The Pioistas made no raids, wrecked no bridges, derailed no trains -- not a single fracas emanated from their side to even momentarily disrupt the American "Get Aggie!" campaign in the North.

Pio del Pilar was now a failed *guerrillero*.

---

[16]*For a summary of the American chase of Aguinaldo from Pangasinan to Ilocos Sur, a long distance of over 200 kilometers within one agonizingly long three weeks, see my* **The Tinio Brigade**, *pages 77-85.*

WARRIORS FOR FREEDOM
The enemy labelled them all "insurrectos" – as if name-calling would cover up the Yanqui's own Anglo-Saxon barbarism.

thirteen

FALL OF THE PIOISTAS

HE WHO HAD PROPOSED *tambang* and *gapang* was left out of the anti-American guerrilla war that raged with fury from the day it was officially sanctioned by Aguinaldo's council of war at Bayambang in November 1899. And he who had been defamed, vanquished and humbled by the enemy was now displaced, disowned and discarded by his own comrades in the Republicano struggle.

When General Luciano San Miguel in Zambales informed the Hongkong Junta on 13 December 1899 that "Pio del Pilar is in San Miguel de Mayumo", he apparently based it on reports which were two months old [1] Obviously, San Miguel did not know that Pio del Pilar had already gone back to Morong with what remained of his failed guerrillas. And San Miguel was unaware that he himself -- as well as Del Pilar -- had been "deposed" from the Central Luzon high command. In January 1900 when Pantalcon Garcia assumed overall leadership as Commanding General of Central Luzon, neither Luciano San Miguel in Zambales nor Pio del Pilar in Bulacan were on Garcia's "official" list of guerrilla commanders in his zone.[2]

Why? In Pio del Pilar's case, was it because he had not been able to carry out Aguinaldo's 21 October orders which probably did not even reach him in the first place? Was it a punishment for having

---

[1]*Luciano San Miguel to Hongkong Junta, in Taylor,* **Philippine Insurrection**, *Volume 5, Exhibit 1023, page 149.*

[2]*The complete line-up of guerrilla zone commanders in Pantaleon Garcia's Central Luzon command were as follows: General Isidoro Torres, southern Bulacan; Colonel Julian H. del Pilar, northern Bulacan; Colonel Pablo Padilla, Nueva Ecija; General Maximino Hizon, Pampanga; General Francisco Makabulos, Tarlac; General José Alejandrino, Pangasinan; and General Tomas Mascardo, Bataan and Zambales. Neither Luciano San Miguel as Zambales commander nor Pio del Pilar as Bulacan commander were recognized by Garcia's Central Luzon headquarters. (See Taylor,* **ibid.**, *Volume 5, Exhibit 1037, page 171.)*

allowed the debacle at San Isidro which may have been really an accident? Was it Garcia's own personal decision -- or had this Aguinaldo adherent acted upon orders from above? Had Aguinaldo finally decided to break all ties of friendship with the once-upon-a-time "Beloved General" of 1896 who had turned recalcitrant by 1899?

For the rest of 1900, guerrillas everywhere would strike fear among and wreak havoc and destruction upon the American forces of occupation. Aglipay would terrorize the Yanquis and their mercenaries in the Ilocos. Lacuna would give them no rest in Nueva Ecija. Torres would take command of all Bulacan. Cailles would score victories in Laguna. Malvar of Batangas and Lukban of Samar would write history. But poor, helpless Pio del Pilar would remain holed up and idle in his hideouts around Manila.

Pio was running out of Pioistas.

What remained of his Pioistas lay hidden in the Antipolo hills -- badly beaten, utterly demoralized, now begging for shelter and food from their more fortunate comrades-in-arms. During the cold Christmas season of 1899 when they had just returned to Antipolo, a pitiable scene unfolds as the once proud Señor Fernando Grey -- his Spanish accent very obvious even in writing -- makes an appeal to the Sandatahan:[3]

[Stationery head: "Fernando E. Grey, Comandante, Jefe de Estado Mayor"]
Antipolo, 19 Diciembre 1899

Sr. Atilano Sta. Ana
Teniente Coronel

Minamahal con caibigan: Ibig co laman matanto con hindi ninyo aco mabibiguian sa cacanin ñg mga sundalo, sapagcat ang isang caban bigas at isang cargan hipon, at sampon piso sa humigit cumulang 300 sancatao ay parang hinipan lamang; sa bagay na ito inaasahanco ang yon casagutan dito sa amin calagayan.

Ang Presidente [Local, i.e., the Mayor] dito ay ayao magbigay at utos dao ni [Lazaro] Macapagal na huag magbigay ñg wala siang orden.

Yto na lamang at magutos cayo, Sr. y amigo.

F.E. Grey

---

[3]**Philippine Insurgent Records**, *"Pio del Pilar Papers", RL-14, Enclosure 370.*

(Grey wants to know if Lieutenant-Colonel Atilano Sta. Ana [of the Sandatahan] can provide food for the soldiers [of Pio's brigade], as a cavan of rice and a bushel of shrimps and ten pesos for more or less 300 men [is this all that is left of the brigade's 12 companies?] disappears in a whiff. Grey also complains about the refusal of the Presidente Local to help, as he claims that he has been instructed by Lazaro Macapagal not to give anything without his orders.)

Colonel Sta. Ana replies the next day to inform Major Grey that he has already sent a cavan of rice and *ulam* (viand), that two more cavans of rice are on the way from Pasig, and that there is a second supply of *palay* (unmilled rice) to follow. To the provisions is added a word of advice. Sta. Ana tells Major Grey to "instruct [Pio's] soldiers not to commit atrocities or crimes so there will be no complaints against us". [4]

The Pioistas stood by and watched as the Republicano forces around them put on their guerrilla show. In the new organizational setup, the Manila-Morong zone came under the jurisdiction of the Department of Southern Luzon -- of which Mariano Trias was Commanding General. Trias, too, like Garcia in Central Luzon, had scratched out Pio del Pilar's name from his own "official list" of guerrilla commanders. Under this setup, General Ricarte was Chief of Operations for Manila, General Geronimo for northern Morong, and the just-promoted General Macapagal for southern Morong.

From the start these guerrilla forces had one common objective: the capture of Manila. That was the very reason why the Sandatahanes (of which Colonel Sta. Ana was one of the principal chiefs) had been given so much importance by the Southern Luzon command, at least in the city itself and its environs. There were persistent rumors in December, when the Pioistas were down and out, that Ricarte was busy mobilizing these Sandatahan units -- particularly the *Armas Blancas* of Tondo and Binondo led by Colonel Lucio Lucas, and Ricarte's own dreaded "Conquering Regiment of the Viper" in Santa Ana and Pandacan led by Colonel Mariano Barroga -- for the final attack. The American high command feared that this "uprising" led by urban guerrillas would be coordinated with simultaneous actions of the regular guerrilla columns from outside the city. General Lawton,

---

[4]**Ibid.**

returning from his northern campaign against Aguinaldo, was ordered to "clean up" the known "insurrecto lairs" in the Morong hills. On 19 December -- to the envy, no doubt, of the Pioistas -- General Lawton was killed by General Geronimo's *tiradores* at the Battle of San Mateo River.[5]

Ricarte decided to take advantage of Lawton's funeral to carry out his plans "to attack the city and [assassinate] General Otis", to quote Taylor.[6] But on the appointed hour, the funeral procession took a different route and not the crowded streets where Ricarte's armed partisans were waiting for the moment to strike -- and his *anarquistas* (the suicide terrorist squad who were to have thrown the bombs) were thwarted and instead were rounded up by the American secret service through their spies. But the Manila "insurgents" sustained their underground activities in the city until the summer months of 1900, and in Pandacan a number of agents of the Manila secret service disappeared and "their fate never definitely ascertained".[7]

All this time, Pio del Pilar may have been inside Manila himself, probably in Pasay where his family lived, or in Pasig where he was known to have a *querida*, or in any of the houses of many friends and comrades in Makati, Guadalupe, Santa Ana or Pandacan. He had not disbanded his followers, and he had maintained communication with them through guerrilla runners who delivered Pio's orders to the men.

There are documents among Del Pilar's "insurrecto papers" which show attempts to reorganize the Pioistas into units of independent guerrillas who were to be called *Tiradores de la Brigada Pio del Pilar*.[8] One document reveals the transformation of Captain Rufino Concepcion's Fourth Company of the First Battalion into two guerrilla squadrons made up of 16 soldados and 10 *rancheros* each -- a total of 26 tiradores to a squadron, or 52 to a column -- under the immediate commands of Lieutenants Nemesio Cuneta and Gregorio Sarmiento.[9] And in Manila itself, Heneral Pio was no doubt working in concert with

---

[5]*Taylor,* **Philippine Insurrection**, *Volume 2, pages 326-327.*

[6]**Ibid.**

[7]**Ibid.**, *page 328.*

[8]**Philippine Insurgent Records**, *"Pio del Pilar Papers".*

[9]**Ibid.**

El Vibora, and maintained his own personal force of urban guerrillas.

But in so far as the headquarters of General Lazaro Macapagal was concerned, the only legitimate guerrilla forces in its territory were its own. And Macapagal may have been referring to the Pioistas when, in March 1900, he ordered the commander of one of his Morong flying columns to "capture those who injure or fight us or have intentions of fighting against us or the independence of our country, the bandits, those who possess arms without licenses, and *the troops of whom I have no knowledge"*. [10] (Underscoring mine.)

Here in Morong in 1900, one sees Cavitismo circa 1897 surfacing again. The novelty this time is of Magdalo fighting Magdalo -- for both Pio del Pilar and Lazaro Macapagal once figured as partisans in the same camp, equally involved in the same conspiracy to eliminate Andres Bonifacio as leader of the Revolution.

One recalls Lazaro Macapagal -- younger -- as the Magdalo commander assigned by the Revolutionary War Council headed by General Mariano Noriel to supervise the "execution" of the Bonifacio brothers. By his own soul-cleansing testimony, Macapagal's grim mission -- accomplished at Mount Buntis (near Maragondon, Cavite) on 10 May 1897 -- was carried out in the name of the Revolution. (Did he feel guilty? For instance, was his order for the capture of the Pioistas, his imagined enemies, a sign of a troubled conscience?)

And Bonifacio's biographers as recent as Alejo Villanueva[11] practically consider Macapagal's role as just another *berdugo* job that only puts Bonifacio's death "in the nature of martyrdom" -- "a summary execution in absolute disregard of the basic requirements of elementary justice, only because Bonifacio was the stumbling block to the [Aguinaldo] Cavite government's pretension to legitimacy." As far as Pio del Pilar's own role is concerned, it can hardly be considered a Judas act since he was not in league with Bonifacio in the first place and

---

[10]*Taylor,* **Philippine Insurrection**, *Volume 2, page 334. In the rhetoric of the Republicano struggle, "bandits" included peasant armed groups such as* Guardia de Honor, Santa Iglesia, Cruz na Bituin, *and* Katipunang San Cristobal -- *as well as the Bonifacistas (men like Emilio Jacinto and Macario Sakay) who carried on their own independence struggle in the name of the Katipunan as the* "Republika ng Katagalugan".

[11]*Alejo L. Villanueva, Jr.,* **Bonifacio's Unfinished Revolution** *(Quezon City: New Day Publishers, 1989), page 63.*

he merely chose between loyalty to the pretender to the revolutionary throne (to whom he was enamored) or shifting that alliance to the Supremo devoured by his own creation -- the Revolution.

In any case, the 1900 Morong internecine war between the two ex-Magdalos as Republicanos was just as bloody as its Cavite archetype. In May, Pioistas arrested Major Eusebio de Rateros -- apparently of Macapagal's command -- on charges of having been "a thief and assaulter of women".[12] From his base in Manila, Pio del Pilar was reported to have "sentenced" the man to be buried alive in the cemetery of Taguig, the town he had allegedly outraged. Another Macapagal henchman, a Comandante Espada, was also reported to have been arbitrarily executed upon orders of Pio.[13]

In turn, the Supremo's executioner must have shouted with joy to hear that at Guadalupe, on 8 June 1900, the American secret police had finally tracked down and captured the sly, foxy Pio del Pilar.[14]

---

[12]**Ibid.**, *page 320. Also Volume 5, Exhibit 1070, page 206.*

[13]**Ibid.**, *Volume 5, Exhibit 1070.*

[14]**Historical Calendar** *(Manila: National Historical Commission, 1970), page 91. Both his Makati marker (for details, see footnote #4, Chapter 1) and his capsuled biography in* **Eminent Filipinos** *(page 207) claim Pio was captured in Santa Ana. The Englishman John Foreman (***Philippine Islands***, page 505) makes this comment on Pio's capture: "Captain Lara of the native [Manila] police took Generals Pio del Pilar and Salvador Estrella prisoners, but was himself assassinated on 4 August [1900]." And Isabelo de los Reyes, sensing the agit-prop value of Lara's "assassination", editorialized that news in the 25 September 1900 of his Madrid-based* **Filipinas Ante Europa***: "The* execution *[my emphasis] of the unfortunate Lara in the center of Manila gives testimony to the vigor and power of the Revolution even in the very capital of the Archipelago, under the cannons of the Americans." (Quoted by Le Roy in* **Americans in the Philippines**, *Volume 2, page 312 footnote.)*

fourteen

EXPATRIATE -- OR EX-PATRIOT?

HE WAS A PRISONER of the Americans at a time covered by an amnesty offer from General Arthur MacArthur, who had succeeded Otis as the American military governor of the Philippines. Pio del Pilar did not lose time in grabbing this opportunity to keep himself out of the old Bilibid Prisons: he took the oath of allegiance to the United States government together with other "insurrecto" Generals who were taken prisoners like himself -- Ambrosio Flores, Venancio Concepcion, José Ignacio Pawa, Francisco Makabulos, and Pantaleon Garcia.

At first, everything looked like it was all for real. Pio behaved, to the American authorities at least, like he was indeed the "reformed insurrecto" he professed to be. And he was even allowed to go out of Manila for the purpose of negotiating the surrender of another Filipino General, Isidoro Torres, who was still fighting in Bulacan. But Taylor, in retrospect, thinks all this was just an act on Del Pilar's part. On Pio's one-man *zarzuela*, Taylor comments:[1]

> *The sincerity of his efforts may be judged by the fact that about 3 July 1900 he wrote Torres from Malolos two letters, one to be read by the American commander there and one to be read only by Torres. In one he told him that he should come in for a conference with the Americans, who had been ordered by General MacArthur to confer with him with respect to a general peace. In the other he told him that he himself was going back into the field as soon as he sent out materials for the manufacture of ammunition.*

Taylor fails to mention Pio's request to Torres that his messenger be granted his wish "to command troops ... at your orders".[2]

---

[1]*Taylor,* **Philippine Insurrection**, *Volume 2, pages 331-332.*

[2]**Ibid.**, *Volume 5, Exhibit 1076, page 214.*

On the reaction of General Torres to these overtures, Taylor says that on 13 August he informed Aguinaldo that "Pio del Pilar, Macabulos [sic] and Buencamino had all written to him urging him to surrender" -- and that "he had written to the first telling him that he should communicate with him through Aguinaldo and he had scorned to reply to the others".[3] In reply to the "peace missives", adds Taylor, Torres "called upon the insurgent generals who had surrendered and taken the oath of allegiance to the United States to again take to the field".[4]

Contrary to what General Isidoro Torres exhorted them to do, most of his fellow Generals -- Tirona, Montenegro, Makabulos and others -- joined the growing number of patriots-turned-*Americanistas* banding together into the Federal Party.[5] Had Pio del Pilar fraternized with this group too, he would have been a free man. But they were as *antipatico* to him as he was abominable to them. And so, although he had sworn "loyalty" to America, he was still among those Filipinos labelled *intransigentes,* or irreconcilables, by the Americans and pro-American Filipinos. And in the roundup of such "insurrecto hardcores" for deportation to Guam in January 1901, it was not surprising at all to find Pio del Pilar among the most prominent ones.[6]

It was a left-handed compliment by the Americans. In this crowd of deportees, Pio del Pilar was among *respectable* company:

---

[3]**Ibid.**, *Volume 2, pages 252-253.*

[4]**Ibid.**, *page 253.*

[5]*The Federal Party was founded on 23 December 1899 in Calle Villalobos of the Manila district of Quiapo. Prominent founding members were Ambrosio Flores, José Salvador Natividad, Francisco Makabulos, Daniel Tirona and Antonio Montenegro among Aguinaldo's former generals; Pedro Paterno, Felipe Buencamino, T.H. Pardo de Tavera, Cayetano Arellano and Florentino Torres among former high officials of the Malolos Republic; Tomas G. del Rosario, Felipe Calderon, Fernando Ma. Guerrero, Ignacio Villamor, Mariano Abella, Manuel Xerez Burgos, José Basa Enriquez and José R. Infante among former Malolos congressmen; and Isabelo Artacho, Clemente José Zulueta, Arturo Dancel and Julio Nakpil among other vacillating types. Taylor translates the party's manifesto and platform, printed in Spanish, as Exhibit 1182 in his* **Philippine Insurrection**, *Volume 5, pages 383-388.*

[6]*For correspondence on the deportation of these Filipino prisoners of war, see Mabini,* **Letters**, *pages 315-327.*

Mabini, the *paralitico* who had been the real brains of the Republica; Ocampo, the fellow delegate to the revolutionary congress who had directed the Manila counterpart of the Hongkong Junta; Almeida, the fearless governor of La Union whom a U.S. military commission sentenced as a "war traitor"; the rich Adiarte Brothers and other patriots of Ilocos Norte who had staunchly backed up Aglipay's guerrillas; and fellow Generals -- Ricarte the Vibora, Llanera the Creole, Hizon the Lunista, De los Santos the Bonifacista -- men of all kinds and persuasions but who were all true *revolucionarios* like Pio del Pilar.[7]

If Pio's integrity as a patriot was ever questioned by comrades, this did not seem to be so in the circle of Guam expatriates who, in an election of officers held on 17 March 1901, chose him President, with 20 out of the 40 exiles voting for him. Could half the population have been wrong in selecting their own Pang-Una in exile?

Said Mabini in a letter to his brother:[8] "Del Pilar after thanking the electors, proceeded to state his lack of qualification for the position inasmuch as he did not know either Spanish or English". Mabini, as the presiding officer, answered Pio that "the majority, in electing him, must have taken into consideration other conditions that made him more qualified [than the other candidates] inasmuch as his lack of knowledge of Spanish or English could easily be supplied with the help of any companion who is in a position to give it to him". One imagines that assembly of radicals seconding Mabini's motion to a man -- with lusty cheers of *Viva Pio!*

Pio del Pilar was chosen over Artemio Ricarte, Pablo Ocampo, Julian Gerona, and Mabini himself.

In Guam, some of the expatriates would die in exile: General Hizon who survived the anti-Lunista purges of 1899, Colonel Barroga

---

[7] *The other deportees, in alphabetical order, were: Joaquin Agramon, Pio Barican, Mariano Barroga, José Buenaventura, Lucas Camerino, Anastacio Carmona, Pedro Cobarrubias, Esteban Consortes, Igmidio de Jesus, Bartolome de la Rosa, Norberto Dimayuga, Doroteo Espino, Julian Gerona, Eulogio Gonzales, Silvestre Legaspi, José Mata, Juan Mauricio, Hermogenes Plata, Cornelio Requiestas, Antonio Prisco Reyes, Alipio Tecson, Simon Tecson, Maximino Trias, Fabian Villareal, and Juan Leandro Villarino. (***Ibid.**, page 322.)*

[8] **Ibid.**, *"Elections in Prison", pages 282-283.*

who had fought under Pio in the Second Zone in 1898 and then under Ricarte in 1899, and Colonel Camerino who had fought side-by-side with Del Pilar in the Cavite campaigns of 1897.[9] Those who survived (including Pio) were amnestied by U.S. President Roosevelt's proclamation of 4 July 1902 -- following the surrender of Malvar -- and they were allowed to return to the Philippines in November of that year, except Mabini and Ricarte. In February 1903 the sickly Mabini finally came in to swear to American rule, but not Ricarte.

Of all the Filipino generals in the hands of the Americans, only El Vibora did not swear allegiance; only The Viper did not give up the Revolution. And back home, he was not alone.

Aguinaldo fell when the exiles had not been in Guam for two months.[10] But the guerrilla war did not end -- not after Malvar gave up

---

[9]*A few words about these unsung heroes. The Pampangueño Maximino Hizon liberated his province from the Spaniards in 1898, commanded a brigade under Luna in the Central Luzon campaigns of 1899, was purged for his Lunista leanings, and re-installed as guerrilla zone commander for Pampanga until his capture in 1900. The Ilocano Mariano Barroga was an 1896 Katipunan veteran who had fought with Pio against the Spaniards and then helped the Vibora in his attempts to organize a* Sandatahan *uprising inside the American lines in Manila until his capture in 1900. The Caviteño Lucas Camerino was another battle-scarred veteran of the "First War" in Cavite who later fought with equal distinction under Generals Noriel and Ricarte until his capture in 1900. These three patriots all died in exile in Guam without renouncing their adherence to the cause of Philippine* independencia.

[10]*Aguinaldo was captured by General Frederick Funston at Palanan on 22 March 1901, through a clever ruse utilizing Macabebe mercenaries disguised as "insurrectos" led by the Spanish renegade Lazaro Segovia. On 16 April, he issued the proclamation calling upon his generals and their forces to lay down their arms. For first-hand accounts on his capture, see Chapter VII of Funston's* **Memories of Two Wars**, *reprinted in* **Historical Bulletin**, *XIII:1-4 (1969), pages 240-270; and Segovia's version,* **The True Story of Aguinaldo's Capture** *(Manila: MCS Publications, 1969). For hindsight views, see especially Agoncillo's* **Malolos**, *Chapter XV ("Operation: Cagliostro"), pages 592-650; and David Haward Bain,* **Sitting in Darkness: The Americans in the Philippines** *(Boston: Houghton Mifflin Co., 1984). For Aguinaldo's activities in Isabela prior to his capture, see Carlos Quirino's edition of the diaries of Simeon Villa and Santiago Barcelona,* **Aguinaldo's Odyssey** *(Manila: Bureau of*

in April 1902, not even after Roosevelt's 4th of July amnesty. Pio came home in November to find Aguinaldo's commanders in the Manila-Morong zone already out of the war. He was probably amused to learn that the renowned Heneral Serio of San Mateo, the nemesis of General Lawton, was now "Teniente Geronimo" of the *Constabularios.*[11] But somewhere in the Morong hills and jungles where Pioistas in their heydays once roamed and ruled, a new people's army was consolidating the warring Katipunero and Republicano factions for a common struggle. General Luciano San Miguel, also unsurrendered, the man whom Aguinaldo deposed from his Zambales command in 1899, had crossed over from Cavite that last quarter of 1902 to take command and carry on the anti-American resistance Malvar had abandoned.[12]

Public Libraries, 1963); and Nick Joaquin's translation of Telesforo Carrasco's military journal, **A Spaniard in Aguinaldo's Army** *(Manila: Solar Books, 1986).*

[11]*For good accounts on Licerio Geronimo, see especially E. Arsenio Manuel,* **Dictionary of Philippine Biography**, *Volume 1, pages 192-195; and Lilia Ramos-De Leon, "The Filipino Geronimo, A Super General, Was the Nemesis of General Lawton",* **Philippine Panorama**, *7 June 1981.*

[12]*Malvar surrendered in Batangas on 16 April 1902 -- which history according to the victors had, through all the colonial years, specified as the date the "Philippine Insurrection" officially ended. The truth is, it did not; for on October of that same year, Filipino forces in Bulacan-Rizal assembled in a council of war in Norzagaray and elected Luciano San Miguel the supreme leader of the Revolution. San Miguel crossed over from his native Cavite to Rizal to formally take command of the resistance forces led by Santos, Guillermo, Sta. Ana, Samson, Cruz, Contreras and others -- on 15 January 1903, according to Constabulary records. On 27 March, San Miguel was killed in action at the Battle of Corral-na-Bato near Marikina. Though he died an authentic hero, colonial history had always classified his fine deed as "bandolerismo" and never honored him even with a biographical sketch other than this feeble blurb in Zoilo M. Galang's* **Encyclopaedia of the Philippines** *(Manila: McCullough Printing Co., 1950, 3rd edition): "LUCIANO SAN MIGUEL. General. Bravely fought and was wounded in Batangas. Hero-like, he exposed himself to danger during the Revolution.* Survived the battles and died in peace [!!!!]. *" (See Galang's Volume 4, page 291. The underscoring and exclamation marks are mine.) For accounts on the San Miguelista movement, see especially* **Report of the U.S. Philippine Commission**, *1903, pages 5, 7-8, 39-42, 54-55, 71-73; Vic Hurley,*

San Miguel died a forgotten hero in March 1903, in a forgotten battle in a forgotten spot near Marikina. But in May, the Bonifacista Macario Sakay[13] emerged to take over the leadership and continue the struggle in the name of Katagalugan -- the "Haring Bayan" of Tondo --

---

Jungle Patrol: The Story of the Philippine Constabulary *(New York: E.P. Dutton and Company, 1938), pages 87-89, 101-104, 106-110; Renato Constantino,* **A Past Revisited**, *pages 251-255; O.D. Corpuz,* **The Roots of the Filipino Nation** *(Quezon City: Aklahi Foundation, Inc., 1989), Volume 2, pages 488-491; my "Himagsikan ng mga Tulisan",* **Diliman Review** *6:3 (1988), pages 27-34; and my* "San *Luciano San Miguel" in* **"Bandoleros"**, *pages 23-45.*

[13]*Macario Sakay, an original or pre-1896 Katipunero, had presided over the "Dapitan" council of Trozo, one of the first branches of the Katagalugan supreme council -- the "Haring Bayan" of Tondo. After the Supremo's death by decree in 1897, he continued to work underground with Emilio Jacinto in the now "outlawed" (and* "contra-revolucionario"*) Katipunan. After Jacinto's death in 1899, outside the fold of Aguinaldo's Republic, Sakay carried on the struggle -- first, in collaboration with diehards of Magdiwang (men like Santiago Alvarez); then, in the grand anti-imperialist alliance of* Katipuneros, obreros, Aglipayanos *and others in the* Partido Nacionalista*; and finally, in his own* Republika ng Katagalugan *of which he was Presidente-Supremo. Sakay's hanging in 1907 had since been a red-letter date for the Philippine Left, past or present.*

For pioneering and richly documented works on Sakay, see José P. Santos, **Tatlong Tulisan**, *and Antonio K. Abad,* **General Macario L. Sakay: Was He a Bandit or a Patriot?** *(Manila: J.B. Feliciano and Sons, 1955). For the "new historiography" viewpoints, see Reynaldo C. Ileto,* **Pasyon and Revolution: Popular Movements in the Philippines 1840-1910** *(Quezon City: Ateneo University Press, 1979), pages 213-244; Constantino,* **A Past Revisited**, *Volume 1, pages 255-261; Corpuz,* **Roots**, *Volume 2, pages 495-497; my "Himagsikan ng mga Tulisan", above cited; and my "Glory at the Gallows", in* **"Bandoleros"**, *above cited, pages 75-111.*

Movie versions of Sakay's life story have been produced 54 years apart by Lamberto Avellana (Filippine [sic] Films, 1939) and Raymond Red (Alpha Omega Productions, 1993). Efren C. Yambot presented it as U.P. play, entitled "Ang Kilabot ng Sierra Madre", in 1972. Published so far but unfilmed is Clodualdo del Mundo Jr.'s (and Herky del Mundo's) "Alyas Raha Matanda", in **Tatlong Dulang Pampelikula** *(Manila: De la Salle University Press, 1992), pages 212-317.*

the supreme council of Bonifacio's deathless Katipunan. And on Christmas Eve of that year, Ricarte himself returned from Hongkong to carry out his own revolution in the style of the Republica. All these movements must have been coordinated by a single central committee in Manila, possibly the Partido Nacionalista.[14] (But it was clear that Sakay was a Katipunero, purely oriented to Katipunan goals, that Ricarte was a Republicano, and that San Miguel was a middle-of-the-roader.) All these movements were classified in the American archives as the "bandit" phase of the Revolution.

Was Pio del Pilar involved in any of these movements?

Ricarte's testimony given during his interrogation in 1904, following his capture, narrates a meeting with Pio del Pilar shortly after he arrived from Hongkong.[15]

> *... at the instance of Pio del Pilar, through Bartolome de la Rosa, I went to visit him at his house in Peñafrancia, Paco ... We held a conference which touched upon the situation as it then was and upon my plans. Pio del Pilar having adhered to them all asked to accompany me, which I did not accept because I did not trust him, and I advised him to remain in Manila until*

---

[14]*The* Partido Nacionalista *was founded during its own Quiapo Assembly on Calle Gunao on 21 August 1901 as a direct challenge to the American-sponsored* Partido Federalista. *Aguinaldo followers were noticeably not among the founding members, who represented radical obrero groups, Aglipayano church militants, underground* zarzuela *theater guilds, diehard Magdiwang Bonifacistas, Bonifacio's old Masonry-Liga-Katipunan circle, and, of course, Sakay's own Katagalugan Katipuneros. It must be emphasized here that this original Partido Nacionalista of 1901 was not the same latter-day "Nacionalista" Party that was to be identified, much later, with Quezon and Osmeña -- the latter was never heir to the former's revolutionary tradition. One of the founders, Lope K. Santos (Aspillera,* **Talambuhay**, *page 44) revealed that the Partido broke up because of differences among the groups loyal to Santiago Alvarez, Pascual Poblete and Macario Sakay. (See also* **Annual Report of the U.S. Philippine Commission**, *1903, pages 39-42; William Brecknock Watson's "The Christmas Eve Fiasco and a Brief Outline of the Ricarte and Other Movements", in Ricarte,* **Memoirs**, *pages 174-175; and Ileto,* **Pasyon and Revolution**, *page 213.)*

[15]*Ricarte,* **Memoirs**, *Appendix K, pages 124-125.*

> *such time as he should see that the people responded [to Ricarte's call for Revolution].*

And in a letter to his associates in Hongkong, dated 25 December 1903, Ricarte wrote: "Pio del Pilar was looking for me yesterday, but in view of the information that has been furnished me by some, I have avoided the meeting. Perhaps I will do so when I am [already] in the battlefield".[16]

Despite Ricarte's doubts, the Hongkong committee must have still considered Pio's participation vital to the movement as Ricarte in January 1904 received a letter from them telling him to "try to reconciliate our cause [differences] with Pio". Ricarte should remember, they advised, that "there must be no antagonism and only union is what constitutes strength".[17]

But in the end, it seems that Ricarte was proven right, if one believes what that chronicler of American empire days, William Brecknock Watson, has to say on Pio's "involvement" in the post-Malvar movement:[18]

> *Ricarte lost no time in looking up his old friend Pio del Pilar, formerly a man as dangerous as himself, a cattle thief and inveterate gambler, but who, politically, then viewed things [already] from a different standpoint. He was no longer the dyed-in-the-wool insurrecto he had once been, but was aiding the authorities very considerably [for a fee?] in putting down attempts to disturb the public peace. Ricarte did not know this to be so, although evidently he had his suspicions. Hence he approached [Del] Pilar as the [Del] Pilar of former days although with some misgivings.*
>
> *On 29 December, a week after his arrival [from Hongkong], he called on him and made a bid for his*

---

[16]*Letter of Ricarte to Manuel Ruiz "Prin", 25 December 1903, in* **ibid.**, *Watson's "Christmas Eve Fiasco", cited in Ricarte,* **Memoirs**, *page 181.*

[17]*Letter of Manuel Ruiz "Prin" to Ricarte, 6 January 1904, in* **ibid.**, *Appendix J, page 121.*

[18]*Watson's "Christmas Eve Fiasco",* **ibid.**, *pages 182-183.*

> *cooperation in carrying out his plans of revolt against the [U.S.] government. [Del] Pilar listened attentively and gave the impression that he was willing, but at the close of the interview, he dispatched an agent of his to the provincial governor [of Rizal] to report what had occurred.*

Pio del Pilar, according to Watson, was made by Ricarte the General-in-Chief for Northern Luzon of his *Ejercito Libertador*. True enough, Pio had nothing to do with Ricarte's only success -- the revolt of a Constabulary company in Vigan -- in what should have been Pio's command.[19] The "Vigan Mutiny" was quelled as quickly as its spark. In fairness to Pio del Pilar, it must be said that he had nothing to do either with Ricarte's capture a few months later in Bataan province.

Ricarte had distrusted not only Pio but Sakay too, with whom he never really united in struggle.[20] They had disagreed mainly on questions of strategy and later events proved that Sakay's was probably more sound. While Ricarte's revolution fizzled out into a failure, Sakay's own Katagalugan movement gained adherents and strength -- from the very people Ricarte would have banked on. "Katagalugan", as the Katipunan of Tondo was named, was the Supreme Council of the Sons of the People -- the "Haring Bayan", as Bonifacio's official seal as Supremo had proclaimed. Noveleta's "Magdiwang" and Kawit's "Magdalo" were only its daughter councils in Cavite. Culi-Culi's "Magtagumpay" to which Pio del Pilar was sworn in as a Katipunero on

---

[19]*Ricarte,* **Memoirs**, *Appendix K, page 127; Hurley,* **Jungle Patrol**, *page 109; and my "Himagsikan ng mga Tulisan", above cited. For a full account of the "Vigan Mutiny", see the official report of Constabulary Captain A.E. Hendryx in* **Annual Report of the U.S. Philippine Commission**, *1904, Part 3, pages 101-105.*

[20]*An exchange of letters between these two radicals is recorded in Watson's "Christmas Eve Fiasco" (Ricarte,* **Memoirs**, *page 182). "Order me at any time", says Ricarte's letter on 29 December 1903 announcing to Sakay his safe arrival from Hongkong. "This government [of Katagalugan] is awaiting for your assistance", replies Sakay on stationery with his official seal as Presidente-Supremo of the Republika ng Katagalugan. Ricarte, of course, had envisioned a different government directed by him, but which had as nominal head "Junta de Amigos" leader Aurelio Tolentino (one of the stalwarts of the Partido Nacionalista).*

the eve of the Revolution, was in principle a section of Katagalugan; but Pio chose to belong to Magdalo. In the internal war of the Katipunan factions in Cavite in 1897, historians forgot that Katagalugan in the persons of the Supremo and his Tondo-Balara (or Manileño) group was itself a faction, the third force in that intramural fight among rebels that in the end both Magdalo and Magdiwang would conspire to abolish.

Magdiwang and Magdalo would dissolve as one into the Republica which would, in the very end, disown Pio and his followers. But Katagalugan, though phased out, was never really liquidated. Having survived the Supremo in 1897 and Emilio Jacinto in 1899, Katagalugan grew once more with Macario Sakay until, in 1904, it was again *The* Revolution, as it had always been since its pre-1896 birth in Tondo. Now Sakay controlled the very Morong hills where the Supremo's intriguers -- Pio del Pilar and Lazaro Macapagal -- had fought each other as soldiers of the Republica.

Would Katagalugan, true to its Katipunan ethics, be willing now to forget the past and forgive a cursed Magdalo like Pio del Pilar for a united struggle to liberate the *Lupang Tinubuan* from the American *imperialistas*?

Among the documents used as exhibits against Sakay during his trial in 1906 was an alleged military order dated 17 May 1904 issued to Pio del Pilar as "Division General" of the Katagalugan forces. He was instructed to enter the town of Teresa "to arrest the *consejal* Maximo Garovillas and all persons concerned with him in detaining our commissioners and as soon as [you have] arrested [them,] you will punish them as provided in Order No. 9 of 10 April 1904, prescribing that the tendon Achilles be cut and the fingers of both hands crushed". Del Pilar was also instructed that "should the town people offer resistance to our troops, [he must] burn all the houses without showing mercy to the inhabitants".[21]

Antonio K. Abad, in his work on Sakay, produces another document which is related to the one previously mentioned:[22]

> *We the undersigned pledge to support, obey and carry out the above orders for the sake of our country and people who love freedom.*

---

[21]*Abad,* **General Macario L. Sakay,** *pages 74-75, 81-82.*

[22]**Ibid.**, *page 32.*

We therefore, accept whatever punishment will be given by the highest command to any one who will disobey this order.

We affix our signatures hereunder:

PIO DEL PILAR
The Division General

Officers:
FORTUNATO MARIANO
CANUTO ESTRELLA
NARCISO ROQUE

Contemporary Constabulary reports, however, neither linked Del Pilar to any of Sakay's guerrilla operations between 1903 and 1906, nor confirmed any guerrilla raid on Teresa led by him. Was the Del Pilar "document" then a mere forgery to add weight to Sakay's death sentence? Or, as Watson said, was Pio "aiding the authorities very considerably" in bringing down the last apostle of Katagalugan to the gallows?

Pio del Pilar in subsequent years would help bring down the off-and-on Ricartista movement to its final end. But he himself had not many years to live. On 21 June 1931, according to his Makati marker, the "Hero of Makati" died in Pasay.

The year before, he had written historian José P. Santos a letter containing these kind words on Macario Sakay:[23]

Sakay may have been a bandit in the eyes of the Americans. That is why they sentenced him to the gallows. But before God, Country and Truth, he was a true makabayan *who deserves to live in the minds of all countrymen for all times.*

---

[23]*See full Tagalog text in Santos,* **Tatlong Tulisan**, *page 36. I did not use Abad's own translation (***General Macario L. Sakay**, *page 33), because I think it is out of context. Abad fails to make the distinction between Pio del Pilar as a Republicano and Sakay as a* tunay na Katipunero. *And here Abad repeats the mistake of other historians who seem unable to grasp this basic contradiction of the Revolution -- but which is simple enough to "new history" exponents like Ileto, who sees the Republicano* and Katipunero *struggles as separate (and, in fact,* contending*) patriot movements. (***Pasyon and Revolution**, *pages 225-227.)*

In those days, anyone good enough to recognize and brave enough to call Macario Sakay a hero, must also be, at heart, a hero.

PATRIOT CALLED BANDIT
Only in the 1970s was Sakay finally given recognition as a Katipunero, genuine and true – not a worthless "bandolero."

AFTERWORD: THE TROUBLE WITH HEROES

In those days, anyone good enough to recognize and brave enough to call Macario Sakay a hero, must also be, at heart, a hero. -- Orli Ochosa's final words on Pio del Pilar, Hero, previous page

I am a part of all that I have met. -- Hero (Ulysses) speaking through Poet (Alfred Lord Tennyson)

I HAVE MET PIO DEL PILAR AND OTHER HEROES, so now they are a part of me, those who have great minds or great courage. That means, if I want to understand me, if I want to make a difference in *my* life, I have to understand my heroes. If you want to understand other people, if you want to make a difference in *their* lives, you have to understand their heroes. You have to read history, of great men of ideas and bold men of action. When you do, I hope it is the *conscious present* coming to terms with the *heroic past*; also the unconscious *present* coming to terms with the revolutionary *present* (the *future* imperfect). (This is Liberation History in so many words; read *Editor's Preface* for more.)

There is another thing you can do: understand yourself. So, understand your heroes. That's the first trouble with heroes: you have to understand them.

As for me, I must now understand mine, and in so doing, hope to show you how to understand yours. So, here's my *other* short list of heroes, the choice mainly based on the fact that *I have something new to say about each of them.* For, of course, I have many heroes, and I cannot possibly discuss them all in this book in which I am only a guest writer. (I must not forget to say thank you to Orli.)

Soledad Lacson-Locsin	Gary Kasparov
José Rizal	Bishop Nikolai
Andres Bonifacio	Raul Roco
Bill Gates	Apo Fidel Ramos
Jesus Christ	Ninoy Aquino
Christopher Reeve	Leticia Ramos-Shahani

Ferdinand Marcos
Erap
Martina Hingis
Sadao Nishibori
Nietzsche
Alfred Yuson
Women Journalists
Crisostomo Ibarra
Mormons
Tiger Woods
Romy Antonio
Lea Salonga
William Henry Scott
Juan Flavier

The other main reason I have chosen the heroes I listed here is that I can assure you *they're* not *too good to be true*. Most of them anyway. (For my *other* short list of heroes, see my *Introduction*.)

LACSON-LOCSIN, NON-TRANSLATOR

One of the newest heroes I have is a lady, Maria Soledad Lacson-Locsin of Talisay, Negros Occidental: She gives us **Noli Me Tangere** which is more a retelling of the story as Rizal would have done it in English. From Spanish to English and yet much of the flavor of the original has been retained; that's the way I feel (no, I don't know Spanish). All the Tagalog translations of the Noli I remember are bad: they inject quaint Tagalog, as if the translators want to impress the reader. In contrast, as this translation makes clear, Rizal's intention was to make his readers aware of ideas, not conscious of words. He was interested not in building your vocabulary but in raising your consciousness, not merely to impress but to convince.

So, a writing translator as hero. Now, Rizal reads superb as he should: *He tells the story with waves following ripples of sentences in a paragraph that ends on a seashore of surprise*. I like that. For you to appreciate that, I quote side-by-side two translations of **Noli**, the same Chapter One: Lacson-Locsin's "A Gathering" and Leon Ma. Guerrero's "A Party" -- see starting next page.

She translated Rizal when she was already very old. The trouble with heroes like Lacson-Locsin is that their heroism comes out rather late. But better late than never.

So, Ma. Soledad Lacson-Locsin's or Leon Ma. Guerrero's? I use both actually. I use the same approach when I read the Bible: I turn to any number of the versions, Catholic or non-Catholic publisher. In this way I am always richly rewarded.

Ma. Soledad Lacson-Locsin's Translation (Bookmark, 1996)[1]

TOWARDS THE END OF OCTOBER, Don Santiago de los Santos, popularly known as Capitan Tiago, was hosting a dinner which, in spite of its having been announced only that afternoon, against his wont, was already the theme of all conversation in Binondo, in the neighboring districts, and even in Intramuros. Capitan Tiago was reputed to be a most generous man, and it was known that his home, like his country, never closed its door to anything, as long as it was not business, or any new or bold idea.

Leon Ma. Guerrero's Translation (Guerrero's Publishing, 1995)[2]

DON SANTIAGO DE LOS SANTOS was giving a dinner party one evening towards the end of October in the 1880's. Although, contrary to his usual practice, he had let it be known only on the afternoon of the same day, it was soon the topic of conversation in Binondo, where he lived, in other districts of Manila, and even in the Spanish walled city of Intramuros. Don Santiago was better known as Capitan Tiago -- the rank was not military but political, and indicated that he had once been the native mayor of a town. In those days he had a reputation for lavishness. It was well-known that his house, like his country, never closed its doors except, of course, to trade and any idea that was new or daring.

---

[1]*José Rizal,* **Noli Me Tangere**, *Ma. Soledad Lacson-Locsin, translator, pages 1-2. She says: "My own personal view is that [translations] should, as much as possible, capture much of the nuances and cadence of the period in which they had been written."*

[2]*José Rizal,* **Noli Me Tangere**, *Leon Ma. Guerrero, translator, first published in London by Longman Group Inc. in 1961, pages 1-2. He says: "I have tried in this version to provide ... the contemporary reader 'the ease of original composition'." The reason Guerrero's translation is longer is because he prefers to explain in the text itself; Lacson-Locsin prefers endnotes (which I did not include here.)*

Lacson-Locsin's Translation	Guerrero's Translation
Like an electric jolt the news circulated around the world of social parasites: the pests or dregs which God in His infinite goodness created and very fondly breeds in Manila. Some went in search of shoe polish for their boots, others for buttons and cravats, but all were occupied with the manner in which to greet with familiarity the master of the house, and thus pretend that they were old friends, or to make excuses, if the need arose, for not having been able to come much earlier.	So the news of his dinner party ran like an electric shock through the community of spongers, hangers-on, and gate-crashers whom God, in His infinite wisdom, had created and so fondly multiplied in Manila. Some of these set out to hunt polish for their boots; others, collar-buttons and cravats; but one and all gave the gravest thought to the manner in which they might greet their host with the assumed intimacy of long-standing friendship, or, if the occasion should arise, make a graceful apology for not having arrived earlier where presumably their presence was so eagerly awaited.
This dinner was being given in a house on Anloague Street, and since we can no longer recall its number, we will try to describe it in such a way as to make it still recognizable -- that is, if earthquakes have not ruined it. We do not believe that its owner would have had it pulled down, this task being ordinarily taken care of by God, or Nature, with whom our government also has many projects under contract.[3]	The dinner was being given in a house on Anloague Street which may still be recognized unless it has tumbled down in some earthquake. Certainly it will not have been pulled down by its owner; in the Philippines, that is usually left to God and Nature. In fact, one often thinks that they are under contract to the Government for just that purpose.

---

[3]*I feel Lacson-Locsin's translation retains much of Rizal's original sequence of ideas, necessarily also his satirical remarks.*

Lacson-Locsin's Translation	Guerrero's Translation
It is a sufficiently large building, of the style prevalent in many parts of the country, situated towards a bend of the Pasig River, called by many the Binondo Creek, which plays, as do all rivers in Manila, the multiple roles of bathing place, drainage and sewage, laundering area, fishing ground, means of transport and communication, and even source of potable water, if the Chinese water hauler or peddler finds it convenient. It is noteworthy that this dynamic artery of the district where the traffic is heavy and entangled, a distance of almost one kilometer, relies only on a one-way wooden bridge rickety for a stretch of six months, and impassable the rest of the year, so much so that during the dry season horses take advantage of this permanent status quo to jump from the bridge into the water below, to the great surprise of the distracted mortals inside the coach who are either dozing or contemplating the progress of the times.	The house was large enough, in a style common to those parts. It was situated in that section of the city which [was] crossed by a branch of the Pasig River, called by some the creek of Binondo, which, like all rivers of Manila at that time, combined the functions of public bath, sewer, laundry, fishery, waterway, and, should the Chinese water-pedlar find it convenient, even a source of drinking water. For a stretch of almost a kilometre this vital artery, with its bustling traffic and bewildering activity, hardly counted with one wooden bridge, and this one was under repair at one end for six months, and closed to traffic at the other end for the rest of the year. Indeed, in the hot season, carriage horses had been known to avail themselves of the situation and to jump into the water at this point, to the discomfiture of any day-dreamer in their vehicles who had dozed off while pondering the achievements of the century.

Lacson-Locsin's translation shows us that the trouble with heroes is when we don't choose our words well to translate their ideas faithfully and well. We have to capture each mind in its own setting.

KASPAROV, NON-WINNER

Gary Kasparov has captured the minds of chess addicts *and* computer nerds. I don't think he's the greatest, but I know he's a hero staking his reputation playing against a computer. The #1 chess player (man) in the world to play the #1 chess player (machine) in the world, in New York -- again.[4] Gary Kasparov (Russian) versus Deep Blue (American), a supercomputer built by IBM. Reuters describes it as:

> *... a re-match between brain cell and silicon and a test of humanity's relationship with computers. ... The key question posed in the contest is whether a machine can dominate a human at chess, the game that for centuries has been considered the ultimate expression of rational thought.*[5]

In the first match in Philadelphia 15 months ago, Deep Blue won the first game. It doesn't matter that it did not win the match. That

---

[4]*Reuters, "Kas to match wits with 'alien' challenger",* **The Evening Paper**, *April 30, 1997, page 16.*

[5]*Reuters, "Kasparov vs Supercomputer: Brain and silicon mix it up",* **The Evening Paper**, *May 2-4, 1997, page 16.*

On the game itself: To say that chess is "the ultimate expression of rational thought" is rational. Chess is pure logic. There are very specific rules to follow (all man-made), so there are very specific ways you can move. The number of combinations of moves at any given time at any given stage of a game is so huge that you would think that, really, logic is the best form of thought. [And that supercomputing is, since the computer can consider 200,000,000 positions in one second, the best medium for thinking.] On the contrary! The very absence of logic is the best form of thought. *Like fuzzy logic. Like intuition. Like prophecy. And best of all: Like faith. The best definition of any word in the world is found in the Bible and it concerns this one: "Faith is the substance of things hoped for, the evidence of things not seen" (Hebrews 11:1,* **New King James Version***).*

victory was stunning and historic.[6]

Reuters reports:

> *The Russian grandmaster, considered by most experts to be the strongest player in the history of the ancient game, eventually won the 6-game contest, but the outcome left him shaken by the feeling that the days of human superiority over machines were numbered.*[7]

Human superiority over machines are numbered? That is a crazy idea. Oh man of little faith! You put too much faith on man. So, I ask again: "Is there intelligent life on earth?"

Gary Kasparov was deadly serious when he thought *that*. In fact, he said, when he lost (again) to Deep Blue in the rematch:

> *Suddenly you know it played like a God for one particular moment. It reminds me of the famous goal [Argentina's Diego] Maradona scored against England in '86. He said it was 'the hand of God.'*[8]

Did you notice? The world chess champion is not enamored with *but* in awe of technology. *Actually, it's the same thing.* He has been reading too many computer magazines or listening to too many

---

[6]*I don't play chess, so what am I doing reading about Gary Kasparov and Deep Blue? I have always been interested in excellence whether or not it comes with the insolence of a champion or the pompous claims of a champion of high tech. (When it comes to chess, I admire Gary Kasparov, especially now that he's learning about technology, but I admire most Bobby Fischer, the one hero of chess that I know. He staked not only his name, his title but everything when he insisted that the ancient rules of chess in world championship games be made modern and changed forever. A renegade thinker, a true hero -- the world laughed at him (but not, I'm glad to say, our very own Filomeno Campomanes, another renegade), sent him to Limbo, and then changed the rules according to the wishes of genius. Gary Kasparov is the world's best chess player? Okay. But he's not a genius, and his own view of one is faulty: He can see genius only when he looks into the mirror.)*

[7]*Reuters, "Deep Blue taps 'human second' for Kasparov rematch",* **The Evening Paper**, *April 3, page 14.*

[8]*Reuters, "Flustered Kasparov: Deep Blue playing 'like a God,'"* **The Evening Paper**, *May 8, page 14.*

computer nerds. Some experts have been predicting that, one day, computers will be as (more) intelligent as (than) people. Since man is the creator of the computer, that is the same as saying man will surpass his own intelligence and become God.

More about that US$ 1 million rematch, listen to the IBM experts saying:

> *"I think the major difference is that in the last match we brought a lot of technology and this time we're going to bring a lot of human input", computer scientist Hsu Feng-Hsiung told Reuters. The "human input" is the addition of grandmaster Joel Benjamin as a full-time adviser.* [9]

Supercomputing doesn't change the fact that computing is really just storing, recalling, comparing, and choosing from a database. It's just superspeed calculation that gives the impression of thinking: we men are so impressionable.

> *IBM says [grandmaster Joel] Benjamin has helped the team augment the computer's ability to look at hundreds of millions of positions per second with a greater appreciation for strategy and the relative value of pieces in certain positions.* [10]

Why is IBM into such a thing as the Deep Blue Project? You might be surprised as I was:

---

[9] *Reuters, cited, April 3, page 14.*

Did you notice? "... in the last match we brought a lot of technology and this time we're going to bring a lot of human input". What that means is that this match is really man versus man, one champion versus one grandmaster aided by chess addicts who happen to be programmers, and the huge memory bank of and instant recall of possible positions by the IBM supercomputer. So what is there left for Gary Kasparov? Strategy, or which is the same thing, deception. Only man is capable of deception. The art of winning is deception.

[10] *Reuters, cited, April 3, page 14. "... the relative value of pieces in certain positions" just about describes chess. Chess, like logic, is positioning. You can win a game, or an argument, if you can create chaos, that is, destroy the logic, that is, the train of thought of your opponent.*

> *... to see how chess can be used to understand computer science applications.*[11] *IBM chose three areas -- data mining, financial modelling techniques, and molecular dynamics -- in which to market the technology developed for Deep Blue ...*[12]

So, the score's the same: *Man wins over man, what else?* The same story in all heroic acts. That's the problem with heroism.

RIZAL, NON-WRITER

José Rizal, the national hero, the genius of the Malay race, is not known to be a great writer, only a great propagandist. That, I say, is a great mistake. He is in fact *on top of the word*.

If you had doubts (or no idea at all) about how good José Rizal was/is as a writer, let me compare him with a most popular writer, nay, a quite famous *author* (they don't call him *writer*): JRR Tolkien. If you don't know him either, you haven't heard of the famous fantasy trilogy, **The Lord of the Rings**. Right now, I'm interested in the first of the trilogy, **The Fellowship Of The Ring**. I have been startled with what I have accidentally found; so, let us compare **Noli** with **Fellowship** using their Chapter 1s; it's definitely hair-raising how they began their stories in entirely different genres but in almost identical central ideas:

JRR Tolkien's Paragraph 1, Chapter 1, "A Long-Expected Party", **Fellowship**:

> *When Mr Bilbo Baggins of Bag End announced that he would shortly be celebrating his eleventy-first birthday with a party of special magnificence, there was much talk and excitement in Hobbiton.*[13]

José Rizal's Paragraph 1, Chapter 1, "A Gathering", **Noli**:

---

[11] *Why didn't they just ask people? It would have been much cheaper. (Ah, but the publicity!)*

[12] *Reuters, cited, April 3, page 14. (See what I mean? This news indicates that even if Deep Blue loses and loses and loses and Gary Kasparov wins and wins and wins, IBM wins and wins and wins too.*

[13] *JRR Tolkien,* **The Fellowship Of The Ring** *(New York: Ballantine Books, 1969), page 43.*

> *Towards the end of October, Don Santiago de los Santos, popularly known as Capitan Tiago, was hosting a dinner which, in spite of its having been announced only that afternoon, against his wont, was already the theme of all conversation in Binondo, in the neighboring districts, and even in Intramuros. Capitan Tiago was reputed to be a most generous man, and it was known that his home, like his country, never closed its door to anything, as long as it was not business, or any new or bold idea.*[14]

Personally, I find Tolkien definitely *boring*, Rizal definitely *wonderful*. Why because Tolkien describes action by non-action words or adjectives ("special magnificence", "much talk and excitement") and leave them at that. Rizal describes by explaining, telling the story. You want, you ache to read on. Incidentally: I have read many of our local (not necessarily inferior) short stories and novels, and they also suffer from what I shall call here the **Tolkien Syndrome**. The Tolkien Syndrome is relying on adjectives for action as well as characterization. It is, I might say, the opposite of way of Hemingway: Let the story describe the action and the protagonists. And it stands in high contrast to Rizal's subtlety and elegance at its best.

JRR Tolkien's Paragraph 2, Chapter 1:

> *Bilbo was very rich and very peculiar, and had been he wonder of the Shire for sixty years, ever since his remarkable disappearance and unexpected return. The riches he had brought back from his travels had now become a local legend, and it was popularly believed, whatever the old folk might say, that the Hill at Bag End was full of tunnels stuffed with treasure. And if that was not enough for fame, there was also his prolonged vigour to marvel at. Time wore on, but it seemed to have little effect on Mr Baggins. At ninety he was much the same as at fifty. At ninety-nine they began to call him* well-preserved*; but* unchanged *would have been nearer the mark. There were that shook their heads and thought this was too much of a good thing; it*

---

[14] *José Rizal, already cited.*

seemed unfair that anyone should possess (apparently) perpetual youth as well as (reputedly) inexhaustible wealth. [15]

José Rizal's Paragraph 2, Chapter 1:

Like an electric jolt the news circulated around the world of social parasites: the pests or dregs which God in His infinite goodness created and very fondly breeds in Manila. Some went in search of shoe polish for their boots, others for buttons and cravats, but all were occupied with the manner in which to greet with familiarity the master of the house, and thus pretend that they were old friends, or to make excuses, if the need arose, for not having been able to come much earlier. [16]

Here Tolkien is more talkative, but Rizal is more effective. Rizal adds details to build the excitement more; Tolkien adds detail of a different nature that throws the first paragraph off. Tolkien continues with his non-descriptive adjectives. So, the phrase "remarkable disappearance and unexpected return" doesn't give me any idea at all what it's all about. An author should tell the story, not describe it -- it is the privilege of the reader to describe it with his heart in his eyes.

JRR Tolkien's Paragraph 3, Chapter 1:

'It will have to be paid for,' they said. 'It isn't natural, and trouble will come of it!'

José Rizal's Paragraph 3, Chapter 1:

This dinner was being given in a house on Anloague Street, and since we can no longer recall its number, we will try to describe it in such a way as to make it still recognizable -- that is, if earthquakes have not ruined it. We do not believe that its owner would have had it pulled down, this task being ordinarily taken care of by God, or Nature, with whom our government also has many projects under contract.

---

[15] *Tolkien, already cited, page 43.*

[16] *Lacson-Locsin, already cited, page 1.*

Rizal sustains my interest, Tolkien loses it. More, Mr. Tolkien. Tell me, what kind of trouble? Rizal's words about what kind of trouble are just right. All the more remarkable because, of course, Rizal was writing under tremendous psychological and intellectual pressure. So, no, the Filipinos are not savages! Now, let me quote Guerrero:

> *For a year Rizal worked in the British Museum on annotations to a history of the Philippines that, he hoped, would establish the ancient dignity and culture of the pre-Spanish Filipinos, denigrated in the monkish chronicles as savages just down from trees. ... In the meantime a Filipino review had once again been issued in Spain by the small colony of expatriates there, and, a master of polemics, he assiduously contributed political articles of remarkable depth and prescience (in one of them he foresaw that within a century the Philippines would fall either to the North American Republic or to Japan, a prophecy which was fulfilled in both respects in less than half the time.)*[17]

José Rizal was thinking beyond his own time. He was always doing that. At a very early age, before he was eight, he already knew that -- though he did not have a name for it -- nationalism was something the Filipinos will have to construct to combat the Spanish colonizers. That's when he wrote "Sa Aking Mga Kababata" (To My Young Friends). In other words, he was too bright for his own good. That was the trouble with José Rizal: he wasn't thinking for his own good, only for the good of his country.

He always wanted to be #1. Another way of putting that is, he always wanted to do his level best in whatever he was doing, even if it meant he wasn't paying attention to what he was supposed to be doing. Remember his mother telling him the moral of the story about the moth and the flame ("Don't be like the moth")? He wasn't listening to his mother; he was listening to an inner voice. He was thinking other thoughts ("What about the flame? How great it would be to die for the great big flame of wisdom!")

---

[17]*Leon Ma. Guerrero, "Two novels that made a revolution", in* **Noli Me Tangere**, *translated by Leon Ma. Guerrero (Manila: Guerrero Publishing), page xi.*

He is the Filipino Christ; he is the greatest hero of the Malayan race; he is one of the noblest men in Asia.[18]

The trouble with him is that he was too brave for all of us. Who would die for his country now? The trouble with José Rizal is that he showed us that Filipinos knew how to die for their convictions, but so far only a handful has proven him correct.

And yet, we don't really have to die physically for our convictions: we could die to ourselves and give up our old life for the new and be born again and be the Christians we are supposed to be:

Generous to a fault.
Forgiving others even when they have not asked for forgiveness.
Storing up riches in heaven, not on earth.
Admitting one's fault when one has to, and that is always.
Looking at anyone and seeing Christ in an ugly face or body.
Seeing that everything works together for the good.
Hearing words of wisdom even from the illiterate.
Feeling confident when you know you shouldn't be.
Looking at a beautiful sunset when you know it's an ordinary sunset, because all sunsets are beautiful, and so are all sunrises.
Seeing everything is lost and rejoicing everything else is not.
Feeling helpless, then realizing now you can let go and let God be helpful.
Being a Christian even when nobody is looking or nobody knows or nobody cares.

It is difficult, nay, impossible, to be a true Christian, that's true. But, Christian, take heart. Lay missionary William Henry Scott, scholar extraordinaire, gives us this advice:

Christmas Sonnet 1972

The curfew marks the ending of the play,
And as the candles, flame by flame, go out,
And darkness stills the last applauding shout,
The players take no bow, but simply lay
Their costumes by and quiet steal away.

---

[18]*Vicente F. Del Carmen,* **Rizal: An Encyclopedic Collection** *vol II (Quezon City: New Day Publishers), 1982, inside book flap.*

The gates are barred, and so there'll be no doubt
In any mind, the callboard's left without
The least announcement of next opening day.
Yet more will follow, Christian, so take heart:
See how the hour is being broken by
A babe too young to know that he will start
A new performance by his Christmas cry
Tonight -- for his small voice will spring the lock,
Pluck out the mortised chain, and split the rock.[19]

Can we make everyday Christmas for ourselves as well as our friends? The trouble with José Rizal is that he was able to do what we can't do for our friends, a Christian in deed if not in name:

> *No one has greater love than this, to lay down one's life for one's friends.*[20]

Ah, but he didn't lay down his life for his friends alone -- he did it also for his enemies. No greater life than his.

BISHOP NIKOLAI, NON-TEACHER

Greater creativity is what we don't realize we need now in the field of education: We worry about the millions of schoolchildren all over the country, and always forget the millions of out-of-school youth, not to mention the out-of-school adults.

In this, truly creative was Danish poet, theologian and Bishop Nikolai Grundtvig (born 1783).[21] It was he who inspired the idea of the Danish Folk High School, one of the greatest educational innovations of all time -- and we never heard of it! It's this teacher in me saying this, having obtained a Bachelor of Science in Agriculture, with major in Agricultural Education. That we never heard of it, or him, doesn't make him less of a hero.

The trouble with us is that we are not so innovative when it

---

[19]*William Henry Scott, "Christmas Sonnet, 1972",* **Chips** *(Quezon City: New Day Publishers), 1987, page 7.*

[20]*John 15:13.*

[21]*Arne Andresen (ed.),* **The Danish Folk High School Today** *(Copenhagen, Denmark: Hojskolernes Sekretariat, 1985. The brochure is my whole source for this section.*

comes to education. The Danish Folk High School has been around for more than 150 years and we have managed to ignore it. "Folk High School" because it's for the folks who can't otherwise go to formal school, or won't. And it's not just about "going to school".

Bishop Nikolai thought long and hard about how to mobilize the Danish people's spiritual strength. He didn't think of founding a church, or a church-based movement (the fashion these days in these islands); instead, he thought of a new kind of school. He had studied at the Trinity College in Cambridge, and he was impressed by the lively exchanges between teachers and students in class and their comradeship outside the classroom. In his mind, the Folk High School was born.

At that time, the world was already into the Age of Romanticism, the beginning of the modern age. Romanticism was a rejection of the Age of Enlightenment and its emphasis on man's own reason. Romanticism extolled creativity. What is creativity but reliance on intuition, reliance on one's own feelings, reliance on inspiration at any time or all at the same time? I am an incurable Romantic.

The Folk High School is really a school without: without walls, without curricula, without dogma, without class distinctions, without limits. The Folk High School is a residency school, but you do not attend classes: you attend to life. With a little help from friends, you create your own curriculum. The idea is for you to know what you want to know, and to give you the environment to learn, to teach yourself, to interact with others: with teachers, with other students, with the rest of the community. Along with whatever fields -- sports, art, technology -- in a short (up to 3 weeks) or long (up to 32 weeks) course which you are after, you learn to be part of the community.

The Folk High School is unique. It is not a high school, and the students interrogate the teachers, not the other way around. And there are no examinations.

The main aim of the Folk High School is, according to Bishop Nikolai, "To enlighten, nourish and develop that human life which may be pressupposed in the Danish Youth". All things considered, in or out of school, human life is the most important. Even in his thinking, Bishop Nikolai already was a hero. The trouble with Bishop Nikolai as a hero is that we cannot duplicate the historical events in his country when his ideas found rich soil: A huge nation (Germany) threatening to engulf Denmark, and Bishop Nikolai saw the necessity to mobilize not only the Danish military might but also their spiritual strength. (More than 30 years later, Denmark did lose Schleswig and Holstein to

Germany.) In the Philippines, there is a separation of Church and State. The trouble with our heroes is if they can't mix school with religion.

ANDRES BONIFACIO, NON-INTELLECTUAL

Apparently, Andres Bonifacio mixed his school of politics with religion -- just look at the Katipunan documents. But sorry, Andres Bonifacio is the #2 hero of the Philippines, not #1. Many people won't accept that fact. I do. His contributions to his country? The *Katipunan*. It was born out of Rizal's *La Liga Filipina* but it's okay, because the one advocated reform, while the other advocated independence, by every means necessary. I would have joined the Liga myself but not the Katipunan, but that doesn't make Bonifacio to me less of a hero. He was a courageous man; without him, there would not have been the Katipunan and the Revolution of 1896. He lost all his battles; he lost everything, including his life. A hero.

The trouble with Bonifacio is that his person has been put in question in a hero-bashing, well-researched history book, **Inventing A Hero**[22] by American historian Glenn Anthony May. While many local historians do not agree with his findings, and I am not a historian, I do find May's arguments very convincing and difficult to refute.

Bluntly, in the first two paragraphs of his book, May tells us:

> *This book tells a bizarre story about a famous man. The man in question is the Philippine national hero Andres Bonifacio, the leader of the Philippine Revolution of 1896, who died almost a century ago. The story concerns the successful efforts of a number of historians and one memoirist to transform Bonifacio in the years since his death.*
>
> *In effect, Bonifacio has been posthumously re-created. He has been given a new personality and a childhood that may bear little resemblance to his real one. Literary compositions have been attributed to him*

---

[22]*Glenn Anthony May,* **Inventing a Hero: The Posthumous Re-Creation of Andres Bonifacio** *(Quezon City: New Day Publishers in cooperation with the Center for Southeast Asian Studies of the University of Wisconsin), 1997, 200 pages. He is a Professor of History at the University of Oregon.*

> *that he almost certainly did not write, and, as a consequence, he has been credited with ideas he did not have.*[23] *Key events in his life have been altered beyond recognition. The national hero who has emerged from this process of re-creation -- the Bonifacio celebrated in history textbooks and memorialized in statues around the Philippines -- is, in reality, something closer to a national myth.*

That is the trouble with being a hero -- your life is subject to the littlest scrutiny.

Glenn May's main thesis is that the documents purporting to show Bonifacio's ancestry and his intellectual outputs are of doubtful origin. He has stories and explanations of how certain historians obtained certain documents have not been scholarly; instead, they have been ridiculous and absurd. One of the historians even claimed to have found the letters of Bonifacio in a hen's nest in Bataan! Another historian was found to have doctored the document he claimed was authentic. Historians Manuel Artigas, Epifanio de los Santos, José Santos, Teodoro Agoncillo, Renato Constantino, and Reynaldo Ileto; memoir-writer Artemio Ricarte; and scholar OD Corpuz, were all found by Glenn May to have been guilty of unscholarly claims about Bonifacio.

The trouble with heroes like Bonifacio is those historians guilty of hero-worship. Hero-worship is "the idealization of an admired man", according to the **Reader's Digest-Oxford Complete Wordfinder** (1994). To idealize is to think of someone as a standard or model of perfection or excellence. Bonifacio was idealized for purposes of cultivating Philippine nationalism after the United States restored independence to the Philippines in July 1946. That is the trouble when you're locked in to one hero. The nationalists wanted a warrior as a symbol, and creating the intellectual Bonifacio wasn't so difficult with a gullible public. We didn't know any better until after 50 years. We admire the nationalists for their inventiveness, but we hate to be fooled.

Metaphors, metaphors. So, Bonifacio's Achilles heel is his

---

[23] *With this one, I disagree. I would revise that to read: "... he has been credited with ideas* he may not have had*". If he is correct in denying Bonifacio's authorship of all the manuscripts attributed to him, it is but logical that even Glenn May does not know what ideas Bonifacio* may *have had, so he cannot know what he did* not *have.*

intellectual credentials: there are none. Glenn May is right -- except for the idea of the Katipunan, Bonifacio's mind is a blank. Well, we can't all be intellectuals.

Still, I am willing to grant that Bonifacio wrote everything people (especially some UP Diliman historians) say he did write:[24]

* The newspaper (**Kalayaan**) article "Ang Dapat Mabatid Ng Mga Tagalog" (What Tagalogs Should Know).

* Poems: "Katapusang Hibik Ng Pilipinas" (The Philippines' Last Plea), "Tapunan Ng Lingap" (Cast Some Compassion, Please), "Ang Mga Cazadores" (The Hunters), "Pag-ibig Sa Tinubuang Bayan" (Love Of Country).

* A proclamation about bravery and persistence, about preparing for more struggle.

* A translation of Rizal's last poem.

* His Decalogue (rules for members of the Katipunan).

* Six letters: two to Mariano Alvarez, head of the Magdiwang Council of the Katipunan and an uncle of his wife, four to close friend Emilio Jacinto (composed between March and April 1897, just before he was executed May 1897 for treason on orders of Emilio Aguinaldo).

So, Bonifacio had intellectual brilliance, not only true grit. But it's all beside the point now. **I don't believe in Revolution anymore.** I hate the sight of blood, including my own. I can't give you the exact date, but I know I lost my faith in Revolution even before 1972.

I did a book review in the late sixties (a memorable day, February 8, Claro Recto's birthday) in college (UP Los Baños) on the bestselling **Anatomy Of A Murder**, of an accused whose defense was self-defense in the form of, if I remember right, *the theory of irresistible impulse*, and I said something like this in conclusion: *Revolution is justified if it is an irresistible impulse, if it is in self-defense.* I rather thought that was a brilliant insight myself.

I meant a *bloody* revolution.

I still read fiction and legal cases, especially those of Louis Nizer, but I don't agree with *that revolutionary position* anymore. Except the Revolution of 1986, which was an irresistible impulse that played out to millions. I am not the angry young man I was, thank God. And I have come to learn that what is legal is not necessarily good, that what is justified is not necessarily moral. In the final analysis, that is

---

[24]*May, cited, page 36.*

the trouble with military heroes: they violate the moral law.[25]

Morality, how many crimes are committed in thy name! Isn't that the underlying message of **Noli Me Tangere**?

RAUL ROCO, NON-PERFECT

He translates his messages into laws, and opinions based on his assessment as a lawyer.

April 1997, Senator Raul Roco proposed what he called a "systematic consensus system" of choosing presidential candidates from among the presidentiables: "Let the people, not political parties, nominate presidential bets". He had previously announced his intention to run for President himself. "There must be a system that will ensure the people's participation -- not through the party itself -- because the Constitution prohibits power-brokering", he said.

He's bright and different. From December 1996 to March 1997, Raul Roco was my hero. His contribution to his country? Quite a few, and they are unmatchable. He is the Senator who masterminded the Women in Nation-Building (WIN) Act, the New Central Bank Act, the abolition of the National College Entrance Examination (NCEE), and the People's Initiative Act -- among other notable acts. The WIN Act punishes discrimination against and harassment of women by men at the workplace. The New Central Bank (Bangko Sentral ng Pilipinas) Act has resuscitated the ailing guardian of monetary policy in the country. The NCEE was an abomination, and its abolition is as welcome as rain after a long hot summer -- I myself stopped believing in IQ or intelligence tests long ago: they test my patience. And the People's Initiative Act is a masterpiece in creativity -- now the people can come up with creative ideas of their own as legislation and fight for it themselves. That's what the PIRMA pushers are doing. You can disagree

---

[25]*After I had written that and he had read it, Orli gifted me with a copy of* **The Art of War, Sun Tzu** *(New York: Dell Publishing, 1983), edited by James Clavell ("author of the best-selling Asian saga consisting of* **Shogun, Tai-Pan, King Rat, Noble House** *and* **Whirlwind***" -- says the blurb at the back of the book). Sun Tzu says, "The art of war is governed by five constant factors, all of which need to be taken into account. They are the Moral Law; Heaven; Earth; the Commander; Method and discipline" (page 9). And I learn: The art of war is deception.*

with what they say, but if you want to be a hero, you will fight to the death their right to say it. That's the problem with man-made laws; they aren't perfect. Do I now blame Raul Roco for having fathered the obnoxious PIRMA in more ways than one? Well, he isn't perfect either.

He's a genius, but that's the problem with a genius: He doesn't know what to do with other people except for them to follow him.

Raul Roco is a follower of poetry. His favorite poet, TS Eliot, said of himself, "I am an Anglo-Catholic in religion, a classicist in literature, and a royalist in politics".[26] A conservative. Eliot's first poem was *The Love Song of J. Alfred Prufrock*, which Raul Roco loves: he wrote a thesis on it. Eliot won a Nobel Prize in Literature, and Roco dreams of it. Roco's art is Constitutionalism, so he has been creative only within the confines of the rule of law and order. That's the problem. He is a conservative inside, an activist outside. You are not my hero anywhere if you are not creative anywhere else. We need a creative leader, not another lawyer. Law is not the way to progress (not even the way to peace): We have too many laws already!

BILL GATES, NON-STOPPABLE

The Law of the Internet covers a multitude of scenes. So, what about an electronic hero, since information has become the new capital, according to management guru Peter Drucker?[27] The best candidate seems to be Bill Gates, co-founder and CEO of Microsoft Corporation. "He is the most famous businessman in the world. Reams have been written about how he [has so far] dominated the revolution in personal computing".[28] He is a hero in the eyes of millions of computer users,

---

[26]*Not credited. "T.S. Eliot", in* **Compton's Encyclopedia,** *cited, 1995, vol 7, page 189.*

[27]*Peter F. Drucker,* **The Age of Discontinuity: Guidelines to Our Changing Society** *(New York: Harper & Row, Publishers), 1969, reprint by National Book Store, Inc., page x. He says, "Knowledge, during the last few decades, has become the central capital, the cost center, and the crucial resource of the economy. This changes labor forces and work, teaching and learning, and the meaning of knowledge and its politics. But it also raises the problem of the responsibilities of the new men of power, the men of knowledge."*

[28]*Walter Isaacson, "In Search of the Real Bill Gates",* **Time,**

including the experts, the nerds and the cyberpunks. Since without Microsoft's products, hundreds of millions of us cannot use the personal computer, Bill Gates is now the richest man in the world![29]

What is Bill Gates' contribution to civilization? He invented Microsoft. Microsoft owns the intellectual property rights to the disk operating system (OS) of your personal computer, and has been raking in millions because of that: you can't run a PC without it. Bill Gates did not invent OS: he bought the rights to it.

Bill Gates also invented planned software obsolescence, copying from that in cars: *the latest is the best*. So, you are advised that Windows is the OS to watch. The latest version of any program is the best. Which goes well with the technical experts' (both local and foreign) wide-eyed much-ado about the latest hardware, the fastest with the most memory, the most gorgeous interface etc. The latest, the fastest, the most: Where does it end, Mr. Gates? Nowhere. "How much money is enough?" John D. Rockefeller, the incomparable millionaire, was asked. His answer? "Just a little more than what you have".[30]

He did not invent Windows; he copied it from the Apple Macintosh, and sold his copy grandly as his own. (Apple's Steve Jobs is the Father of the Personal Computer Revolution and no other: he proselytized for it against all odds and despite minds like Bill Gates'.) The trouble with some heroes who cry software piracy is that they can sell small ideas big but that they are also capable of great intellectual -- not to mention commercial -- software piracy! There's your hero.

The Intel chip (say, *Pentium*) and the software that go with it (mostly from Microsoft), do not make up the only magnificent way to compute. IBM, Apple and Motorola have teamed up to create *PowerPC* in direct competition with the Intel 486 or 586 (the Pentium). Discovery! PowerPC is cheaper, faster, and more energy-efficient;[31]

January 13, 1997, page 31. Isaacson is the Managing Editor of Time; in 1993, he was the leader of the team that created Time Online, *according to the Editor-in-Chief of* **Time**.

[29]*Norman Pearlstine, "To Our Readers",* **Time**, *January 13, 1997, page 3.*

[30]*Quoted by David C. Churbuck, "My chip is faster than yours",* **Forbes**, *April 25, 1994, page 162.*

[31]*Tom Thompson; "PowerPC performs for less",* **Byte**, *August 1993, pages 56 ff. This is the cover story of the issue. Tom Thompson is one of the Senior Technical Editors (At Large) of* **Byte**.

and IBM and Apple have software that are better than Microsoft's. But having the stranglehold on the industry, this is how Microsoft (Bill Gates) has "dominated the revolution in personal computing".

The trouble with heroes like Bill Gates is that they think they have the monopoly of truth.

APO FIDEL, NON-FAITHFUL

The specter of the monopoly of the truth is also hounding Apo Fidel Ramos. He is one of the heroes of the Edsa Revolution, of course. And so are you, if you were there. And so am I; in the morning of February 25, I walked from Guadalupe Bridge to Channel 4 and then lingered on; I was there the whole day; in the evening, I went home, same old place, and the Marcoses went to Hawaii, new home.

Many would argue and say that there was no Edsa Revolution at all, no People Power Revolution that February in 1986. What do they want: a bloody revolution? We showed the world a Revolution did not have to be bloody. To overthrow a dictatorship, all you need are some braver souls -- heroes -- to start the Ball of the Revolution rolling.

Aside from the overthrow of the Marcos dictatorship, what is Apo Fidel's contribution to his country? Infrastructure. The roads, bridges & systems. The infrastructure of peace: the coup plotters and the Muslims all have accepted peace as an option. (Someone else had said it better: "There is no way to peace. Peace is the way!") The infrastructure of energy: no more power blackouts. The infrastructure of hope: he is mainly responsible for restoring the faith of the Filipino in himself. Even the APEC are convinced that Apo Fidel has done his country proud. He has followed the beatings of his own heart.

Is his travelling abroad several times (29 as of the latest count) heroism? It is, since he is staking his reputation. People are calling him just another of our opportunist Presidents, but in truth we need foreign investments in the country. Like the $4 billion power plant by Shell Corporation in Batangas.[32]

Tom Thompson and Bob Ryan, "Apple, IBM bring PowerPC to the PC", **Byte**, *April 1994, pages 44 ff. Bob Ryan is one of the Technical Editors (State of the Art/Features) of this computer magazine owned and published by McGraw-Hill Inc.*

[32]*Marichu Villanueva, "Ramos: UK visit very productive",* **Philippine Star**, *June 22, 1997, front page.*

The trouble with the brains behind Apo Fidel, the brains behind PIRMA (not necessarily the same) is that they think they have the monopoly of truth, and they have made a lot of noise in view of that. They think what Apo Fidel has done is enough to make him as the one indispensable next President of his country.

The trouble with heroes is their over-zealous admirers.

JESUS, NON-REASONING

I am an ardent admirer -- if I may use the term -- of Jesus of Nazareth, the carpenter's son, an authentic hero. This is the one who became not only a great teacher but the most charismatic teacher who ever lived. "Follow me", he said to Peter and Andrew, "and I will make you fishers of men".[33] And at once, they let go whatever they were doing and followed him. That means he inspired blind faith in you. Of course, *faith* is always blind; otherwise, it's called *reason*. That is what is wrong with Jesus as hero of faith: You cannot understand him unless you believe in him *first*.

When he grew up and gained the enlightenment we all seek, the folks from Nazareth asked:

> *Where did this man get such wisdom and mighty deeds? Is he not the carpenter's son? Is not his mother named Mary and his brothers James, Joseph, Simon, and Judas? Are not his sisters all with us? Where did this man get all this?*[34]

They would not accept him as he was; in other words, they doubted him. The trouble with heroes of this kind is that they are not honored in their own country.

Was Jesus the Son of God? Millions have difficulty accepting that. In fact, millions have difficulty just following the two greatest commandments (Jesus' summary of The Ten Commandments) without believing that this was the Son of God talking:

> *You shall love the Lord, your God, with all your heart, with all your soul, and with all your mind.*

---

[33]*Matthew 4:19 (New American Bible, 1991)*

[34]*Matthew 13:54-56 (New American Bible, 1991)*

> *This is the greatest and the first commandment. The second is like it: You shall love your neighbor as yourself. The whole law and the prophets depend on these two commandments.*[35]

Jesus was the ultimate hero, dying for others, for those who loved him and those who hated him. The trouble with this kind of hero is that his is a difficult act to follow.

NINOY, NONE BUT THE BRAVE

Another tough act to follow was Ninoy Aquino. When his assassination was announced over the radio past noon that day, September 21, 1983, I said "Sonababitch!" in Tagalog, in pure, unadulterated hate. I had admired Ninoy ever since I noticed he was babbling about and bubbling over with his ideas and dreams for the Filipinos. He was my hero: young, always with ideas irrepressible if not original. He dared, and did well. He was a bright star in many a dreary political night. He was a counterpoint; he was a one-man opposition party. And many believed in him; I believed in him. That's why they killed him. Did I go to his funeral? No, Sir, sorry. *I was afraid.* After that, we learned that his was the longest funeral march in our history. In fact, the bravest funeral march in all history, and I wasn't there. Either we are not all made of sterner stuff, or we are not all angry at the same time.

Ninoy Aquino was at his best when he was fighting and speaking, both and at the same time. He couldn't stand still; he couldn't keep his mouth shut. He must have had the worst time of his life when they shut him in prison, all by himself, because he could fight but he couldn't speak.

Between Ferdinand Marcos and all the rest of you fellows, Ninoy was the best Upsilonians ever. He fought and died for his country, not abandon it in its years of bereavement and bedevilment. He could crack jokes like a dictator could crack people. and the people loved him for it.

The trouble with Ninoy was that he was too sure of himself before Marcos caught up with him, and that was the only time when Ninoy caught up with himself. Finally, he found the power of God he

---

[35]*Matthew 22:37-40 (New American Bible, 1991).*

never found before. Ninoy. They called him *Superboy*, and that he was. No one will be like him again.

CHRISTOPHER REEVE, NON-SUPERMAN

And no one will be like Superman/Superboy. He was my hero for a long, long time. "Justice, Freedom, and the American Way!" he shouted with the *Justice League*. I liked him better when he was just Superman. For years I didn't get tired following up the stories of how he would survive any dastardly plan to destroy him by exposing him to kryptonite.

And of course the children and I were watching *Lois & Clark* on TV until last year when Superman became a victim of a lightning strike -- it was a stormy day when lightning struck our TV set (a gift from my mother-in-law), and we decided against buying a new one. (Too many commercials.) Goodbye, Superman.

My favorite Superman is not Dean Cain (of *Lois & Clark*) but Christopher Reeve of Superman (The Movie). When he survived a spinal cord injury in a horse riding accident two years ago, he vowed he will walk again -- and donated money for research on his condition. On April 15, still paralyzed from the neck down, he received a star on the Hollywood Walk of Fame witnessed by some 500 fans, along with wife Dana and four-year-old son Will.[36] He said, "If we keep giving our scientists the funding they need for research, soon I will stand here in front of the star". The star meant that his has been acknowledged as a bright Hollywood name. Also on hand were Glenn Close and Jane Seymour, who star in Superman's directorial debut, "In The Gloaming". Close said of Superman, "The most human of humans, a man with great beauty ... and a man who refuses to let go of his dreams".

Superman and Christopher Reeve now are metaphors that get told again and again: Heroes always have an Achilles heel or some weakness, even the best of them. Still and all, it doesn't make them less of a hero; sometimes, it makes them more. So I say of Reeve: *My hero!*

---

[36]*Reuters, "'Superman' Reeve gets star on Hollywood Walk of Fame",* **The Evening Paper**, *April 16, 1997, page 2.*

MANANG LETTY, NON-HYSTERICAL

Being sister to the President, Leticia Ramos-Shahani comes from Asingan, Pangasinan (our town). Cousin to Ferdinand Edralin Marcos on the Valdez side, when Marcos last dictated that he won the February 1986 Snap Elections, Manang Letty denounced the act in so many words, and I said to myself, "So, there is an honorable man from my hometown after all". I didn't expect a she. *My hero!*[37]

I heard Manang Letty speak early this month (May) at the UP School of Labor & Industrial Relations (SOLAIR) in Diliman, Quezon City, and she surprised me.[38] She said, "Let not our folklore and traditions just be intellectual preoccupations; rather, let's study how we can use what happened to us, how our history can help strengthen us, so that our country can be stronger as it enters the millennium that is coming".

She mentioned Gregorio Aglipay and Artemio Ricarte as having come from Batac. Two authentic Filipino heroes. She said her brother and she had childhood memories of Gregorio Aglipay, their neighbor, who as a Catholic priest had the courage and leadership to secede from Rome and found his own church, the *Iglesia Independiente Filipina*. This church was the first to use *Ilocano* to say mass. So, she said, "Folklore and history can be used to give a people a sense of national identity". She spoke of an "inner culture, a sense of security, a sense of identity that we will not exchange in the face of a superior foreign culture". She spoke of the Solid North as "not so much a political allegiance but a sense of identity. If you lose that as a collective, you're lost". She also said:

> *We have to accept globalization. But we have to fight the negativism. Taiwan* bawang, *for instance,* mas

---

[37]*I am not gender-conscious, sorry.*

[38]*The occasion was the Pambansang Komperensya Sa Folklore At Panitikan (National Conference On Folklore & Literature), the theme being "Folklore And History: The Philippine Revolution, The Working People, And National Renewal". National Renewal: that was why the Senator was there, because of her Movement for National Renewal. Sponsors of the Conference were UP SOLAIR, Literary League of the Philippines Inc., and Philippine Folklore Society Inc. She spoke at the Isabelo delos Reyes Auditorium at the Andres Bonifacio Hall.*

malaki, mas mura: Papano na yong Ilocano bawang?[39]
Let us improve our performance. We have to be able to create the very conditions in our own backyard to come up to world class standards. We have to put in the moral and cultural dimensions if you want the economic and political to succeed.

The trouble with Manang Letty is her listeners -- there seems to be too few.

MARCOS, NON-HISTORICAL

On the other hand, there were many rapt listeners of Ferdinand Edralin Marcos, a spell-binding orator. He was my hero when he ran for President and won the first time, in 1965. "This nation can be great again!" was his winning battlecry. That was when he defeated Diosdado Macapagal, the Ilocano beating the Pampango. If you're not Ilocano, you don't know what it means when an Ilocano beats anyone. Years and years later, what did Leticia Ramos-Shahani say about the Solid North? "It is not so much a political alliance but a sense of identity. If you lose that as a collective, you're lost". I'm an Ilocano, and I just know that; Manang Letty just knows how to put that exactly in words.

So when the Solid North finds its hero, as it did in Apo Ferdie, he becomes a winner more than you understand why. I read his book **For Every Tear A Victory**, written by Hartzell Spence but, of course, authored by the Real Macoy, and, reading between the lines (I read the book twice), I can sense that he wanted to become President when he was a young boy yet. So, he didn't start to get ideas when he had succeeded himself as President and couldn't run another time: He never liked to be anywhere but the top. He wanted always to be #1, and what could be the #1 #1 but the President of the Philippines? He was good enough to be #1, and he proved it by being #1 in the bar exams that year when he stood accused of assassinating his father's mortal enemy, and he was behind bars all the while that he was reviewing.

So I voted for him in 1965, and he became President. He was good. He gave us the North Diversion Road. He gave us the South Super Highway. He gave us infrastructure. He gave us Miracle Rice.

---

[39]*Taiwan garlic, for instance, bigger, cheaper. What happens to the Ilocano garlic?*

And he gave us a new sense of greatness.

The trouble with heroes like this is that they get more than they give. First, he began to *get ideas* -- then *more*. How much more? Much more than a billion dollars, which brought down the economy of the country he was trying to bring up. He thought he was historical, that he could write history all by himself.

Macapagal has been buried at the Libingan ng mga Bayani in Fort Bonifacio, while Marcos' remains *remains* in limbo. So, in death, the Pampango beats the Ilocano. Does this hurt the Solid North? Yes. And yes, the Solid North denounced the Great Ilocano long ago, in February 1986. The paradox of power.

CRISOSTOMO IBARRA, NON-CONVENTIONAL

His creator denounced the Great Occupying Spanish Forces (of good and evil). Crisostomo Ibarra is the hero in José Rizal's **Noli Me Tangere**, the book that changed the Filipinos and, by extension, other Asians: for the first time, they began to feel as one nation.

I have always admired Crisostomo Ibarra, not because he had a beautiful and sweet sweetheart in Maria Clara (**Noli** is the novel where the boy didn't get the girl in the end), but because of his crazy idea that the Filipinos needed education first and more than anything else, if they wanted to become independent. I suspect that it wasn't plain education, but education toward a national identity was what he had in mind. If you can't identify with a national something, how can you act as one people?

Walking, Crisostomo Ibarra was looking at Bagumbayan:

> *He was thinking of the man who had opened the eyes of his intellect, and made him understand what was good and just. True, the ideas inspired in him were few, but they were not vain repetitions: they were convictions which did not pale before the brightest focusing lights of progress. That man was an old priest, and the words he told Ibarra when he said goodbye, still resounded in his ears.*
>
> *"Do not forget that if knowledge is the patrimony of humanity, it is inherited only by those who have the heart", the old man reminded him. "I have tried to transmit to you what I have received from my*

> *teachers; the riches I have endeavored to augment as much as I could, and I am passing it on to the following generation. You will do the same with those who come after you, and you can triple it, for you are going to very rich countries." He added, smiling: "They come in search of gold; go to their country to look for that other gold which we lack. Remember, however, that all that glitters is not gold." That man had died in Bagumbayan.*[40]

The trouble with Crisostomo Ibarra is that his dream died in him, because he was impatient.

ERAP, NON-EXPERT

Filipinos are very patient, nay, very forgiving, with Joseph "Erap" Estrada, a hero to millions, including PhDs of UP Los Baños. He isn't an expert in anything, but he has charisma. "Charisma", says my favorite, the **American Heritage College Dictionary** (1993), "is a rare personal quality of leaders who arouse fervent popular devotion and enthusiasm". It is also animal magnetism, personal charm. It has nothing to do with intelligence or achievement or erudition or wisdom. It has something to do with people identifying themselves with him.

And why not? The moviegoers have a movie star in him. He was as popular a movie hero as his *kumpadre* (soul brother) Fernando Poe Jr., and they are still both popular in their own different ways. No matter that Erap has made many silly mistakes and committed so many sins against the sensibilities of people, to put it mildly. We are a forgiving people most of the time, yes we are. We even vote our coup plotters to the Senate.

Los Baños has an advocate in Erap, a few of his advisers being UP Los Baños consultants. If he becomes President, how can they be far behind? They would be heroes for the President. The trouble with scientific heroes is that they have faith only in numbers or statistics; when any of their equations result in a high or perfect correlation: "When A happens as B happens, C happens" -- they like to call that *scientific* knowledge. That's *oversimplifying* things! There's only one

---

[40]**Noli Me Tangere**, *Ma. Soledad Lacson-Locsin's translation, pages 67-68.*

thing to say about science or statistics: Grossly imperfect.[41]

Mormons, Non-Gods

Did the Mormons have the perfect religion *and* the perfect software? Before the WordPerfect Corporation with its extremely popular word processing software also called *WordPerfect* passed from one owner to another, WordPerfect was created, owned and managed by the Mormons. No wonder the address was Salt Lake City, Utah, the city that Mormons built.

About the Mormons, here are some odd details:[42]

Certain ceremonies are performed only within the temple in Salt Lake City to which non-Mormons are religiously kept out.

Missionaries are sent to all the corners of the earth, charge to their own family's account, to preach their message of salvation.

Mormons believe that God had originally evolved from mankind; therefore, men could become gods themselves. The three persons of the Trinity are three separate beings. They practice baptism of the dead. They do not believe in a place of eternal punishment.

Mormons call themselves Christians but consider other Christian churches in error. At one time or another, the Mormons practiced polygamy. Joseph Smith, the founder and first leader, may have had as many as 50 wives.

By this short, biased account, I say the Mormons indeed look like villains. Otherwise, the Mormons are heroes for having fathered *WordPerfect*, one of the most successful software of all time. Also one of the best. It gained millions of users without the Mormons using dirty business tactics, unlike its main rival. Millions liked, nay, loved WordPerfect's exuberant flamboyance, its nonconformist attitude (if a program has attitude) which it showed by disregarding tradition (the way of *WordStar* by MicroPro and *Word* by Microsoft). The graphics

---

[41] *Haven't you heard the neat joke about statistical methods? It goes like this:* A man took water and wine on Monday; he got drunk. He took water and beer on Tuesday; he got drunk. He took water and rum on Wednesday; he got drunk. He took water and vodka on Thursday; he got drunk. Therefore, water made him drunk! *Much of science is like that.*

[42] *Not credited, "Mormons",* **Compton's Encyclopedia,** *cited, vol 15, pages 583-584.*

were superb and the fonts positively alluring.

The trouble with heroes like the Mormons and their software is that, like Microsoft and its software, they didn't leave well enough alone: The Mormons allowed WordPerfect to become too powerful (gargantuan) it now caters to the rich and does not champion the man on the PC anymore.

HINGIS & WOODS, NON-HARASSED

Champions both! She was 16 when Martina Hingis became the youngest women's tennis champion this century end of March 1997,[43] about the same day Editor & Publisher Krip Yuson called me by phone and said he was accepting me as a columnist of **The Evening Paper**. But that's not the reason she is one of my heroes. One is that she's "awesome", as another champion, Monica Seles, the vanquished, put it. There's another reason. This is Monica Seles speaking:

> *She's just a better player at this point than I am, so there's nothing to feel sad about. ... She just took charge of all the points, which I'm not used to. ... [About the pressure of playing to win,] it doesn't seem a burden to Martina at all. She's having a great time. Everything is happening very fast, and I think she's [handling] it great. She really is enjoying tennis out there so much, and it shows in her game.*[44]

I admire her because she is one of the few champions and near-champions in sports who enjoy what they're doing. They mind the pleasure, *not* the pressure.

> *"I've never had so much fun out there", says Hingis. ... "If you play well, you know you can beat almost everybody in the world. It's great to go out there and play in front of 10,000 people." ...*
>
> *An avid horsewoman, Hingis travels with "my boots and pants" in hopes of a joyous ride. [Not only that.] Rollerblades also fit into the suitcase and*

---

[43]*AP, "Hingis blitzes Seles at Lipton",* **The Evening Paper**, *March 31, 1997, page 14.*

[44]*AP, cited, page 14.*

residents on Key Biscayne have stopped and started as the Swiss miss skates by.

"I can't be all the time here at the courts", Hingis said. "It would just get crazy if you would spend all the time on the site. For me, it's important to do something else."[45]

Just like Tiger Woods, at 21 the youngest golfer ever to win the Masters title. It was his third try in fact, but he was undaunted. He said, "I don't care what anyone else says -- as always. I just came here to win. I'll try to be patient as possible".[46] And he did, and he was.

The Augusta National Golf Club where the Masters was played was touted as "the early leader" in the game because it is a most difficult course, where "wild winds, fast greens bring misery".[47]

So, what happened was record-breaking history; not only that, it was literally a mind-boggling achievement:

By winning the Masters by 12 strokes at Augusta at age 21, Woods rewrote the record books and caught the imagination of young and old, male and female, black and white.[48] *The* **BBC***'s Peter Allis said Woods' feat transcended sport and could only be compared to the precocious talents of Mozart and Chopin. Several papers described his mastery of the tough Augusta course as reducing it to pitch and putt. By outplaying a field that included greats such as Jack Nicklaus, Arnold Palmer, Gary Player, Tom Watson, Seve Ballesteros, Nick Faldo and Greg Norman, he appeared to change the whole concept of the game.*

"It seemed clear that he was staking his claim to the kind of greatness that rewrites the rules book and redefines the dimensions of a sport", the **Guardian**

---

[45]*Reuters, "Hingis rules tennis world",* **The Evening Paper**, *April 1, 1997, page 16.*

[46]*AP, "Faldo vs Woods: The best of two generations meet",* **The Evening Paper**, *April 10, 1997, page 16.*

[47]*Reuters, "Augusta National is early leader in Masters",* **The Evening Paper**, *April 11-13, 1997, page 16.*

[48]*Tiger Woods is an American Black.*

said.

"It is not the money or the flashing smile which dazzles", said the **Daily Mail**. *"It is the sheer breathtaking talent of a youngster who, in one weekend, changed the face of his chosen sport.*[49]

Seles called Hingis' win "awesome"; in turn, Nick Faldo, three-time winner of the Masters, called Tiger Wood's performance "phenomenal". Woods is an example of, "Where there's a will, there's a win. Where there's a giant will, there's a giant win". The trouble with heroes like Martina Hingis and Tiger Woods is that it's difficult to be like them, being heroes in whatever we do, and doing it brilliantly.

SADAO & ROMY, NON-WASTERS

Brilliant is the brainchild of Sadao Nishibori, Japanese, creative man, President of Ein-Engineering Company, a hero in recycling.[50] He is a back-to-the-basics fellow. A few basics from him: (1) That which you call waste is a resource. (2) You can create resource based on other resources. (3) Air is a better way to clean materials than water. (4) The most economical way to make resource is to use physical force.

Nishibori makes "plastic wood" out of discarded vinyl and scrap wood. In Japan, some 200,000 tons of vinyl is discarded every year by farmers alone. He has developed a method of removing chemicals and mud that cling to the material. He crushes the vinyl into small pieces, puts them into his "cleaning separator", and blows air into the machine. "The resultant shock abrasions removes the dirt from the vinyl", he says.[51]

He may have gotten his idea from the Philippines. He may have been working with the RP-Japan Reforestation Project, which Japan funded. It was based in Carranglan, Nueva Ecija. I know about this Project because I was Chief Information Officer of the Forest Research Institute (FORI) at that time, and FORI had a Research Station there,

---

[49]*AP, "The roar that was heard around the world",* **The Evening Paper**, *April 16, 1997, page 14. Which means, when you do your best, it makes a qualitative difference.*

[50]*Takahiro Takesue, "Japanese Now Intent on Recycling",* **Pacific Friend**, *June 1996, page 23.*

[51]*Takesue, cited, page 23.*

and I went out to the fields to gather information and photographs for our publications. So, I saw it too:

> *Nishibori saw 21 years ago how forests in the Philippines were being cut down one after another. Unless something was done, the rain forests would all be lost. Since then, he has invested ¥5 billion in researching technologies for recycling scrap wood.*

The trouble with heroes like Sadao Nishibori is if we ignore them because they were once the barbarians of Asia in World War II.

Not to be outdone (except in material wealth) is Romy Antonio, Filipino. He has a mind as curious as a child and as rich as the soil he works with. In fact, he has discovered, among other things, that an *organic soil* (my term) can be created based on waste materials simply by mixing them together -- and wonder of wonders, you can use the soil mixture right after mechanical mixing: Where by other means you can have an organic fertilizer in 15 days (and they say that's *fast*), here you can have an organic soil in 15 minutes (that's fantastic!). To see is to believe. And there is no smell of rotting matter. How good is the soil? I have seen it myself; for instance, his organic soil can make carpet grass grow faster and yield much more from the same area. And that's only the beginning of the wonders of his organic soil. The trouble with heroes like Romy Antonio is when we look down on them just because they happen to be only high school graduates.

NIETZSCHE, NON-BARBARIAN

We are *not* barbarians? Man must be careful not to assume the air of superiority, which Nietzsche saw very clearly in his own time. He was a brilliant man, this German poet and philosopher (1844-1900), born in Saxony, a province of Prussia. His political thoughts shook his own (19th) and our (20th) century. It was he who saw that man had become so obsessed with his own genius, mostly that of self-satisfied Europeans, proud of civilization's accomplishments with and mastery of science, technology, politics and economics; for them, "God is dead" or, "belief in the Christian God has become unworthy of belief".[52]

Upon his death, nobody knew that Nietzsche's own sister,

---

[52]*Not credited, "Friedrich Nietzsche",* **Compton's Encyclopedia**, *cited, vol 16, page 307.*

Elisabeth, rewrote his writings to reflect her own anti-Jew and nationalistic ideas. So, for a time, his name was associated with fascism. In fact, Nietzsche did not believe in the state, and, like Carlyle, did not believe in democracy either. Instead, he believed in the "will to power" and the superman, the one who shucks conventional or traditional (Christian) morality and creates his own values.[53]

I like Carlyle's heroes better than Nietzsche's superhero. I also believe that, indeed, with the halo around the heads of men of science (technology, mostly), *science has become a religion*. With scientists and their believers more fanatic than witch-hunters, they have gone on to proclaim not that "God is dead" but worse than that: "God never existed except in the imagination of the superstitious".

That's superstition! Scientists claim there is no God because no one can prove the existence of God. Well, can scientists disprove it? In the first place, science and faith are two different ways of looking at the world. If the scientists insist that theirs is the only right and reasonable way, I say that *science is superstition.* The trouble with scientists as heroes is if they become superstitious themselves.

LEA SALONGA, NON-SELFISH

Because they are not up to their necks in a science that survives on superstition, the young can be heroes in their own chosen fields. For instance, in the arts, in music. Why is it that Filipino singers are now riding the crest of the airwaves even in the United States? Jaya hits Top Ten. Jocelyn hits #1 in the billboard charts, a first. All because of one hero we have had: Lea Salonga. She is the one who broke the camel's back; hers is the face that launched a thousand Flips, if you don't mind the mixed metaphor. The Filipina is now being noticed. She's very good, in fact, she's phenomenal. She starred in the long-running **Miss Saigon** stage play in London and won top acting honors and the hearts of the British. She starred in the Broadway adaptation of **Miss Saigon** and won top acting honors and the hearts of the Americans. This girl is sensational. Of course, the world has been wondering whether all Filipinos were as good as Lea Salonga is. And of course we all are. If we all do our homework. If we all have heart, if we all have faith. If we are all prepared when it is time for us to be a hero.

---

[53]*Not credited, "Friedrich Nietzsche", cited, page 307.*

I remember the time she won the London acting award. We were all very proud of her, and what did she do? She sent a brief message to all Filipinos. The message said: "Please stop that crab mentality" so that we can all be as good as the best in the world. The trouble with heroes like Lea Salonga is that they are honored in other countries first.

YUSON, NON-NOVELIST

Alfred Yuson has written a strange book, **Great Philippine Jungle Energy Cafe** (Diliman, Quezon City: UP Press, 1996, 231 pages), and I'm not surprised that Maria Teresa Martinez-Sicat of UP Diliman dismisses it in two words, that it has "impotent charm".[54] She sees a failure in "unifying the past and the present". The trouble with heroes like Krip Yuson is that they bewilder even doctoral candidates.

I too was stupefied; I too felt stupid. When I first read that book, I said it was a big disappointment, and I told Orli exactly that (he had lent me his copy). But I gave Krip Yuson the benefit of the doubt; one reason was that at that time he had just accepted me as one of the opinion columnists of **The Evening Paper**, where he was Editor & Publisher.[55] It was my way of saying "Thank you" -- if I could see something to praise about his book; otherwise, I'll just keep my mouth shut (he had no way of knowing I had seen the book).

Then, it dawned on me, reading what others said about the book. In his excitement, all in one breath, Franz Arcellana called it *magic* and *music* and *poetry*. More soberly, Nick Joaquin said it was poetry. And I did a review of it in a completely different light; when you read it, you will be surprised to see that *Krip's book actually succeeds in unifying the past and present*.[56] And I dare add: Krip's

---

[54]*Maria Teresa Martinez-Sicat,* **Imagining The Nation In Four Philippine Novels** *(Quezon City: University of the Philippines Press), pages 91-121.*

[55]*My columns appeared under the serial title* **Th!nk**, *and I wrote about pollstergeists (like those of the Social Weather Station), Levi's as good for people and presidents, Bataan defenders as April Fools, Darna and the Dewey Decimal Syndrome etc. I was appearing three times a week. It was good while it lasted. The paper folded up May 13, 1997. Some good things don't last.*

[56]*Read my book review, "Aggravation! Discovering the*

book is history, and it is Liberation History. (For a discussion on Liberation History, see *Editor's Preface*.)

Right now, I'm looking at Krip's book in yet another light. Everyone is a hero in his own right -- Ferdinand Marcos, Ferdinand Blumentritt, Emilio Aguinaldo, Leon Kilát, Nick Joaquin, José Rizal, Andres Bonifacio, Nonoy Marcelo, David Cortez Medalla, Bencab, Franz Arcellana, José Garcia Villa and many others. What Krip Yuson has done really is make his own heroes write a *novel* novel.

What he did was an Alfred Yuson. The trouble with heroes like Krip is that we can't always be original.

SCOTTY, NON-NATIONALIST

Before there was Alfred Yuson, before Ambeth Ocampo, there was William Henry Scott who was as white as the next American you meet, and as brown as the next Filipino you see: his heart was in Sagada, Bontoc, where he served as missionary for many years.

Scotty was a historian as he was a missionary; he taught us our history as no one had done before. Scholar that he was, he exposed the Hoax of Kalantiaw and the Hoax of Maragtas -- he proved that the forger José Marco was both Kalantiaw *and* Maragtas.

Scotty also exposed us to the fact that we need not lament the loss of pre-Hispanic Filipino literature just because the incendiary Spaniards burned what they didn't like, including souls, if not bodies. Instead, he showed us how we can capture gold nuggets from unlikely unhistorical soils like correspondences.

The trouble with heroes like Scotty is that we can't choose our parents. The trouble is also that it takes a non-Filipino to see what is best for the Filipino.

Scotty was not only a nationalist; he was an internationalist, inside him and outside. Reading Confucius, he gave us these thoughts:

> *If a man cultivates himself, his household will be well ordered;*
> *If households are well ordered, proper human relationships will be observed;*
> *If proper human relationships are observed, the state will be well governed;*

---

wonder in us", **Philippine Daily Inquirer**, *June 13, 1997, page d2.*

If the state is well governed, the nation will be at peace;
If the nation is at peace, universal harmony will be established;
If universal harmony is established, Heaven will be pleased.[57]

Scotty was unique. His mind was global, his act was local. There is an interesting story about him, and which reveals yet to me another hero.

When Professor Bonifacio S. Salamanca was Dean of UP College Manila (which became UP College of Arts and Sciences), he appointed Dr. William Henry Scott *Professorial Lecturer in History*, "to teach any course of his choosing, including Philippine history."[58] But that's preposterous! Scotty is American, so what's his business teaching Philippine history?

Salamanca was warned, "You are doing something illegal in your College."[59] But he was undaunted. He knew there was no law prohibiting such an appointment, no rule preventing a White from teaching Brown History. He also knew Scotty's qualifications: He was currently teaching at Saint Andrew's Theological Seminary and Trinity College; he had a bachelor's degree from Yale University, and a doctorate in history from the University of Santo Tomas. For his doctoral dissertation, he studied prehispanic source materials for Philippine history, and successfully defended it before a panel of eminent and well-known historians: Teodoro Agoncillo, Horacio de la Costa, Marcelino Foronda, Nicholas Zafra, and Gregorio Zaide. The manuscript was subsequently published as a book by the UST Press in 1968, and which has been revised by the author and published by New Day.[60]

Salamanca risked both reputation and position -- therefore, he is an authentic hero -- to inject into the University of the Philippines, and the whole country, a higher quality of scholarship in terms of

---

[57]*William Henry Scott,* **Hollow Ships On A Wine Dark Sea** *((Quezon City: New Day Publishers), 1976, page 114.*

[58]*Bonifacio S. Salamanca, "Foreword", in William Henry Scott's* **Prehispanic Source Materials For The Study Of Philippine History**, *revised (Quezon City: New Day Publishers, 1984), page v.*

[59]*Salamanca, cited, page v.*

[60]*William Henry Scott,* **Prehispanic Source Materials For The Study Of Philippine History**, *revised (Quezon City: New Day Publishers, 1984), 196 pages.*

searching, reading, analyzing and writing in Philippine history. A precious gift. In fact, he praises Scotty to high heavens; of Scotty's **Prehispanic Source Materials**, he says:

> *Anyone who enjoyed [and profited from] the 1968 edition of [Scotty's] book will naturally find leafing through the present edition a more rewarding experience, incorporating as it does the findings in the literature on Philippine prehistory which have been published during the fifteen years since 1968, and of his own archival research. This edition, like the earlier one, is an excellent piece of scholarship. [Scotty's] meticulousness, patience and industry are simply astounding. I might also add that, perhaps, only he among contemporary Filipinologists could have written this work, which draws from such scholarly disciplines as anthropology, archaeology, geology, history, linguistics, paleography and paleontology, fields of study in which he seems to possess equal interest.*[61]

He is the greatest Filipino non-Filipino historian. The trouble with Scotty as hero is that his color (white) gets in the way of emulation. He was born on the wrong side of the Pacific.

So, where do we look for more heroes from here?

WOMEN JOURNALISTS, NON-PARTICIPANTS

We can look for more heroes among journalists in the print and broadcast media. And they need not lay their life on the line when they walk their beats.

Today, when local (and foreign) journalists report on current events, they do it as if they are apart from the scene, as if they are not part of the story they are telling. When did humanity declare that those who report on it are not part of it?

"An esteemed colleague of mine has written," says Tad Szulc, that "journalism is the first draft of history."[62] Why can't our

---

[61] *Salamanca, cited, pages v-vi.*

[62] *Tad Szulc,* **Then And Now** *(New York: William Morrow and Company, Inc., 1990), page 7.*

journalists be heroes and take care that *that* first draft is a good one they can be proud of in some future time, or, at least, not be ashamed of what they are doing when their family asks?

In fact, we are all guilty of lack of heroism, not only the journalists, but they have the awesome power of the press that they don't share with anyone else, so what Benedetto Croce says applies mostly to them:[63]

> *It is even stranger to find that instead of accurately and profoundly analyzing social diseases of the kind we have just mentioned or of similar kinds, or isolating them in a sort of ideal hospital, so that they can only harm those who are already incurably contaminated, people commonly turn to blaming historical thought or historicism for the generating of these diseases, by promoting fatalism, by dissolving absolute values, by sanctifying the past, by accepting the brutality of facts as facts, by applauding violence, by recommending quietness, and, in fact, by removing the impetus and confidence from creative forces, by blunting the sense of duty, and by disposing men to inactivity and lazy compromise.*

Journalist-heroes are not only those who get killed for their reportage. Dying is easy; it's the heroic living that's difficult. Journalistic heroes are like Deedee Sytangco and Luchie Cruz-Valdez who probed the merits of the proposed computerized system of voting and found it wanting. The trouble with journalists as heroes is that they can easily hide behind a cloak of objectivity: "I was only reporting what I saw and heard." Like scientists, they can't admit that they are biased.

In any case, we can borrow from Ernest Hemingway who once said, "Anyone who thinks writing is easy is a fool." *Anyone who thinks journalism is easy is a fool.*

FLAVIER, NON-DOCTOR

And anyone who thinks healing is easy is a fool. Ask Senator Juan Flavier who used to be your favorite doctor in the barrios,

---

[63] *Benedetto Croce,* **History As The Story Of Liberty** *(Lanham, Maryland: University Press of America, 1984), page 43.*

although he wasn't there only to treat your physical ailments. The more potent potion he brought wasn't magic at all; it was called *Rural Reconstruction*.

He wrote the bestselling **Doctor To The Barrios** and other books. To him, the Philippine Rural Reconstruction Movement (PRRM) was a hero; the International Institute of Rural Reconstruction (IIRR) was a hero, and so was the founder, James Yen. He devoted that one book to these heroes.

He became a folk hero (that's why you voted him Senator) when he wrote about ordinary folks, about the *taga-barbaryo*, **My Friends In The Barrios**. The heroes are: Poldo, a boy of many skills. *Pareng* Tonying, farmer-businessman, a pillar of the community. *Aling* Sepa, family planning assistant. *Mang Senting*, partner in pig-raising. *Ka* Berong, *arbularyo*. *Aling* Rosing, unschooled but wise, a woman for all seasons. *Tata* Poloniong, interpreter of life. *Atibapa*.

The trouble with heroes like Juan Flavier is when they forget the little heroes who made them the bigger heroes.

LOOKING FOR MORE HEROES

We need to look for more heroes, but we have to be careful. So, considering the more obvious examples: Are Pio del Pilar, Andres Bonifacio, and José Ma. Sison[64] heroes? Yes, because they were truly fighting evil with their own life at stake. No, because they were fighting evil with evil, hate with hate. The easiest thing to do is to hate. It is easy to fight with the moral principle in the head and hate in the heart, but there is no virtue in it:

> *Do not let your love be a pretence, but sincerely prefer good to evil. Love each other as much as brothers should, and have a profound respect for each other. Work for the Lord with untiring effort and with great earnestness of spirit. If you have hope, this will make you cheerful. Do not give up if trials come; and keep on praying. If any of the [brothers] are in need you must share with them; and you should make hospitality your special care.*

---

[64]*Marxists would, of course, argue that Marxism is scientific. A debatable point.*

> *Bless those who persecute you: never curse them, bless them. Rejoice with those who rejoice and be sad with those in sorrow. Treat everyone with equal kindness; never be condescending but make real friends with the poor. Do not allow yourself to become self-satisfied. Never repay evil with evil but let everyone see that you are interested only in the highest ideals. Do all you can to live at peace with everyone. Never try to get revenge; leave that, my friends, to God's anger. As scripture says:* Vengeance is mine -- I will pay them back, *the Lord promises. But there is more:* If your enemy is hungry, you should give him food, and if he is thirsty, let him drink. *Thus you heap red-hot coals on his head. Resist evil and conquer it with good.*[65]

Above, I have quoted in length to forestall any out-of-context interpretation. The message is clear: The trouble with heroes is when they try to conquer the bad with a halo in their head and blood in their hands. I like Goethe who was a hero to Carlyle because he "appealed ... to persons of head and heart".[66] As did the man from Nazareth who, in just one short sentence, summarized the Ten Commandments:

Love your enemies!

But we prefer vengeance. We don't get mad; we get even. We prefer justice, which is vengeance in disguise. So we nurse our hurts. So we continue to feel that we do not deserve our hurts. And of course we are right: we do not deserve our hurts. But who gave us those hurts? It was we ourselves, because we refuse to forgive *and* forget, because we are selfish in the sense that when we give we expect something in return in the form we like in the time we expect. Selfish love, I say:

> *We do not realize it, but we love those whom we love much too much, so much so that we don't have any love left for others. We exhaust ourselves in our love for our beloveds, including ourselves, that we have no energy left to see Jesus in the ones we see as our enemies, who may turn out to be the ones we love. Our love exhausts us, so our hate easily overwhelms us.*

Now comes Maximo V. Soliven, Publisher of **The Philippine**

---

[65]*Romans 12:9-21,* **Jerusalem Bible.**

[66]*Behnken, cited, page 49.*

Star, lover of freedom, essaying about the assassination of Danny Hernandez and the drug menace, angry, calling for heroes:

> *Only a ruthless government crackdown, personally led by General Ramos, Interior Secretary Bobby Barbers, Defense Secretary Renato de Villa, and the chiefs of both the police and the Armed Forces, can combat this menace. Only our police (outside of those already corrupted by the spreading virus) and our military have the firepower, at this stage, to match and overpower the drug challenge.*[67]

No! With all its law-enforcing agencies -- the FBI, CIA, DEA, NSA and the state police apparatus -- not even the greatest nation on earth can arrest the drug menace anywhere in America. For law is not the answer, neither is it law enforcement. Not even Mayor Alfredo Lim's "Danger: A drug pusher lives here. Keep out!" spray-painted on the fence of the pusher's house -- the Signs of the Times.

Why not? Because the drug menace was not spawned and not created and is not being cultivated by the drug lords and drug pushers and drug farmers but by our own materialism, dialectical or not. For our riches are of this world. Where our treasures are, there our hearts lie also.[68] Until we ourselves get rid of the world *inside* ourselves, we will never get rid of the drug menace outside the door, or inside.

If we don't do anything, we could get rid of the world *outside* ourselves. Robert Frost says it well:

Fire And Ice

Some say the world will end in fire,
Some say in ice.
From what I've tasted of desire
I hold with those who favor fire.
But if it had to perish twice,
I think I know enough of hate
To say that for destruction ice
Is also great
And would suffice.

---

[67]*Max Soliven, "By The Way",* **Philippine Star**, *June 6.*

[68]*Luke 12:34.*

We must start with us; the family must start with the family, I must start with me; you must start with you.

And you must *begin with love*; you must be a hero of love. Above all, remember: "If you are angry, let it be without sin.[69] Hate the evil act, love the actor. Hate the malice of the entrepreneur, love the entrepreneur. Hate the bad program, love the programmer. To do any of that calls for heroism, not militarism, not militantism.

The Philippines, an emerging tiger. Remember when you think APEC: *Pacific Century or not, we need more than economic heroes* to make a better history than we have had so far. I like Linda Bicksler in her letter to the Editor of **Fortune**, as I too am wary of economics:

> *Ideology is not the exclusive property of the religious right. All sides are ideological, even big business. Business is the ideology of power. When Shakespeare echoes the Bible in asking, "What is a man?" business answers the question in measurable terms - dollars and cents, supervision over others. It is the religion of control. Might not economics, as an ideology, be as frightening as any other? Born-agains are not anti-achievement; they are against an ideology that declares the sum value of a man to be economic.*[70]

So the present catches up with the past. So we go back to where we started: "Has Makati found its hero in Pio del Pilar?" Yes! He is a hero one can be proud of at his most heroic hour (this book, pages 37-38):

> *Pio del Pilar's greatest battle was, perhaps, the defense of Bacoor on 16 February 1897. Here he was in command of the rebel advance lines together with Colonels Mariano Noriel and Agapito Bonzon. The defense of Bacoor was a joint effort of the Magdalo and Magdiwang forces, and among its defenders were*

---

[69]*Ephesians 4:26 (New American Bible, 1984).*

[70]*Letters to Fortune,* **Fortune**, *March 6, 1995.*

Andres Bonifacio's personal troops from Tondo and Balara under General Lucino de la Cruz. Although the rebels suffered heavy losses, particularly at Zapote Bridge where the ilustrado-engineer General Edilberto Evangelista died in action, the Filipinos never abandoned their trenches. Finally, General Pio del Pilar led his Magtagumpay troops in a brilliant flanking action, hacking and firing their way into the very lines of the enemy and engaging the Spaniards in what was probably the fiercest running fight ever recorded in the history of the "first war". And that night -- almost all night -- Aguinaldo and his Pio del Pilar stayed awake deliberating on their next moves.

Even Antonio Luna praised Pio del Pilar when he heard of the latter's military exploits with only bolos for his men. *My hero!*

But we need even more heroes from today than from the past. Specifically, we need more of those whose heroism is based on the essentials. If there is any single lesson from all this talk about heroes, it is this: *We must go back to the basics.*

Like, the question of responsibility is basic. "Carlyle," says Behnken, "puts the ultimate responsibility for history and human destiny squarely on men's shoulders, not on God's."[71] You can disagree with that, but it doesn't absolve you from responsibility.

But do be careful about responsibility. Here's a true anecdote on me; I have shared this in one of our Living Word Group sessions of the Bukás Loób sa Díyos Los Baños District community.

I used to brag:

"I taught myself how to write, and I'm one of the best; I taught myself how to edit, and I'm one of the best; I taught myself how to do word processing, and I'm one of the best; I taught myself how to do desktop publishing, and I'm one of the best; I taught myself programming, and I'm very creative. You see, I'm a self-made man."

The perfect retort to that is this:

"Excellent! That relieves God of a great responsibility!"

---

[71]*Behnken, cited, page 6.*

My worp has an *Autosave* feature, and that's a clue: we must save ourselves *ourselves*. "What is the biggest room in the world?" a wag asks, and answers his own question: "The room for improvement". So, looking for heroes now, I look at us. I look into the mirror first, then I look at you. I see only one trouble when *when* we look for heroes, we overlook ourselves.

And so we may led heroic lives, and so we must. And what if we fail? We can be assured, as John Skow says, writing of the new book **The Promise Of Rest** (last in a trilogy) by the novelist Reynolds Price, to whom, being incapacitated by cancer, writing is an act of heroism: "Grace and seriousness are enough."[72] Amen.

FRANK A. HILARIO
LOS BAÑOS, LAGUNA, JULY 30, 1997

---

[72]*John Skow, "Staring down loneliness"* **Time**, *June 5, 1995, page 52.*

GLOSSARY

Aguinaldista, a diehard for Emilio Aguinaldo, who wrested control of the Revolution from Andres Bonifacio, founder of the Katipunan and Supremo; and they became mortal enemies of each other. (See **Bonifacista**). The term thus indicates that even in the face of a common enemy (first the Spaniards, then the Americans who were wilier), partisanship was intense at the expense of a united opposition, ultimately at the expense of the Revolution. We ask: **Why is it that the Revolution is devoured by its own children?**

Alsa balutan literally means "pack things up and leave". In the context of the 1897 factional war among rebels in Cavite, it was a snide remark which native Caviteños applied to all individuals or groups (and, maybe, especially to Andres Bonifacio and his Tondo-Balara Katipuneros) who had evacuated from Manila and other places to seek the safety of "Cavite Libre" (*Cavite Liberated*). Katipuneros in Cavite were enjoying victory after victory in their battles.

Americanistas were those Filipinos (Creoles, mestizos or Indios) who collaborated with the American military and civil authorities, either as mercenaries or civil officials, as opposed to the so-called **insurrectos** who fought and resisted American aggression. The truth of the matter is that we Filipinos are more Americanista than ever before: Just look at the way we dress, the cars we drive, the values we hold dear, the language of our book. (Compare with **Filipinos**.)

Americano is a term used to refer to *white Americans* -- as opposed to Negro, which in turn was how both white (and brown) Americans referred to Blacks in general.

Anarquista is, literally, an *anarchist*. It is used here to refer to the underground suicide squad of Artemio Ricarte, the group who at one time went out to assassinate General Elwell Otis, Military Governor, Americano. There was anarchy from the American side too; what do you expect in a war?

Antipatico refers to *one with quite displeasing manners, antipathetic*. In those days, the feeling was mutual: Some leaders of the Revolution were strongly averse to the company of Pio del Pilar as he was to theirs.

Armas Blancas (literally, *Invisible Army*) was the collective name given to the "phantom army" of Katipunan veterans who were organized as reserves in the Republicano Army, apart from the **Sandatahanes** (or *Bolo Corps*) which, though not carrying rifles, was really an integral part of that army, serving as auxiliaries.

Autonomistas vs Independistas were those *pro-autonomy* against those who were pro-independence, for a State within the United States as against a free Philippines. The Autonomistas (like Paterno and Buencamino) were in the Republicano government (also called the Malolos Republic) who openly favored annexation to the United States, as opposed to the Independistas (like Mabini and Luna) who stood for nothing short of freedom from any colonial master, Spanish or American.

Bakang Batangas is *Batangas cattle*, known for its quality meat, much sought after inside and outside the province, then and now. The "rival" meat is **Bakang Pangasinan**. The high quality comes from the grass given and the **toyo** (by-product of milling rice: fine hulls inseparable from fine grains) mixed with water (which makes a protein-rich diet) and force-fed by bamboo tube to the animals. It's the feed that makes the difference.

Bamboo cure was one of several torture methods practiced on Filipinos by both the Spaniards and the Americans (or should it be, more properly, by Filipinos in the service of colonial masters on their compatriots?). It took the form of clamping sensitive parts of the body using split bamboo. Among the variations were **water cure** and **rope cure**. (See related note on **Macabebes**.)

Bandit was the derogatory term used by the American colonial masters, Yanqui soldiers and their cohorts among Filipinos, to refer to any Filipino revolutionary, as if name-calling would erase the fact that the rebels were fighting for national liberation from the colonizer.

Bandolerismo is *banditry*. Among other atrocious things, the American colonizers were guilty of name-calling. For a history cum treatise on the subject of bandolerismo, read Orlino A. Ochosa, **"Bandoleros": Outlawed Guerrillas of the Philippine-American War, 1903-1907** (Quezon City: New Day Publishers, 1995, 165 pages). (See also related note on **Bandit**.)

Batallon Primero (*First Battalion*). Pio del Pilar was conscripted into the Spanish Batallon Primero, and he didn't like it. He wanted to be his own leader, not merely a soldier. On short notice, Capitan Lorenzo Protacio conscripted him out of the Spanish Army.

Batang Makati is now, as then, *someone born and bred in Makati*. Pio del Pilar was a native of Makati (of Culi-Culi, now renamed Pio del Pilar in his honor). **Batang Tondo** is someone born and bred in Tondo. Both terms indicate belonging to peer groups in a defined geographical area sharing common dreams and aspirations.

Batang Tondo. *See note on* **Batang Makati**.

Beloved General is a term of endearment used by Presidente Emilio Aguinaldo on Pio del Pilar and Gregorio del Pilar, because they deserved it. Pio won battles for his Presidente while Goyo became his personal defender and hatchetman and in fact gave up his life so that his Presidente may not be captured.

Berdugo is *executioner*. In the Filipino context, a berdugo is one who is not merely ordered to execute someone but is himself eager to do it. Was Macapagal a berdugo?

Bonifacista, a *partisan of Bonifacio*, i.e., of the Manila-Morong Katipuneros (most especially those of Tondo and Balara) who belonged to the Katagalugan Council and the few Magdiwangs of Cavite who did not join the Republicano forces. They were diehard rebels with a cause who resolutely supported what they were fighting for, and some of them (like Jacinto and Sakay) gave up their lives in order not to give up *their* struggle.

Bordadera, an *embroiderer*, as Pio del Pilar's mother was said to be. Did she have a direct hand in his son's Magtagumpay Council's flag design? This was the most symbolic of all Katipunan Council flags.

Brains of the Katipunan refers to Emilio Jacinto. **Brains of the Republica** refers to Apolinario Mabini. Jacinto and Mabini, although almost 10 years apart in age, had much in common aside from being "brains" of two distinct revolutions. They were both, to begin with, ilustrados originated from the masses: one was born in the slums of Tondo, the other in a Batangas nipa hut. They were obsessed with Law and Government and both would take up writing as means of articulating their thoughts; one gave the Katipunan its "Bible" (the *Kartilla*), the other gave the Republica its "Commandments" (the *Decalogo*). They were both patriots and revolutionaries, though one was *Katipunero* and the other *Compromisario*. And both possessed a headstrong character that made one to choose to lead a humble life rather than play along with the abusers of his friends, the other to prefer a lonely exile rather than work for the deceivers of his people. In the days of Independencia, when Aguinaldo officially abolished (outlawed?) the Katipunan and proclaimed its transformation as the Inang Bayan itself, the "brains' in Malolos invited his earlier and younger counterpart to help in the making of Republicano history, but the true Bonifacista declined to go. *Sayang*. With their minds in sync, transcending personalities and group interests, these two heroes might have changed the unenlightened course of the Revolution and together deserved to be called the **Brains of the Revolution**.

Brigada Pio del Pilar is the *Pio del Pilar Brigade*, the officers and soldiers who fought under and with General Pio del Pilar alone and no other. They were willing to give up their lives for their country -- and for Pio del Pilar. They were notorious but they were victorious.

Bungo is Tagalog for *skull*, the symbol in the flag of Mariano Llanera, Nueva Ecija's leader Katipunero. His "Skull Flag" had a white skull and crossbones against a black background.

Burguesos are the *bourgeoisie*. The Malolos Congress was full to the rafters with members of the bourgeoisie that there was no room for a representative of the masses.

Cabo (Corporal) was a *non-commissioned officer's rank* which was below a **Sargento** (*Sergeant*) and above a **Soldado** (*Buck Private*). Cabo Leoncio Cayetano saved Pio del Pilar's life from the Guardia Civil.

Cajero or **Pagador** is *Cashier* or *Paymaster*. Captain Lorenzo Protacio, the one who bailed Pio del Pilar out of the Spanish Army's draft, later became Paymaster of the Pio del Pilar Brigade.

Capitan (Captain) in its military sense is a rank below a **Comandante** (*Major*) and above a **Teniente** (*Lieutenant*). As a civilian title during the last days of the Spanish regime in the Philippines, it was used as short for **Capitan Municipal** (now **Mayor**), as in *Capitan Tiago* or *Capitan Kulas*. Under the Revolutionary Government and later during the early years of the American regime, **Capitan Municipal** was superseded by **Presidente Local** (*which see*). It was Capitan Santiago Coronado of Mandaluyong who introduced Pio del Pilar to **filibusterismo** *(which see)*.

Carta anonima is an *anonymous letter* with malicious intent, a poison pen. According to Pio del Pilar, Andres Bonifacio forced him to accede to his (Bonifacio's) plan to secede from the Aguinaldo Government by showing him anonymous letters, presumably derogatory to his character.

Castigado is when one gets *reprimanded* or *punished* for an offense or misdemeanor. The two Civil Guards who tortured Pio del Pilar were chastised; for punishment, they were sent to the frontlines to fight the Moros.

Cavitismo was a pejorative label, popularized by Nick Joaquin/Quijano de Manila, to describe that *extreme regionalism displayed by*

Caviteños towards other regional or provincial Filipinos during the entire revolutionary phase. At its worst, it was manifested in such infamous events of the Revolution as Bonzon disgracing the Lakambini of the Katipunan, Macapagal liquidating the Supremo, and Janolino disobeying and later murdering Luna. At its best, it was Aguinaldo himself during his glorious 1896-1897 Cavite and Batangas campaigns, Bonzon redeeming himself in two great battles at Zapote River (against the Spaniards and later against the Americans), Camerino dying unsurrendered as an exile in Guam, San Miguel carrying on the fight after Malvar, and Montalan holding high the Katipunan ideals with Sakay until 1906.

Cazadores means, literally, *hunters*. In the Spanish Army in the Philippines, they were the Infantry's "Special Forces". In one battle, in another war, *American* "cazadores" became "big-game hunters" shooting at the helpless Filipino soldiers trying to cross the Pasig River; they were like sitting ducks.

Colegio refers to both the *school* and the *course*; five years of colegio led to a Bachelor of Arts. One of Pio del Pilar's laments was that he never even entered colegio.

Comandante. See note on **Capitan**.

Comisario is *Commissary* or *Deputy*. Captain Fernando Caruncho was Comisario to Pio del Pilar.

Compadre is *comrade* or *cosponsor* (godfather both to the same child). **Comadre** is the *female* form. **Compañero** is *companion* or *partner*. Compadre expresses kinship (including in-laws), while compañero expresses friendship. Blood is thicker than water.

Compañero. See note on **Compadre**.

Comprovinciano (*provincemate*) is someone who hails, at least, from the same region, if not from the same province.

Consejal is *Municipal Councilor.*

Constabulario is *Constabulary, the Spanish police.*

Contra-revolucionario (*counter-revolutionary*) was how Bonifacio and Aguinaldo (and their respective partisans) accused each other. Later, after Bonifacio's liquidation, Aguinaldistas typically used the term to discredit all anti-Republicano dissenters -- such as the "true Katipuneros" of the groups of Bonifacio, Jacinto and Sakay, as well as the **Guardia de Honor**, **Santa Iglesia**, **Cruz na Bituin** and other peasant or plebeian brotherhoods.

Diputado is *Deputy or Representative.* Pio del Pilar was deputized as Representative of Negros Oriental, which did not elect a delegate to the Malolos Congress.

Ejercito Libertador was the *Liberation Army*, as Ricartistas regarded their military organization, from the time their leader, Ricarte the Vibora, first returned from exile in 1904. He designated Pio del Pilar General-in-Chief of his Liberation Army for Northern Luzon.

El Vibora. *See* **The Viper**.

Evangelista trenches were so-called in honor of their creator in the Cavite battlefields, General Edilberto Evangelista, in 1896 a new engineering graduate from the University of Ghent in Belgium, who joined Aguinaldo's Magdalo Army and became Lieutenant-General. The trenches spelled victory for the Cavite defenders. The Zapote River Line especially made good use of those Evangelista trenches, which impressed even the Spanish General Lachambre in 1897, as well as the American General Lawton in 1899.

Filibusterismo and **Filibustero.** By definition, **filibusterismo** is hiring soldiers *(**filibusteros** or mercenaries)* for a private military action, especially in a foreign country. In the context of the Philippine Propaganda Movement, filibusterismo was fighting peacefully against Spanish abuses in the country. In the second novel of José Rizal, **El Filibusterismo**, the story comes close to the original meaning of the term: Simoun tries to manipulate events to enrage Filipinos enough to stage an uprising against the Spaniards.

Filipinas is **Inang Bayan** (*which see*).

Filipinos, in its original context, were those Spaniards born in the Philippines -- as opposed to **Indios**, the native "Filipinos". After the Secularization and Propaganda movements led by pure or mestizo Spanish Filipinos fizzled out into failures, Andres Bonifacio's Katipunan -- predominantly Indio -- introduced (or re-introduced) the substitute word **Tagalogs** (*Filipinos*) for all natives and **Katagalugan** for the country (*Filipinas*). *Filipinas/Filipinos*, in the context of **nation** became "official" during the 1898-1899 **independencia** days and after.

First War and **Second War** refer to the *wars of liberation against Spain*, or the first phase of the Philippine Revolution, and it was divided only by the brief interruption of the Biyak-na-Bato truce. An entirely different war -- and a much longer, costlier one -- was the Philippine-American War that the enemy chose to call "insurrection" (and, to Agoncillo, a mere "imbroglio") which broke out in February 1899 and lasted until 1902, if we limit it to Aguinaldo's and Malvar's protracted Republicano struggle; until 1906, if we extend it to San Miguel's and Sakay's renewed Katipunan struggle; until the "peace time" decades if we include the unsurrendered Ricarte's stoical but quixotic struggle; and until the present if we refer to the continuing, unfinished Philippine Revolution.

Friendly relations, so-called. Towards the end of the Philippine-Spanish War, the Americans were driven to these islands by what they declared as *Manifest Destiny* for the Philippines. Subsequently, they claimed friendship with the Filipinos at the expense of the Spaniards; in fact, they were plotting against the interests of everybody else. Internationalism?

Gapang (literally, *crawl*) is a clandestine military maneuver, moving stealthily in order to avoid detection by the enemy whom one wishes to attack in surprise.

Great Plebeian is an honorific title given to Andres Bonifacio, indicating that he was a *commoner*, that he was one of the masses.

Guardia Civil *(Civil Guards)* was the local police or constable force during the Spanish colonial era in the Philippines. Civil Guards were guarding the interests of the colonial masters.

Guardia de Honor (*Guard of Honor)* took roots as a "clerico-fascist" anti-Katipunan association instigated by the friars. This is where they made a mistake. Infiltration by revolutionary or masonic agents led to its mutation as a patriot movement by 1898, and Guardia leaders like the Del Prado brothers of Pangasinan were exemplars of this transformation, although there were also elements, like the Patajo faction of La Union, who became mercenaries of the Americans. Republicano repression later led to its anti-Aguinaldo stance, and yet, the Guardia de Honor as a whole remained true to the cause of the Revolution, which was abandoned by the Republicanos. Vicente del Prado, among other Guardia leaders, was hanged by the Americans for such intransigence.

Guerrillero is a *guerrilla.* Guerrilla warfare, as a method of fighting against an established government or invading forces, was popularized by the Spaniards in their own Spain during their resistance against the conquering French legions of Napoleon Bonaparte. The fighters were called guerrilleros (guerrillas). As a guerrilla, Pio del Pilar won brilliantly (as he was a good military leader); he also lost ignominiously (he wasn't always good).

Gunita refers to *memories* or *reminiscences*. The book **Mga Gunita ng Himagsikan** (*Memoirs of the Revolution*) was Emilio Aguinaldo's recollections of his experiences as Generalissimo of the Philippine

Revolution, and which was published in 1964.

Haring Bayan (*Head Council*) was, to Andres Bonifacio and Emilio Jacinto and their followers, the **Katagalugan** Supreme Council of Tondo, which the Supremo's stationery head described as "**May-tayo nang Kataastaasang Kagalang-galang na Katipunan nang mga Anak ng Bayan** at unang nag-galaw nang panghihimagsik" -- "Builder of the Highest & Noblest Brotherhood of the Sons of the People and prime mover of the Revolution". Teodoro Agoncillo distorted the phrase by saying Bonifacio referred to himself as the "Hari ng Bayan" (Head of the Country).

Ilustrado literally means *enlightened*. Broadly speaking, in the context of the turn-of-the century Philippines, any university-educated Filipino was an ilustrado, and he was, as even now, treated with respect by the illiterates.

Imperialista (*imperialist, in favor of empire)*. The Americans came to the Philippines with their dreams of empire, calling it "Manifest Destiny".

Inang Bayan (*Motherland)*. To all the anti-Spanish and anti-American nationalists and to Bonifacio, Jacinto and their Katipuneros specially, it was clear that the motherland was neither **Madre España** *(Mother Spain)* nor Mother America but **Filipinas**.

Independencia (*Independence)* was the cause, the goal, the *raison d'etre* of the Philippine Revolution, as far as the exponents and sympathizers of the Republica were concerned. General Antonio Luna's revolutionary paper **La Independencia** (*which see*) resolutely stood for this aspiration: to be for autonomy was to betray it. The period from the declaration of Independence on 12 June 1898 to the breaking out of the Philippine-American War (as provoked by American aggression) on 4 February 1899, was referred to as "those independencia days". Ironically, those were also the days when the Katipunan was abolished by Aguinaldo's decree, the Katipuneros outlawed, and their **Kalayaan** (*which see*) repressed.

Independistas. *See note on* **Autonomistas.**

Indios. *See note on* **Filipinos.**

Insurgent and **Insurgent Records.** The Philippine Insurgent Records, compiled by John R.M. Taylor, were documents captured from Filipino rebels, who were officially labelled insurgents by the American authorities. Insurgents are those who rise in rebellion against civilian authority in a popular but limited movement; the Americans, therefore, were name-*calling*, to downplay the widespread support to the Revolution of 1896. (See related note on **Revolution**.) Even Teodoro Agoncillo, the noted Filipino historian, mouths the line of the colonialists when he calls the Filipino warriors insurgents in his book **Malolos: The Crisis of the Republic**.

Insurrection. A synonym for *insurgency*; see **Insurgent**.

Insurrectos (*Insurgents*), meant to be pejorative, was how the American aggressors viewed all Filipinos who resisted American advances; their government was labeled **Insurrecto Government**, their forces **Insurrecto Army**, their documents the **Insurrecto Papers**, and the Philippine-American war itself **The Philippine Insurrection**. All incorrect and self-serving, to say the least. All references to those words in this book are, therefore, always enclosed in quotation marks. In this book, another correct term used for some of them is **irreconcilables** -- they could not reconcile Revolution with collaboration. (See also **Intransigentes**.)

Intramuros, the *Walled City of Manila*, was the seat of Spanish power in the Philippines from the days of Legazpi to the **zarzuela surrender** (which see) of the Spanish government to the Americans on 13 August 1898. In the siege of Manila in 1898, Intramuros was the single main objective of the Generals of all the four Manila zones of Aguinaldo's Revolutionary Army -- and their failure to capture it as the symbolic seat of power led, partly, to Pio del Pilar's estrangement from Aguinaldo. That was because Pio del Pilar was willing and ready and in place -- but unable to pounce on the enemy because Emilio Aguinaldo wavered: he believed in the benevolence of the Americans more than the intelligence of Pio del Pilar, or his information about the treachery of the Americans. Coming to know that sad fact, other Generals were similarly disaffected.

Intransigentes *(Intransigents)*. After the weakening of Aguinaldo's resistance against the Americans, and especially after the Presidente himself called for acceptance of the American rule after his capture, all those who continued to radically oppose American colonialism were lumped as irreconcilables or intransigentes. The intransigence found no better exemplars than those patriots exiled (because they refused to pledge allegiance to Mother America) to Guam, which included Mabini, Ricarte and Pio del Pilar -- or those who stayed in the mountains to keep on the struggle, which included Malvar, San Miguel and Sakay.

Junta de Amigos literally means *Council of Friends*. In the context of the Philippine military anti-American resistance (1899-1906), **amigo** was not friend (as it should be) but its exact opposite, enemy, meaning all Filipinos who did not belong to the "insurrecto" army but who responded to American aggression in some other way in their own way, while professing friendship to them. **Junta de Amigos** was an anti-American urban guerrilla group in Manila during the early 1900s, made up of pre-1896 Katipunan veterans led by the dramatist-patriot Aurelio Tolentino "Azul". Necessarily, this group would be tapped as a mass base for the Ricartista movements from 1903 to 1915.

Kalayaan is *freedom* from colonialism, oppression. It was the original independence goal of the Katipunan for which every true *Anak ng Bayan* was exhorted to spill his blood and give up his life if necessary. The present **Araw ng Kalayaan** (Independence Day, which is the object of centennial celebrations for 1998), commemorates not the *genuine* Kalayaan the Katipuneros (Bonifacio and Jacinto, especially) nurtured in their hearts and minds, but the Republicano idea of **independencia** (*which see*) -- independence "under the protection of the great North American nation", as Aguinaldo's official proclamation of independence at Kawit recorded for posterity. Aptly, the newspaper of the Katipunan, which Jacinto edited, was named *Kalayaan*. And if it did not stand for *Katipunan* or *Katagalugan*, could the ancient Tagalog script "K" in Bonifacio's war standard have also stood for *Kalayaan*? Perhaps, the difference of meanings of the Katipunero Kalayaan and the Republicano Independencia lies in this: it was *taus-puso* (heartfelt) for all true Katipuneros, but merely *bukang-bibig* (lip service) for most Republicanos. In this case, the bourgeois-ilustrado-Creole Antonio Luna who edited **La Independencia** was as Katipunero as the plebeian-ilustrado-Indio Jacinto who edited *Kalayaan* for his radical independence stand. And, in contrast, Aguinaldo's conviction for what he proclaimed in 1898 can be measured by the ease with which he accepted and even endorsed SURRENDER in 1901.

Kastila is *Spanish*, *Spaniard*. Though it referred to pure-blooded Spaniards born in the Spanish Peninsula (and thus were called **Peninsulares**) or in the Philippine Islands (**Insulares**), the term was usually extended to Spanish-looking mestizos. Such was the reason why Creole rebels like Pepito Leyba and Pedro Janolino (the Kawit Captain who led Luna's murderers) were nicknamed "Kastila".

Katagalugan (*land of the Tagalogs*). As the concept word of Andres

Bonifacio and Emilio Jacinto in their writings concerning the Katipunan, it referred to all Filipinos as *Tagalogs* (also *Katagalugan*). "Sa salitang 'Tagalog', katutura'y ang lahat nang tumubo sa sangkapuluang ito; samakatuwid, Bisaya man, Iloko man, Kapangpangan man ... ay Tagalog din." For the same reason, the very first Sanggunian of the Katipunan -- that of Tondo -- was named "Katagalugan" and it was, theoretically, the Supreme Council, the Kataastaasang Kapulungan, the **Haring Bayan** (which see). It is in the light of Katagalugan -- as the continuing Katipunan of 1899-1906 after Jacinto's death -- that Sakay's struggle should be viewed, and not the "bandolerismo" as it was interpreted and preached by the Americans and those others who didn't know any better, or who decided to shut up for their own good.

Katipunan is short for **Kataastaasang Kagalang-galang na Katipunan ng mga Anak ng Bayan**, the brotherhood founded by Andres Bonifacio and friends on the night of 7 July 1892, the very day José Rizal was exiled to Dapitan and his own association (*La Liga Filipina*) -- of which Bonifacio and his Katipunan cofounders were also members -- was dissolved. Distinction must be made between this Katipunan (its original, i.e., pre-1896 members, were fond of referring to themselves as "ang mga tunay na Katipunan") from the Katipunan reactivated later during the 1900s by Emilio Aguinaldo and his Republicano Generals in support of their guerrilla war against the Americans. The true Katipunan -- led first by Bonifacio, then Jacinto, and finally by Sakay -- was for all intents and purposes dissolved by the Republicano Government by means of Aguinaldo's decree of 10 July 1898. By that decree, Katipuneros were virtually condemned as **contra-revolucionarios** or, worse, **bandoleros**. On this matter, the theme of the book, **Katipunan: Isang Pambansang Kilusan** (Quezon City: Trinitas, 1994), edited by Ferdinand Llanes, which makes no distinction at all between the 1896 Katipunan and the 1900 Katipunan -- whose concepts of Independencia/Kalayaan were worlds apart -- is, therefore, a sweeping and misleading one, to say the least.

Katipunero *refers to any member of the Katipunan.*

Katipunization (*noun*) **and Katipunize** (*verb*)**.** The process and act of converting someone to the ideals and aspirations of the Katipunan. Coined by Gregorio F. Zaide in his works on the Katipunan and the Philippine Revolution.

Laguna de Bay is literally translated *Lagoon of Bay* or *Lake of Bay* (or

Bae) after that ancient Katagalugan lakeshore town which was in the past the capital of Laguna and which would have been the "war capital" of the Katipunan in the course of its libertarian struggle. This lake really is part of other lakeshore towns of Laguna and Morong (now Rizal) provinces. One of the steamers of the Spanish fleet (which the US armed forces later commandeered) was named *Laguna de Bay*.

La Independencia (*Independence*) was the name of the revolutionary newspaper edited by General Antonio Luna. In its editorial staff were such brilliant names as Fernando Ma. Guerrero, Cecilio Apostol, José Palma, Epifanio de los Santos and Rosa Sevilla (later Alvero). Among its printers was Hermenegildo Cruz, later a big name in the **obrero** movement, who led the first strike in labor history against certain policies of **La Independencia**.

La Liga Filipina *(Philippine League)* was founded by José Rizal on 3 July 1892 in Tondo, to continue the work for reforms, as a result of the shift of activity of the Propaganda Movement from Europe to the native land. The nature of the **Liga** is perhaps best expressed in the characters of three of the more prominent members: José Rizal himself, Apolinario Mabini and Andres Bonifacio. Rizal was for peaceful reforms, Bonifacio was for radical change, and Mabini was for somewhere in-between. When Rizal is exiled and silenced in Dapitan only a week after the Liga has been founded, we find Bonifacio organizing the revolutionary **Katipunan**, and Mabini trying hard for a real compromise by forming the **Compromisarios** (Compromisers). While Rizal and Bonifacio both died for the ideals they believed in, Mabini became a statesman both in war and in peace. He deserved to be called the Brains of the Revolution.

Ladron and Leader of Ladrones (*bandit* and *leader of* bandits). Pio del Pilar was called a leader of thieves and accused of ruling with a strong hand by the Americans and, apparently, by some other leaders of the Revolution. What do you expect from your enemies or those jealous of your victories? Also, is there any other way to lead in a war except by a strong hand?

Liwanag is the *Light* or *Enlightenment* which, in the context of the Katipunan struggle, was the guiding light that illuminated the "true path" to the attainment of **Kalayaan** (which see).

Lunista is one who is *pro-Antonio Luna*, especially someone who is willing to die for this hero.

Lupang Tinubuan is the *land of one's birth*, one's nativeland.

Macabebes were natives of *Macabebe*, Pampanga, once-upon-a-time a Kapampangan kingdom whose original subjects were believed to have migrated from the South Americas. During the Revolution, "Macabebe" became a byword for treason because of the mercenary tradition of the town and its menfolk, being perennial "Volunteers" for the Spanish Army and, later the original "Scouts" in the U.S. Army. Some of the ruthless torture methods, like the "water cure" and the "bamboo cure" (which see), were attributed to them.

Madre España is *Mother Spain* as distinct from **Inang Bayan** (*which see*).

Magdalo is, literally, to *succor* and was the name designated for one of the two provincial councils of the Katipunan in 1896 Cavite, the other being **Magdiwang** (*to celebrate*). Magdalo was also Emilio Aguinaldo's own *nom de guerre* as a Katipunero. Aguinaldo claimed he derived the name from his patron saint, Santa *Magdalena*.

Magdiwang. See note on **Magdalo**.

Magtagumpay (*to win*) was the name given to the Katipunan chapter of Culi-Culi in San Pedro Makati, of which Pio del Pilar **Pang-Una** (Leader) was Secretary.

Malolos Republic is the Republicano government led by Emilio Aguinaldo.

Malvarista is *someone who is pro-Miguel Malvar, a hero of Batangas.*

Manileño is someone born or raised in Manila.

Manu-mano means *hand-to-hand.* In an earlier manu-mano combat, Julian Paguia lost, but Pio del Pilar saw his potentials as a fighter and made him his own second-in-command.

Medico is Spanish for *Doctor*, good for the physical wounds. For psychological and moral wounds, each of us is a doctor; so, physician, heal thyself!

Mesticillo is someone who has *foreign blood but is not half-breed.*

Mestiza is the *feminine* of *mestizo*. Pio del Pilar's mother was a mestiza of the Castañeda clan.

Mestizo is a *male half-breed*. Eugenio Blanco was a Pampango mestizo who was a leader of Macabebe mercenaries; Juan Gutierrez was an Ilocano mestizo who showed brilliance as an officer of Pio del Pilar in the attack and capture of Guadalupe.

Mi Presidente (*My President*), is a term used in fondness for Emilio Aguinaldo, President of the First Philippine Republic, by his "Beloved Generals", favorites like Pio del Pilar and Gregorio del Pilar. Goyo died for "Mi Presidente" defending Tirad Pass, while

Pio was deposed by the same for real or imagined insolence.

Monte is *a game of chance.*

Naquintos is a corruption of the Spanish *quinta*, which means a military draft or conscription. Pio del Pilar didn't like the idea of serving in the Spanish Army against his will and wanted out.

Noli Me Tangere (*Touch Me Not*), or **Noli** for short, was the first novel of José Rizal, intended not to be incendiary but to illuminate the minds of the ilustrados and burguesos to think as one people and seek peaceful change with Madre España. That partly explains why it was written not in Tagalog or English but in Spanish. As it turns out, **Noli** is a grossly underrated work in terms of how well it is written. (*See* **Afterword** for some proof of the matter.)

Nuestra Señora de la Paz y Buenviaje is *Our Lady of Peace and Good Voyage*, the patron saint of the parish of Antipolo.

Obrero is *worker*, from **obra**, which is *work*.

Original Katipunero refers to any one of the founding members of or early joiners to the Katipunan. Pio del Pilar was not an original Katipunero, but he proved to be one of the best military leaders of the revolutionaries.

Pagador. *See note on* **Cajero**.

Palay is the *rice plant* itself or *unmilled rice grains.*

Pang-Una means *Leader, Foremost,* or *First*. Pio del Pilar gave himself the Katipunan name *Pang-Una*, and he proved worthy.

Paralitico is *paralytic. See also* **Sublime Paralytic**.

Partido Federalista (*Federal Party*) was the exact opposite of the **Partido Nacionalista** and may be considered the original Philippine Statehood USA movement. (Compare with **Partido Nacionalista**.)

Partido Nacionalista (*Nationalist Party*) refers not to the Nacionalista Party we are familiar with, but to the original radical political front uniting Bonifacio-leaning Magdiwangs (represented by Santiago Alvarez) with original pre-1896 Katipuneros (Macario Sakay), budding obrero groups (Pascual Poblete), Aglipayano church militants (Valentin Diaz), underground theater guilds (Aurelio Tolentino), and others -- in short, the "Left" of the Revolution. (Compare with **Partido Federalista**.)

Pioistas were the followers of Pio del Pilar, *the officers and soldiers who composed* the **Brigada Pio del Pilar**.

Plaridel is an anagram of "Del Pilar" and was used by Marcelo H. del Pilar as one of his noms-de-plume as editor and writer of the Propaganda mouthpiece, **La Solidaridad** (*Solidarity*).

Presidente Local was *head of the town or municipality* during the Spanish period.
Presidente refers to *President* Emilio Aguinaldo as Head of State of the First Philippine Republic.
Principal refers to any member of the voting-class **principalia** of the Spanish regime.
Pro-Republicanos refers to the Caviteño Magdalos and Magdiwangs (together with their non-Caviteño allies) who conspired as a group to vote out Bonifacio and the Katipunan at the 1897 Tejeros bloody mess, in favor of Aguinaldo and a "republican" form of government. Aguinaldo's Republicanos later advocated Philippine independence "under the protection" of the United States -- and that is what, until today, we are proclaiming.
Propagandista is *propagandist* or *agitator*, used here to mean an advocate of the Propaganda Movement of the 1880s. Pio del Pilar claims that he was a propagandist of José Rizal, distributing some copies of his book (no title given) when it was a crime against the Spanish authorities to do so. He says he learned **filibusterismo** *(which see)* from this experience.
Pueblo means *town* or *municipality*.
Querida (literally, *dear one*) is in common usage in the Philippines for a "mistress" or "the other woman" and carries a social stigma. Querida Monica was Pio del Pilar's "ever-beautiful mistress".
Quilez is a *two-wheeled horse-drawn vehicle*, usually without covering and smaller than a calesa. The name is said to be in honor of the native of Vigan (Ilocos Sur) who invented it.
Rayadillo is the *cotton uniform with thin blue lines (raya)* of the Spanish Army, later adopted for their own use by Aguinaldo's Revolutionary Army.
Rebel is one who refuses to swear allegiance to or who opposes by force a ruling authority or constituted government.
Republica, Republicano and **Republika. Republica** is used here to mean Aguinaldo's **Republica Filipina**, as differentiated from Bonifacio's **Haring Bayang Katagalugan** which became **Republika ng Katagalugan** under Sakay in the 1900s, the use of Republika being a concession to the Republicano holdouts of Montalan, Felizardo, Oruga and others who provided the mass base for the Katagalugan forces. Similarly, **Republicano** *(Republican)* is used in contra-distinction to **Katipunero** *(which see)*.
Reseña Veridica *("True Version")* is short for Emilio Aguinaldo's

memoirs published in 1899, fully entitled **Reseña Veridica de la Revolucion Filipina**. A one-man's testimony.

Revolucionario as a general term refers to all the *veterans of the Philippine Revolution*. As a polarization word, as Reynaldo Ileto points out in his book **Pasyon and Revolution**, it separates Aguinaldo's **Republicanos** from Bonifacio's *"true"* **Katipuneros**.

Revolution, First Revolution and Second Revolution. The Revolution of 1896 came to be so-called because it was a mass attempt to change the existing government (Spanish). That was the First Revolution, otherwise known as the Philippine-Spanish War. Then the Americans came and established their hegemony on us by tricking our forefather-revolutionaries. The brave hearts among the Filipino leaders did not give up the struggle and declared the Americans the new enemy. That was when the Second Revolution began, otherwise known as the Philippine-American War. (*See also* **First War** and **Second War**.)

Ricartistas were *pro-Artemio Ricarte*, who was one of the leaders of the Revolution. Loyalty to the Revolution could not be expressed by the ordinary soldier except as loyalty to a leader and to be willing to die for that leader (and, therefore, one's country).

Salvadoristas were followers of the Pampango prophet-hero Felipe Salvador, head of that politico-religious brotherhood called **Santa Iglesia** (Holy Church), that fought under Aguinaldo's Republicano Army in 1898-1899, on its own as an independent anti-Republicano guerrilla army against the Americans, and later as part of the unconquered Vibora's Liberation Army that "terrorized" Central Luzon, especially Pampanga and Nueva Ecija, until Salvador himself was captured and hanged in 1910.

Salvajismo is *savagery*. Pio del Pilar was accused of savagery time and again. Question: Is it possible to be a great military leader without savagery?

Sandatahanes. *See note on* **Armas Blancas**.

Sanggunian is *council* or *committee*, as in **Kataastaasang Sanggunian** (Supreme Council) and **Sangguniang Bayan** (Provincial Council).

Sargento. See note on **Cabo**.

Segunda Zona (*Second Zone)*, one of four Filipino zones in Manila, was commanded by General Pio del Pilar and later by General Artemio Ricarte. The zone covered San Pedro Makati, Paco, Pandacan, Guadalupe, Pasig, Taguig and Pateros. Pio del Pilar proved to be the most successful of the zone attackers and defenders.

Segundo Jefe. *Second in Command,* or *Vice-Chief.*
Señores is *Gentlemen*, such as those in the Malolos Congress.
Sinangag is the *native fried rice*, made from leftover *rice, usually sauteed in lard with garlic and seasoned with salt. The mention of it in Grey's letter indicates that rice is in short supply. Filipinos prefer white, newly cooked rice.*
Soldado. See note on **Cabo**.
Special ties refers to the *special relations* General Pio del Pilar had with Presidente Emilio Aguinaldo who was happy with his "Beloved General" for quite a number of successful, even brilliant, military operations. In the same sense, Philippine-American relations was going to be forever special.
Sublime Paralytic refers to *Apolinario Mabini*, who had polio and therefore his legs were useless but his mind was a driving force of the Katipunan.
Sugod! is the Tagalog form of **Avance!** which appears to be the stance of General Pio del Pilar in his Makati statue (see back cover).
Tagalogs. See note on **Filipinos**.
Tambang is an *ambuscade*, especially favored in guerrilla warfare.
Teniente del Barrio is, literally, *Barrio Lieutenant*, the village headman (now Barangay Captain) in the country.
Teniente. See note on **Capitan**.
Tila. See **Tirad Pass**.
Tirad Pass is the Ilocos mountain pass east of Candon (Ilocos Sur) in the lower Cordilleras, where General Gregorio H. del Pilar and his Bulakeño Brigade sacrificed their lives in 1899 defending Presidente Emilio Aguinaldo. **Tila** is properly **Tirad** (literally, pointed), The Igorots (because they cannot pronounce the "r") and the Spaniards used **Tila**, while the Ilocanos used **Tirad**, the correct name.
Tiradores means *sharpshooters*, as in General Geronimo's **Tiradores de la Muerte** ("Deadly Sharpshooters").
Titulo *is literally,* title *or certificate of graduation* from a college or university; its holder is considered **titulado**.
Tres colores is the *tricolor* or the Filipino flag, which has three colors.
True Katipuneros are the *original, pre-1896 cadres of the* Katipunan who remained steadfast to the sacred ideals of independence (*see also* **Independencia** and **Kalayaan**).
Ulam is *dish or viand*, a particular food other than rice, as may be differentiated from **sabaw** (soup) and **matamis** (dessert).
Uprising is a *limited resistance to authority*. This is how the Americans

were belittling the armed (and unarmed) struggles of the Filipinos against their colonizer.

Valiente means *valiant, brave.* Isidoro Carmona was known far and wide as a valiant one as he got wounded again and again in battle after battle.

Vibora. *See* **Viper**.

Viper is **El Vibora**, the appellation that an Ilocano General liked attached to his name: Artemio Ricarte Vibora. Ricarte says he derived his alias from the Bible where Jesus sends out his disciples as sheep to the midst of wolves and that, therefore, they should be gentle as doves and wise as vipers. A viper is a venomous serpent (snake) with a thick heavy body.

Viva Pio! Long live Pio! An imagined greeting of the Guam exiles when they elected him their President, despite his objections.

War traitor. If you fought against the Americans, you were a war traitor. The patriot Lucino Almeida, who was civil governor of La Union under the Malolos Republic, was tried and sentenced by a US military commission as a war traitor, for which he was deported to Guam together with Mabini, Ricarte, Pio del Pilar and others.

War, First War and Second War. See note on **Revolution**.

Yanqui is the Spanish form of *Yankee*, used, at best, to signify lack of affection. *(See also* **Americano**).

Zarzuela is a *musical comedy*, a heritage from Spain. It is a stage play popularized in the early American empire days by nationalist dramatists like Aurelio Tolentino and Severino de los Reyes, replacing the Spanish-era **moro-moros**. In this sense, a one-man zarzuela is play-acting or masquerading.

Zarzuela Surrender refers to the "surrender" of Spain to the United States after the mock Battle of Manila. At that time, the Filipino rebels were winning (read this book! if you haven't) and, for the coup de gráce, were waiting for the right time, while the Americans were two-timing!

BIBLIOGRAPHY

Abad, Antonio K. **General Macario L. Sakay: Was He a Bandit or a Patriot?**. Manila: J.B. Feliciano and Sons, 1955.

Abella, Domingo. **The Flag of Our Fathers.** Manila: Milagros Romualdez Abella, 1977.

Agoncillo, Teodoro A. **Revolt of the Masses: The Story of Andres Bonifacio and the Katipunan.** Quezon City: U.P. Press, 1956.

Agoncillo, Teodoro A. **Malolos: The Crisis of the Republic.** Quezon City: The U.P. Press, 1960.

Agoncillo, Teodoro A. **The Writings and Trial of Andres Bonifacio.** Manila: Bonifacio Centennial Commission, 1963.

Agoncillo, Teodoro. "General Luna Reconsidered". **Solidarity**, March-April 1976.

Agoncillo, Teodoro. "On Distorting Historical Facts". **Solidarity**, January-February 1977.

Aguinaldo, Emilio. **Reseña Veridica de la Revolucion Filipina.** Tarlac: Imprenta Nacional del Zacarias Fajardo, 1899.[1]

Aguinaldo, Emilio. **Mga Gunita ng Himagsikan.** Manila: Cristina Aguinaldo Suntay, 1964.

Alejandrino, José. **The Price of Freedom.** Manila: M. Colcol Press, 1949.[2]

Almario, Virgilio S. **Panitikan ng Rebolusyon(g 1896): Isang Paglingon at Katipunan ng mga Akda nina Bonifacio at Jacinto.** Manila: Sentrong Pangkultura ng Pilipinas, 1993.

Alvarez, Santiago. **The Katipunan and the Revolution: Memoirs of a General.** Quezon City: Ateneo University Press, 1992.[3]

Alzona, Encarnacion. **Julio Nakpil and the Philippine Revolution.** Manila: Carmelo & Bauermann, 1964.[4]

---

[1]*For English translations, see* **The Philippine Social Sciences Review** *(May 1941), pages 179-223;* **Historical Bulletin** *(January-December 1969), pages 278-- 313; and Taylor's* **The Philippine Insurrection**, *Volume 1, pages 443-448 and Volume 3, pages 4-27.*

[2]*This is the memoirs of General José Alejandrino translated from the original Spanish,* **La Senda del Sacrificio** *[1933] by his son José M. Alejandrino.*

[3]*Translated from the original Tagalog,* **Ang Katipunan at ang Paghihimagsik** *[1927], by Paula Carolina Malay.*

[4]*With the autobiography of Gregoria de Jesus.*

Archer, Jules. **The Philippines' Fight for Freedom.** London: Crowell-Collier Press, 1970.

Arcilla, José S. "The Fall of Manila: Excerpts from a Jesuit Diary", **Philippine Studies** 37 (1989).

Arias Rodriguez, Manuel. **Vistas Fotograficas Sobre de la Revolucion.** Manila, 1897.[5]

Aspillera, Paraluman S. (ed.). **Talambuhay ni Lope K. Santos.** Manila: Capitol Publishing House, 1972.

Ataviado, Elias. "The Forgotten Filipino Military Heroes of the Philippine War for Independence", **The Journal of History**, Volume V, Numbers 1 and 2 (1957).

Baclagon, Uldarico S. **Philippine Campaigns.** Manila: Graphic House, 1952.

Bain, David Haward. **Sitting in Darkness: The Americans in the Philippines.** Boston: Houghton Mifflin Co., 1984.

Baja, Emmanuel. **Our Country's Flag and Anthem.** Manila: Juan Fajardo Press, 1928.

Blount, James. **The American Occupation of the Philippines.** New York: G.P. Putnam's Sons, 1912; Manila: Malaya Books, 1968.

Brillantes, Gregorio C. "*That* War with the Americans", **Philippines Free Press**, 12 June 1965.

Castillo, Erwin. "The Life and Times of a Minor Myth", **Asia-Philippines Leader**, 16 June 1972.

Castillo, Erwin. "The Revolution in Cavite", **Sunday Inquirer Magazine**, series of 28 May, 4 June and 11 June 1989.

Castillo, Erwin. **The Firewalkers.** Pasig (Metro Manila): Anvil Publishing, Inc., 1992.[6]

Concepcion, Rod F. "Generala", **Women's Home Companion**, series of 28 March, 4 April, 11 April, 18 April and 25 April, 1990.[7]

Constantino, Letizia R. **Recalling the Philippine-American War.** Quezon City: The Education Forum, 1989.

Constantino, Renato. "Origin of a Myth", **Graphic**, 17 April 1968.

---

[5] *Picture collection.*

[6] *A historical novel on the "bandit" phase of the Revolution in Cavite.*

[7] *A historical narrative on Laguna's rebel heroine of '86, "Henerala" Agueda Kahabagan.*

Constantino, Renato. "Roots of Subservience", **Graphic**, 12 June 1968.
Constantino, Renato. **The Philippines: A Past Revisited.** Quezon City: Tala Publishing, 1976.
Constantino, Renato. **History: Myths and Reality.** Quezon City: Karrel, Inc. [1992?].
Corpuz, O.D. **The Roots of the Filipino Nation.** Quezon City: Aklahi Foundation, Inc., 1989, Volume 2.
Cortes, Rosario Mendoza. **Pangasinan 1901-1986: A Political, Socio-Economic and Cultural History.** Quezon City: New Day Publishers, 1990.
Cruz, Isaac C. Cruz.**General Gregorio H. del Pilar: Idol of the Revolution.** Bulacan, Bulacan: Samahang Pagkalinangan ng Bulacan, 1985.
Daroy, Petronilo Bn. "Cry, Slaughter!" **Graphic**, 14 June 1972.
Daroy, Petronilo Bn. "Imperialist Gore", **Graphic**, 23 August 1972.
De Achutegui, Pedro S. and Miguel A. Bernad. **Aguinaldo and the Revolution of 1896: A Documentary History.** Manila: Ateneo dc Manila, 1977.
De los Santos, Epifanio. Letter to the Editor, **Philippine Magazine**, 13 April 1926.
De Los Santos, Epifanio. **The Revolutionists: Aguinaldo, Bonifacio and Jacinto.** Manila: National Historical Commission, 1975.
Del Mundo, Clodualdo Jr. and Herky del Mundo. "Alyas Raha Matanda", in **Tatlong Dulang Pampelikula**. Manila: De la Salle University Press, 1992.
Del Pilar y Castañeda, Pio. **Biografia.** Ms., Manila. 1929
De Olivares, José and William S. Bryan (eds.). **Our Islands and Their People.** St. Louis, New York: N.D. Thompson Publishing Co., 1899.
Dery, Luis Camara. "From Insurrecto to Bandido", in his **From Ibalon to Sorsogon** (Quezon City: New Day Publishers, 1991).
Dery, Luis Camara. **The Army of the First Philippine Republic.** Manila: De la Salle University Press, 1995.
Devins, John Bancroft. **An Observer in the Philippines.** Boston: American Tract Society, 1905.
Fast, Jonathan, and Jim Richardson. **Roots of Dependency: Economic Revolution in 19th Century Philippines.** Quezon City: Foundation for Nationalist Studies, 1979.
Faust, Karl Irving. **Campaigning in the Philippines.** San Francisco: Hicks-Judd Company.

Fernandez, Leandro. **The Philippine Republic.** New York: Columbia University Press, 1926.

Foreman, John. **The Philippine Islands.** Hongkong: Kelly and Walsh, Ltd., 1906.

Funston, Frederick. **Memories of Two Wars.** New York: Charles Scribner's Sons, 1911.

Gagelonia, Pedro A. **The Filipino Historian: Controversial Issues in Philippine History.** Manila: Far Eastern University, 1970.

Galang, Zoilo M. **Encyclopaedia of the Philippines.** Manila: McCullough Printing Co., 1950, 3rd edition, 10 volumes.

Garcia, Mauro (ed.). **Aguinaldo in Retrospect.** Manila: Philippine Historical Association, 1969.

Garcia, Pantaleon. **Maikling Ulat ng Himagsikan.** Manila: José Paez Santos, 1930.

Gealogo, Francis A. "Ang mga Taong Labas, ang Kabayanihan, at ang Diskurso ng Kapangyarihan sa Kasaysayan", **Diliman Review** 38:1 (1990).

Ginzberg, Robert N. "Damn the Insurrectos!" **The Military Review**, January 1964.

Givens, J.D. **[War] Scenes Taken in the Philippines.** no publisher, 1912, unpaged.

Gleeck, Lewis E. **Laguna in American Times: Coconuts and Revolucionarios.** Manila: Historical Conservation Society, 1981.

Gleeck, Lewis E. **Nueva Ecija in American Times.** Manila: Historical Conservation Society, 1981.

Gleeck, Lewis E. **The American Half-Century: 1898-1949.** Manila: Historical Conservation Society, 1984.

Gleeck, Lewis E. **The American Governors-General and High Commissioners in the Philippines.** Quezon City: New Day Publishers, 1988.

Guerrero, Amado. **Philippine Society and Revolution.** Manila: Pulang Tala Publications, 1971.

Guerrero, Milagros. "Provincial Elites During the Philippine Revolution", in **Philippine Social History** (Quezon City: Ateneo de Manila University, 1982), edited by Alfred McCoy and Edilberto de Jesus.

Gwekoh, Sol H. "Hero of Mandaluyong", **The Manila Times**, Hall of Fame Series (1966).

Herrero y Sampedro, Ulpiano. **Nuestra Prision en Poder de los Revolucionarios Filipinos.** Manila: Imprenta del Colegio de Santo Tomas, 1900.

Historical Calendar. Manila: National Historical Commission, 1970.

Hurley, Vic. **Jungle Patrol: The Story of the Philippine Constabulary.** New York: E.P. Dutton and Company, 1938.

Ileto, Reynaldo C. **Pasyon and Revolution: Popular Movements in the Philippines 1840-1910.** Quezon City: Ateneo University Press, 1979.

Ileto, Reynaldo C. "Toward a Local History of the Philippine-American War: The Case of Tiaong, Tayabas (Quezon) Province, 1901-1902", **The Journal of History**, VII:1-2 (January-December 1982).

Ileto, Reynaldo C. "Orators and the Crowd: Philippine Independence Politics, 1910-1914", in **Reappraising an Empire** (Cambridge: Harvard University Press, 1984), edited by Peter Stanley.

Ileto, Reynaldo C. **Critical Questions on Nationalism: A Historian's View.** Manila: De la Salle University, 1986.

Joaquin, Nick. **A Question of Heroes.** Makati: Ayala Museum, 1977.

Joaquin, Nick. **The Aquinos of Tarlac.** Manila: Cacho Hermanos, 1983.[8]

Joaquin, Nick. (tr.). **A Spaniard in Aguinaldo's Army.** Manila: Solar Books, 1986.

Joaquin, Nick. **Culture and Society.** Manila: Solar Books, 1988.

Jocano, F. Landa. "Ideology and Radical Movements in the Philippines: An Anthropological Overview", **Solidarity** 102 (1985).

José, Vivencio R. **The Rise and Fall of Antonio Luna.** Quezon City: The U.P. Press, 1976.

José, Vivencio R. "The Bankruptcy of the Subjectivist Conception of History". **Solidarity**, September-December 1976.

Kalaw, Teodoro M. **The Philippine Revolution.** Manila: Manila Book Company, 1925. Mandaluyong (Rizal): Jorge B. Vargas Filipiniana Foundation, 1969.

---

[8]*See especially "Part One: The General" for an account on Gen. Servillano Aquino and the Revolution in Tarlac and Central Luzon.*

Kalaw, Teodoro M. **Life and Death of a Boy General.** Manila: National Historical Commission, 1974.[9]

Kane, Samuel E. **Life or Death in Luzon.** New York: Grosset and Dunlap, 1933.

Karnow, Stanley. **In Our Image: America's Empire in the Philippines.** New York: Random House, 1989.

Kasandugo (pseud). **Ang Katipunan at si Gat Andres Bonifacio.** Typescript, not dated, in the National Library.

Kelly, Amzi B. **The Killing of General Noriel.** Manila: Historical Conservation Society, 1987.[10]

Lapeña-Bonifacio, Amelia. **"Seditious" Tagalog Playwrights: Early American Occupation.** Manila: Zarzuela Foundation of the Philippines, 1972.

Larkin, John A. **The Pampangans: Colonial Society in a Philippine Province.** Berkeley: University of California Press, 1972.

Laurie, Clayton D. "The Philippine Scouts: America's Colonial Army, 1899-1913", **Philippine Studies** 37 (Second Quarter, 1989).

Le Roy, James A. **The Americans in the Philippines.** Boston: Houghton Mifflin Co., 1914, Volume 2.

Legarda, Benito J. "The first shot that triggered the Philippine-American War in Feb. 1899 was fired in Balic-Balic, not San Juan: A neighborhood chronicle", **Mr. & Ms. Magazine**, series of 2 & 9 February 1988.

Llanes, Ferdinand. **Pagbabalik sa Bayan: Mga Lektura sa Kasaysayan ng Historiograpiya at Pagkabansang Pilipino.** Manila: Rex Book Store, 1993.

Llanes, Ferdinand (ed.). **Katipunan: Isang Pambansang Kilusan.** Quezon City: Trinitas Publishing, Inc., 1994.

Lucian, Justin. **A Soldier's Letter.** Manila: De la Salle University Press, 1995.

Lumbera, Bienvenido. "Aguilar, Abad at Gatmaitan: Tatlong Manunulat sa Pakikibaka (1900-1912)", **The Philippine Collegian Folio**, First Semester (1970-1971).

Luna, Ma. Pilar S. "General Artemio Ricarte y Garcia: A Filipino Nationalist", **Asian Studies** IX:2 (August 1971).

---

[9]*Translated from the original Spanish,* **El Heroe de Tirad** *[1933], by Marcelino A. Foronda.*

[10]*Original 1916 title:* **General Mariano Noriel, Innocent.**

Luzviminda (pseud.). "Pahalaw na Salaysay sa Kabuhayan ni Agueda Esteban at De la Cruz", **Bulletin of the Philippine Historical Association** I:1 (July 1957).

Mabini, Apolinario. **The Philippine Revolution.** Manila: Loyal Press, 1935.

Mabini, Apolinario. **Letters.** Manila: National Heroes Commission, 1965.[11]

MacArthur, Arthur. **Annual Report of Major-General Arthur MacArthur,** U.S. Army, Commanding, Division of the Philippines. Manila, 1901. Vols. I and II.

Manuel, E. Arsenio. **Dictionary of Philippine Biography.** Manila: Filipiniana Publications, 1957, Volume 1.

Martinez-Sikat, Maria Teresa. **Imagining the Nation in Four Philippine Novels.** Quezon City: U.P. Press, 1994.

Matatag (pseud.). **History of One of the Initiators of the Philippine Revolution.** Manila: National Historical Institute, 1988. Translated by O.D. Corpuz.[12]

May, Glenn Anthony. **A Past Recovered: Essays on Philippine History and Historiography.** Quezon City: New Day Publishers, 1987.

May, Glenn Anthony. **Battle for Batangas: A Philippine Province at War.** Quezon City: New Day Publishers, 1993.

Medina, B.S. **The Primal Passion.** Manila: Centro Escolar University, 1976.

Medina, Isagani R. **Cavite Before the Revolution (1591-1896).** Quezon City: [U.P.] CSSP Publications, 1994.[13]

Miller, Stuart Creighton. **"Benevolent Assimilation": The American Conquest of the Philippines.** New Haven, Connecticut: Yale University Press, 1982.

Minutes of the Katipunan. Manila: National Historical Institute, 1981.

Misa, Arturo Ma. "Emilio Jacinto as the Meat Merchant", **Sunday Times Magazine**, 6 June 1972.

---

[11] *With a preface by Carlos Quirino and original annotations by Teodoro M. Kalaw.*

[12] *"Matatag" was the Katipunan war name of General Antonino Guevarra of Laguna.*

[13] *See especially the Chapter on "Tulisanismo", pages 59-106.*

Ocampo, Ambeth R. **Looking Back.** Pasig (Metro Manila): Anvil Publishing, 1990.

Ocampo, Ambeth R. **Aguinaldo's Breakfast and More "Looking Back" Essays.** Pasig (Metro Manila): Anvil Publishing, 1993.

Ocampo, Ambeth R. **Bonifacio's Bolo.** Pasig City: Anvil Publishing, 1995.

Ocampo, Ambeth R. **Talking History: Conversations with Teodoro Agoncillo.** Manila: De la Salle University Press, 1995.

Ochosa, Orlino A. "Gen. Luciano San Miguel: A Rebel to the End", **Mirror Magazine**, 27 November 1965.

Ochosa, Orlino A. "Himagsikan ng mga Tulisan", **Diliman Review** 36:3. 1988.

Ochosa, Orlino A. "Big Black Brother: Remembering David Fagan, A Black Guerrilla in the Philippine-American War", **Diliman Review** 36:4 (1988).

Ochosa, Orlino A. "Emilio Jacinto *Pingkian*", **Diliman Review**, 37:3. 1989.

Ochosa, Orlino A. **The Tinio Brigade: Anti-American Resistance in the Ilocos Provinces, 1899-1901.** Quezon City: New Day Publishers, 1989.

Ochosa, Orlino A. "The Bravest Men: Caviteños, Cavitismo, and Lawton's Cavite Campaign". Ms. Paper read at the Annual Seminar of the Philippine Historical Association, Fort Santiago Shrine, Manila, 24 November 1992.

Ochosa, Orlino A. **"Bandoleros" -- Outlawed Guerrillas of the Philippine-American War, 1903-1907.** Quezon City: New Day Publishers, 1995.

Otis, Elwell S. **Report of Major-General E.S. Otis, U.S.V., Commanding, Division of the Philippines, Military Governor, September 1, 1898 to May 5, 1900.** Washington: Government Printing Office, 1900.

Pecson, Geronima and Maria Racelis. **Tales of the American Teachers in the Philippines.** Manila: Carmelo and Bauermann, 1959.

Philippine Historical Committee. **Pio del Pilar Historical Marker.** Makati: Philippine Historical Committee, 1976.

Philippine Historical Papers 1952-1953.[14]

---

[14]*These are bound manuscript compilations of local histories of all towns in the Philippines kept at the National Library.*

Philippine Insurgent Records. "Pio del Pilar Papers", RL-14, RL-15 and RL-16, National Library Filipiniana and Asia Division Rare Books Section.[15]

Quirino, Carlos. **The Young Aguinaldo.** Manila: Regal Printing Co., 1969.

Quirino, Carlos. **Filipinos at War.** Manila: Vera-Reyes, Inc., 1981.

Quirino, Carlos. **Who's Who in Philippine History.** Makati (Metro Manila): Tahanan Books, 1995.

Quirino, José A. "Three Faces of the Hero: A Legend of the Vibora", **Philippines Free Press**, 8 June 1968.

Ramos-De Leon, Lilia. "The Filipino Geronimo, A Super General, Was the Nemesis of General Lawton", **Philippine Panorama**, 7 June 1981.

Reports of the Philippine Commission. Washington, D.C.: Government Printing Office, 1903 and 1904.

Reyes, Pedrito. **Pictorial History of the Philippines.** Manila: Capitol Publishing House, 1951.

Ricarte, Artemio. **The Hispano-Philippine Revolution.** Yokohama: self-published. 1926.

Ricarte, Artemio. **Memoirs.** Manila: National Heroes Commission, 1963.

Riggs, Arthur Stanley. **The Filipino Drama (1905).** Manila: Intramuros Administration, 1981.[16]

Robinson, Albert G. **The Philippines: The War and the People.** New York: McClure, Phillips and Company, 1901.

Robles, Eliodoro G. **The Philippines in the Nineteenth Century.** Quezon City: Malaya Books, 1969.[17]

Ronquillo, Carlos (ed.). "Ang Paghihimagsik Laban sa Espanya" (Kantahing Pulube), **Renacimiento Filipino**, 7 and 14 June 1911.

Rosca, Ninotchka. "Rayadillo and Toledo Steel", **Asia-Philippines Leader**, 12 June 1971.

---

[15] *"Philippine Revolutionary Papers" is the file entry for the* **Philippine Insurgent Records**, *which are original documents captured from "insurrectos" during the Philippine-American War.*

[16] *With an introduction by Doreen Fernandez.*

[17] *With an introduction by Teodoro Agoncillo.*

Roth, Russell. **Muddy Glory: America's "Indian Wars" in the Philippines 1899-1935.** West Hanover, Massachusetts: Christopher Publishing House, 1989.

Salamanca, Bonifacio S. **The Filipino Reaction to American Rule, 1901-1913.** Quezon City: New Day Publishers, 1984.

Salazar, Z. A. **Ang Pagsalakay ni Bonifacio sa Maynila.** Quezon City: Miranda Bookstore, 1994.

Santos, Angelito L. **Looking out for Indio Jones: An Essay on Philippine Nationalism and Culture.** Quezon City: Foundation for Nationalist Studies [1991?].

Santos, José P. **Tatlong Napabantog na "Tulisan" sa Pilipinas.** Tarlac: José Paez Santos, 1930.

Saulo, Alfredo B. **The Truth about Aguinaldo and Other Heroes.** Quezon City: Phoenix Publishing House, 1987.

Schirmer, Daniel B. **Republic or Empire: American Resistance to the Philippine War.** Cambridge, Massachusetts: Schenkman Publishing Co., 1972.

Schumacher, John. **Revolutionary Clergy.** Quezon City: Ateneo University Press, 1982.

Scott, William Henry. "A Minority Reaction to American Imperialism: Isabelo de los Reyes", **The Journal of History**, VII:1-2 (January-December 1982).

Scott, William Henry. **Ilocano Responses to American Aggression 1900-1901.** Quezon City: New Day Publishers, 1986.

Scott, William Henry. "Guerrilla Padre", **National Midweek**, series of 1 & 8 June 1988.

Scott, William Henry. **Union Obrera Democratica: First Filipino Labor Union.** Quezon City: New Day Publishers, 1993.

Segovia. **The True Story of Aguinaldo's Capture.** Manila: MCS Publications, 1969.

Serrano, Leopoldo R. "News from up Front as Seen by the [Malolos] Republic's Reporters", **Sunday Times Magazine**, 2 January 1962.

Sexton, William T. **Soldiers in the Sun.** Harrisburg, Pennsylvania: The Military Service Publishing Co., 1939.

Sheridan, Richard Brinsley. **The Filipino Martyrs.** London: The Bodley Head, 1900; Manila: Malaya Books, 1971.

St. Clair, Francis. **The Katipunan, or the Rise and Fall of the Filipino Commune.** Manila:Tip. "Amigo del Pais", 1902.

Steinberg, David Joel. "An Ambiguous Legacy: Years at War in the Philippines", **Pacific Affairs**, XLV:2 (1972).

Storey, Moorefield and Marcial P. Lichauco. **The Conquest of the Philippines by the United States, 1898-1925.** New York: G.P. Putnam's Sons, 1926.

Sturtevant, David. "Guardia de Honor: Revitalization with the Revolution", **Asian Studies**, IV:2 (1966).

Taylor, John R.M. **The Philippine Insurrection against the United States.** Pasay City: Eugenio Lopez Foundation, 1971-1973. 5 volumes

Villa, Simeon. "The Flight and Wanderings of General Emilio Aguinaldo from Bayambang to Palanan: A Diary", in **Historical Bulletin**, XIII:1-4 [1969].

Villaroel, Hector et al. **Eminent Filipinos.** Manila: National Historical Commission, 1965.

Watson, William Brecknock. "The Christmas Eve Fiasco and a Brief Outline of the Ricartista and Other Similar Movements", in Artemio Ricarte's **Memoirs** (which see).

Welch, Richard E. Jr. **Response to Imperialism.** Chapel Hill: University of North Carolina Press, 1987.

Wilcox, Marrion. ed., **Harper's History of the War in the Philippines.** New York: Harper and Brothers, 1900.

Wildman, Edwin. **Aguinaldo: A Narrative of Filipino Ambition.** Boston: Lothrop Publishing Co., 1901.

Willis, Henry Parker. **Our Philippine Problem: A Study of American Colonial Policy.** New York: Henry Holt and Co., 1905.

Wolff, Leon. **Little Brown Brother.** New York: Doubleday, 1961. Makati: Erehwon Press, 1971.

Worcester, Dean C. **The Philippines: Past and Present.** New York: McMillan Company, 1914. 2 vols.

Yap-Diangco, Robert T. **The Filipino Guerrilla Tradition.** Manila: MCS Enterprises, 1971.

Zaide, Gregorio F. **History of the Katipunan.** Manila: Loyal Press, 1939.

Zaide, Gregorio F. **The Philippine Revolution.** Manila: Modern Book Company, 1954.

Zaide, Gregorio F. **Great Filipinos in History.** Manila: Verde Book Store, 1970.

INDEX

DATE

SUBJECT

A

D

K

L

M

Y

Z

Other Centenary Books By New Day

Babaylanism in Negros: 1896-1907; Cullamar, Evelyn Tan
"Bandoleros" --- Outlawed Guerrillas of the Philippine-American War, 1903-1907; Ochosa, Orlino A.
Battle for Batangas; May, Glenn Anthony
Bonifacio's Unfinished Revolution; Villanueva, Alejo L. Jr.
Exemplar of Americanism; Sullivan, Rodney J.
Filipino Martyrs; Sheridan, Richard Brinsley
Filipino Reaction to American Rule, 1901-1913; Salamanca, Bonifacio S.
From Ibalon to Sorsogon: A Historical Survey of Sorsogon Province to 1905; Dery, Luis Camara
George Ade's "Stories of Benevolent Assimilation"; Gianakos, Perry
History of the Mountain Province; Fry, Howard T.
History of the Religious Revolution in the Philippines: 1850-1940; Vaño, Manolo
Ilocano Responses to American Aggression 1900-1901; Scott, William Henry
In Time of Hesitation: American Anti-Imperialists and the Philippine-American War; Bresnahan, Roger J. (ed.)
Inventing A Hero: the Posthumous Re-Creation of Andres Bonifacio; May, Glenn Anthony
Kangkong 1896; Alabado, Ceres
Mandate in Moroland; Gowing, Peter G.
Manila Workers Unions, 1900-1950; Tria-Kerkvliet, Melinda
Pampangans, Colonial Society in A Philippine Province; Larkin, John A.
A Past Recovered; May, Glenn Anthony
Presbyterian Missionaries in the Philippines: Conduits of Social Change (1899-1910); Kwantes, Anne C.
Rage in the Hearts; Leveriza, Jose P.
Tinio Brigade: Anti-American Resistance in the Ilocos Provinces, 1899-1901; Ochosa, Orlino A.
Union Obrera Democratica; Scott, William Henry
The United States and the Philippines: A Study of Neocolonialism; Shalom, Stephen R.
We Thought We Could Whip Them in Two Weeks; Trafton, William Oliver
White Apos: American Governors on the Cordillera Central; Jenista, Frank L.

Orli

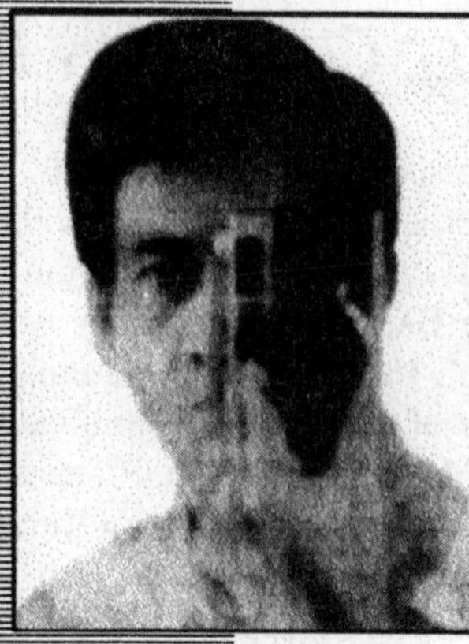

Frank

Two friends, both Ilocanos, he from Vigan and he from Asingan; single and married; both Virgos, he September12 and he September 17; both began as copywriters of Pacifica in the mid-70s and have since graduated from their rural naivetes to other naivetes and, having met again after 22 years, talking of heroes and history, shifting to the sophistication of language as a tool for understanding how to express either the sublime or the paralytic, shifting from the art of the vulgar to Zen and the art of motorcycle writing: you rev up and let go; now agreeing and disagreeing, trying to elevate history to the level of the masses, where it all began, where it all begins. In other words, in this book, these two boys are trying to tell us in one voice: we are all heroes -- or should be.